Spatializing Internatioi

What exactly does politics mean in the age of the Internet?

Spatializing International Politics investigates the ways political activists use the Internet to network, mobilize and gather information. In this innovative book, Jayne Rodgers argues that we need to think about ways to bring the politics of transnational activism and information communication technologies, such as the Internet, into our broader interpretative frameworks.

Rodgers takes spatial theories drawn from the work of Henri Lefebvre and applies them to real political practices. The book includes case studies of transnational activism in order to examine how individuals, organizations and institutions can be better understood as political actors and can address key questions such as:

- Does the Internet provide new forms of political practice?
- Does this technology really give political power to the disenfranchised?
- Does more information mean more politics?

This volume is a valuable resource for both scholars of politics seeking an understanding of the role of the Internet and other media in political mobilization. It will also be indispensable for those researching global media and communications, and looking for information on how these technologies are applied in the political arena.

Jayne Rodgers is a Lecturer in International Communications at the University of Leeds, where she teaches global media and international politics.

Routledge advances in international relations and global politics

Spatializing International Politics

Analysing activism on the Internet

Jayne Rodgers

Routledge
Taylor & Francis Group

LONDON AND NEW YORK

First published 2003
by Routledge
2 Park Square, Milton Park, Abingdon, Oxfordshire OX14 4RN

Simultaneously published in the USA and Canada
by Routledge
711 Third Avenue, New York, NY 10017

First issued in paperback 2015

Routledge is an imprint of the Taylor and Francis Group, an informa business

© 2003 Jayne Rodgers

Typeset in Sabon by LaserScript Ltd, Mitcham, Surrey

British Library Cataloguing in Publication Data
A catalogue record for this book is available from the British Library

Library of Congress Cataloging in Publication Data
Rodgers, Jayne, 1961–
    Spatializing international politics : analysing activism on the
internet / Jayne Rodgers.
        p. cm.
    Includes bibliographical references and index.
    1. Internet–Political aspects. 2. Cyberspace–Political aspects.
3. Political activists. 4. Internet users. 5. Social movements.
6. Protest movements. 7. Social action. I. Title.

HM851.R63 2003
303.48'33–dc21

                                                                2003000638

ISBN 13: 978-1-138-87440-4 (pbk)
ISBN 13: 978-0-415-25592-9 (hbk)

For Shirley, lovely little mum-thing

Contents

Acknowledgements

In keeping with one of the themes of this book, there are people who have made 'formal' and 'informal' contributions to it. Most of them, in the spirit of relationality that the book pursues, play more than one role: the colleagues who play a social role and the friends who, sometimes inadvertently and/or drunkenly, offer intellectual guidance. Most important in terms of content are the activists who provided time for interviews, emails and telephone chats to give me an insight into their actions, intentions and the obstacles they face. Some, at their request, remain anonymous: unnamed but not unacknowledged. Others – Anni Rainbow, Dave Webb, Stacey Fitz, Glen Tarman and Jim Carey in particular – I am happy to thank warmly and openly.

My colleagues at the Institute of Communications Studies at the University of Leeds are wonderful and I've had a lot of support from my workmates while I've been writing this. Some of this has been in the form of high-level research meetings and some has been in the form of cheap lunches. The best bits have, of course, involved both. So thanks to Phil Taylor, Robin Brown, Katrin Voltmer, Graham Roberts and David Gauntlett. Christine, Isobel and Tricia haven't been directly involved but they help other bits of life run smoothly and deserve a box of chocolates each, at the very least. Cindy Weber offered grown-up, sensible advice – thanks to her too.

There's a growing academic community interested in this stuff and the chance to be involved in conferences, workshops, seminars, etc. with them is one of the perks of the job. My lovely friends in the BISA IR/International Communications Working Group make play and professionalism seem like the same thing sometimes. Our legendary worldwide business meetings are more fun and more productive than work should be. Thanks to Chris May, Des Freedman, Gillian Youngs, Robin (again) and Marianne Franklin for all that. Anyone who is interested in the work of the group (there *is* work involved but we do it in cool places and make sure it's both intellectually and socially rewarding) should email me on f.j.rodgers@leeds.ac.uk for details.

My strange and lovely family people – Mum, Sally, Helen, Steve – have been, well, strange and lovely and very supportive. Bibi the kid is a wonderful thing so thanks to her for our snuggly nights in with the West Wing, Johnny Cash and her rubbish jokes. Thanks finally to my great mates Alan, Angie, Cathie O'Hoolie, Cathie the Painter, Colin, ET ('DT'), Nic, Spobbie ('media breakfast?'), Netski (parallel lives, or what?), Tooth and the rest – love, kisses and that kind of thing to them all.

Introduction

Research for this book originated with an analytical dilemma, namely how to analyse complex and overlapping phenomena in International Relations (IR). Looking at the role of the Internet in international politics (complex issue number one) and its implications for non-state actors (number two), it became clear that the frameworks available within the field, though broad and diverse, were not really adequate for the task. Hence the book swiftly moved from being an analysis of the ways some non-state actors use the Internet to one which questions how a discursive hegemony can impose constraints on the ways we understand and interpret practices that fall outside of our usual remit. As use of the Internet has continued to expand and a rise in transnational activism has become apparent, these issues have come to prominence in the discipline.

This book is based on the premise that the increasing complexities of international politics – of which the Internet and activism are only two related aspects – mean that it is necessary to push our conceptual boundaries and attempt to find new ways of thinking about theorizing the field. At the heart of this book, then, is an endeavour to find new ways of addressing complex issues in IR. With this, five key areas that may help to achieve this have been identified and are woven as themes through the book. The first of these relates to analysis of the Internet, a communications technology whose role in international politics has become increasingly significant in recent years. Some have argued that this technology is radically transforming the ways politics can be conducted and, by implication, what political practices are and how they can be understood. Others have suggested that the cost of access and the skills required to use the Internet make it little more than a toy with which rich kids can play with politics and pornography. Whatever the real effects of its introduction into the political arena – and these won't be fully appreciated for some time yet – it's clear that the Internet is having a profound impact on how we perceive and conceive of social and political relations on local and global scales.

I declare my own position on this from the outset: the Internet is having a profound impact on social and political relations, though not uniformly, certainly not equitably and not necessarily for the greater good. This may not be a revolution, but the scale, scope and reach of the Internet offer new dimensions to human interactions and, as a consequence, create a need for analysts to carefully consider how they address these. As with most audience analysis, assessing the real scale of Internet use is proving a virtual impossibility. The International Telecommunications Union (ITU) points out that measurement and analysis of the number of host domains, modem access, subscription figures, licensing policies, tariffs, online traffic and data transfers all offer variations on the scale of Internet use (Minges 2002: online). Even where all of these factors are taken into account, there is no common international standard for defining the terms and the results their analysis generates (ibid.) One media analysis organization suggests that there were around half a billion people with Internet access in the home by 2002 (Nielsen 2002: online). Workplace access is assumed to make these numbers greater still.

Without being blasé about the iniquities of the Internet, it is possible, by whatever measures, to suggest that this technology has both a fairly wide reach – the ITU suggests around one hundred and thirty countries and rising (Minges 2002: online) – and that access is continuing to grow. As a consequence, there are new and important questions about the relationships between the Internet and politics, many of which have yet to be adequately addressed. Does the Internet provide new forms of political practice or is it simply adding a technological dimension to the old ones? Does this technology really give political power to the disenfranchised? Does more information mean more or better forms of political communication? These and related questions will be touched upon in this book.

The second key issue addressed here relates to the dominant spatial discourses underpinning the study of international politics. IR has been the subject of many discursive variations and mutations in its history. The hegemony of state centrism has had the greatest longevity, but postmodern, post-colonial, globalization, gender-aware and civil society perspectives, among others, have all offered differing dimensions to the debates on power and political legitimacy in IR. All of these developments have served to enrich the field of study and broaden its scope. There have been, however, few theoretical advances that have developed new ways of addressing relationships between actors, institutions and practices in international politics. The book is designed, at least in part, to address these gaps in spatial theorizing in the discipline.

Third, despite the apparent rise in the number of the number of transnational political actors in recent years – or at least the recognition of this group as a legitimate object of analysis in IR – it remains very difficult when studying international politics to analyse the actions of individual, non-elite actors and of social collectives. Whether the world is viewed as globalized, supra-nationalized or state-oriented, entrenched notions of power and political process in IR continue to militate against anything beyond a superficial understanding of non-state actors as political agents in their own right. The third objective of this book is to contribute to the development of interpretative frameworks which address the *relationality* of political actors and actions. That is, viewing a wide range of actors as politically significant, and their actions as intrinsically related, the book seeks to find ways of addressing instead of ignoring these links.

A fourth objective of this book is to provide some *evidence* on how the Internet is being used by non-state actors in the international political arena. If nothing else, the Internet has proved its effectiveness as a tool for international – though perhaps not yet truly global – networking. In this respect, Internet technologies have provided a more effective, more efficient tool for those engaged in, or wishing to become engaged in, politics than any previously available. Research into the ways some large non-governmental organizations (NGOs) and other, looser forms of political association like activist collectives have been using the Internet provides valuable information in two areas: how the technology is being applied and what these actors perceive its value to them to be. Much is made of the Internet's role in events such as anti-capitalist protests, but research into the *strategies* used in the application of the technology by non-governmental organizations and other non-state actors remains limited. The fourth aim of the book, then, is to look at some of the ways non-state actors are actually using the Internet to influence governments and other political players.

The book's final, and most important aim, is to develop a theoretical approach which can be applied to non-state political actors to help demonstrate and interpret the effects of change. The change in this case, of course, is the introduction of the Internet. The spread of communications technologies and the rise in transborder activity – social, political and economic – mean that our conventional topographies of political agency are in urgent need of revision. What happens when an organization starts to use websites for information provision and for email petitions? How do organizations mobilize web surfers to engage in political actions? Do activists represent themselves in new ways on the Internet? Are networks created, extended or transformed in some way when the Internet is adopted as a tool of political agency?

Rather than simply providing quasi-quantitative responses to these questions, this book draws on the work of Henri Lefebvre to find new ways of viewing the field on international politics. Lefebvre's theories of spatiality are used because, despite the impact of his work in raising awareness of the intellectual constrictions of conventional spatial politics, there have been few attempts to apply his theories to political practice. Taking some of his key concepts on space, this book adopts the premise that the way politics is *spatialized* in IR is problematic and that it is possible to develop new theoretical approaches which may help to '*un-spatialize*' or '*de-spatialize*' the field.

It does not attempt to provide a new 'lens' through which to view political interactions. We can perhaps see the dominant spatialization of IR as the application of a state-centric lens, as a state-dominated topography or as a hierarchy of power relations where all actors are defined through their relations with states. Beyond this, newer conceptualizations, such as globalization and the global civil society approach offer different but equally potentially limiting ways of framing international politics. It suffices at this point to say that this book is about finding new ways of spatializing international politics by deconstructing some of the inbuilt hierarchies that have become legitimized over time. While some literature on the limitations of the spatial logic of the discipline exists (see Niemann 2001; Walker 1993; Youngs 1996b), the book represents the first attempt to *apply* spatial theories to specific transnational practices and, in doing so, illustrates how they can be used as an alternative mechanism for interpreting political practices.

The key elements of the task outlined in the points above – condensable to relationality, use of the Internet by social movement actors and the application of spatial theories – are threaded through the book. Related issues, such as the role of gender theorists in promoting change in the landscape of political analysis, are also addressed. In developing its methodology, the book aims to contribute to the development of gender-aware theorizing in IR, by demonstrating the significant contribution feminist theorists have made to the development of spatial awareness in the discipline. In addition, attempting to develop a relational approach may permit analysis of non-state political actions as significant in their own right, an approach which most extant categorizations of power and legitimacy in IR appear unable to provide.

Chapter 1 addresses the nature of spatial theorizing both in IR and in other disciplines. It highlights ways in which discursive constructs impose conceptual boundaries and examines the work of spatial theorists who have challenged how academic disciplines legitimize some spaces over others. The chapter explores spatial theorizing in general, looking at the historical assumptions on space that have underpinned much academic analysis. Also examined are the specific forms of spatial boundaries in IR and, in particular, the ways the territorial imagination has historically framed how international political practices can be understood and interpreted. The chapter addresses, too, the increasing links between social and political practices, wrought in part by the Internet and its use by NGOs and other activists, arguing that the spatial frameworks that we have used in the past are ill-suited to analysis of contemporary interactions in the international arena.[1]

Chapter 2 draws upon the work of feminist theorists to illustrate how the dichotomous logic of much academic endeavour curtails opportunities to address complex practices, by marginalizing a wide range of largely non-institutional actors and practices. The feminist work examined is valuable in exposing entrenched conceptions of the legitimacy of some political spaces and practices within the discourse of IR. Feminist theories on discursive boundaries in the analysis of political practices are a useful element in the examination of spatial ontologies. It is argued that feminists and other scholars have contributed to processes of re-spatialization of the discipline's discourse in recent years and that IR is no longer so deeply entrenched in a state-centric conceptualization of politics as was once the case. It is argued too, however, that we have not yet found ways to evade the dichotomous hegemony of thought that still positions non-state actors as 'other' in the political arena.

Chapter 3 focuses on the Internet, highlighting the characteristics that render it qualitatively different from other forms of communication. The chapter provides a brief analysis of the nature of this form of communication, identifying the specific differences between this and other media. In particular, it considers the ways information is exchanged using Internet technology. As the Internet allows a greater degree of control over access to and exchange of information by comparison with other media, these phenomena are suggested to represent 's/elective' forms of communication. It is this 's/elective' feature that is potentially of greatest significance to analysts of the functionality of the Internet, as the sender–receiver relationship between communicators is more dynamic, and more user-led than many other communications media permit. The chapter goes on to analyse the changing nature of audience construction, arguing that, with the use of this form of technology, audiences potentially have much greater control over which information they wish to access and exchange. Again, this would appear to demonstrate the need for new theoretical approaches which have the flexibility to interpret multi-layered, multi-dimensional interactions.

Chapter 4 is concerned with non-state actors – who they are, how they become involved in political protest and how their networks, – both off and online – evolve. The Internet should be seen as a *tool* of political activism, not as the genesis of it; social movements existed long before the Internet did. This chapter looks at what political protest actually is: is signing an e-petition to George Bush Junior any more or less 'political' than participating in a street demonstration against the World Trade Organization in Seattle, for example? Questions about whether our understanding of protest is changing are raised and the role of the Internet as a key feature of contemporary activism is considered. While it is widely assumed that the Internet is of more use than the mass media to movement activists, how it is applied in the field of contentious politics as a means of promoting engagement needs to be explored.

Chapters 5 and *6* provide case study material on activist use of the Internet. The term 'activist' in this context covers a wide range of actors, again challenging neat spatial categories. Some activists are members of transnational NGOs, others are individuals opting in and out of different movements and collectives. The four case studies used cover actors who are part of transnational social movement organizations (TSMOs) (see Smith *et al.* 1997), those who are not affiliated to 'formal' movements (see McAdam 1996: 2) and a range of actors in between. The case studies in *Chapter 5* look at what can be termed 'structural challenges'. The first centres on the online strategies of large transnational NGOs in generating support and seeking influence on the global political stage. The second looks at the rationale behind alternative online media, examining how these loose collectives[2] seek to challenge mass media representations of politics, providing information with different framings of the actions of governments, commercial organizations and activists.

The case studies in *Chapter 6* come from a slightly different angle. All of the protests and campaigns researched for this book can be considered normative in their intent. The two cases in this chapter, though, look in detail at issue-led protest, as opposed to those posing structural challenges. One looks at campaigns against the US government's missile defence shield. These protests have a strong normative underpinning – pacifism and antipathy toward the militarization of space. These concerns have, for the activists involved, a universal resonance. The different sites planned to house the missile shield, however, are geographically and culturally diverse. Consequently, the local applications of Internet technology differ quite significantly. Similarly, but with a focus on multinational corporations (MNCs), protests against genetically modified (GM) foods demonstrate the multiple dimensions of global campaigning. Again, different local contexts influence how activists network and the campaigns they become involved in. Perhaps most importantly in this case, it is clear that *political* activists see *economic* actors – in the form of agro-business companies – as key players, rather than the governments and international organizations who regulate GM products.

All of the case studies provide insights into how political activists – formal and informal – are spatializing politics. They also supply clear evidence on the role of the Internet in information gathering and exchange processes, in providing opportunities for innovative campaigning and in extending networks of communication and interaction. They also help us to interpret the strengths and weaknesses of a global networking tool in the mechanics of social movement politics. To explore how these issues can be addressed as politically legitimate within the discourse of IR, *Chapter 7* returns to the spatial theories of Lefebvre. Evidence from the case studies is interpreted under the headings 'spatial practice', 'representations of space' and 'spaces of representation', demonstrating the inter-relationships between actors, practices and the material environment.[3]

The book's concluding chapter draws together the key issues from the preceding chapters, arguing that the application of spatial theories has much to offer the discourse of IR. The complexities of contemporary politics are such that a flexible framework, applied within an open discursive structure, can help us to interpret the actions, interactions and relationality of a wide range of diverse actors. No less than seven ways that this approach can enhance the study of international politics are identified and avenues for further research are considered in conclusion.

A final note on the structure of the book: the themes of spatialization, social movements, activism and the Internet are threaded through each of the chapters. If there appears to be a wholly linear logic to the chapter outline given here, I apologize. Each chapter can be read as a discrete entity; the central issues are threaded through them all, though.

1 Space in international relations

Introduction

This book is about the ways we interpret politics. Its central claim is that our understanding of what constitutes politics is limited by what we imagine politics is or can be. As a consequence, we need to develop new ways of conceptualizing political processes. This much is straightforward. If, for example, we perceive states to be the most significant actors in international politics, we create hierarchies that position other actors, groups and organizations in a subordinate position in relation to them. Similarly, a belief that transnational networks form the most important arena of international politics would invoke a particular perception of hierarchical power relations between actors.

Such simplistic conceptualizations of politics have, of course, been widely challenged. Real or imagined globalization, the rise in the number of international institutions and non-governmental organizations, a growth in transnational activism and the spread of communications technologies all contribute to a sense that the arena of politics is complex and multi-layered. Given the multi-faceted relations between political actors, a need to develop interpretative frameworks that allow us to adequately account for the many actors, practices and multi-way associations and interactions that now constitute 'the political' is evident. Although there has been wide acknowledgement that politics have become increasingly multi-faceted, pre-existing interpretative hierarchies tend to impose limits on attempts to address changing political relations, by over-emphasizing, under-playing or excluding some actors, practices and concepts.

Particular types of space have traditionally been privileged in social and political theory, imposing constraints on meanings and definitions of social and political practices. Hidden or implicit discursive boundaries frame academic endeavour and the boundaries they invoke are particularly significant in the study of world politics. The complexities of global relations evidently operate at myriad levels and it is argued in this chapter that many of the boundaries mapped in IR can have the effect of reducing the effectiveness of much research in the discipline by marginalizing or excluding some significant actors and practices.

Academic disciplines identify the terrain upon which their subject-matter should be plotted, and scholars negotiate this terrain to produce their analyses. The spatial ontologies upon which these terrains are based map out the most significant features of each discipline, emphasizing some actors, issues and practices over others.[1] Discursive closure – the fixing of limits on appropriate subject-matter in academic disciplines – is an aid to coherence but is unhelpful in producing satisfactory analysis of complex material. All academic analysis requires some form of discursive closure; it would be impossible, and probably undesirable, to analyse everything and the actions of everyone. What are called into question here are the particular boundaries established in IR as the discursive core for analysis of international politics.[2] Situating the state as central to analysis has a certain convenient logic, of course. As sources of data, perspectives for comparative analysis and so on, states are a useful starting point. To embody them as the central site of meaning for this information is, however, problematic, as it strips away the layers – of culture, inter- and intra-agency power, race, gender and so on – which can afford it context.

That academic disciplines construct particular terrains upon which to conduct their analysis is clear. That these terrains may or may not reflect the way the world functions is also fairly self-evident. What is problematic is the issue of how to move beyond a set of assumptions that no longer reflects the world as we know it. Although the study of international politics has made important advances in recent years with the study of globalization, transnational activity, civil society and so on, there remains the under-pinning of a map of power, and in particular of state power, which none of the debates on political practices above, below and beyond the state have been able to eradicate.

It is suggested in this chapter that an understanding of the multiple constructions of space is crucial to the analysis of political activity. This is because the complexity of contemporary political relations requires methods of interpretation that can conceive of a range of actors and practices as related, rather than as discrete and separable. For example, policy on debt in less developed countries may be made by national governments, with reference to the work of NGOs, the agendas of international organizations, the state of the global economy, the experience of grassroots organizations and knowledge of local or regional circumstances. None of these issues is separable from the others, though some may have greater or lesser impact in particular circumstances. As Dahlgren puts it: 'we must certainly keep in focus the practical business of politics, yet also acknowledge the origins of people's political views in the intricate spaces of their everyday lives' (2001b: 40). It is in an endeavour to find ways of encompassing this relationality – or 'mixity', as Massey puts it (1999: 43) – of actors and issues that the spatial theories outlined in this and later chapters are explored and applied.

The concept of spatiality is fairly abstract. A brief, catch-all definition such as the one that follows is designed to encapsulate the bare bones of it, forming a foundation for the much more detailed analysis undertaken in the rest of the chapter. Spatiality can be seen as a metaphoric characterization of spheres of activity, opportunity structures and agendas, which have the effect of creating boundaries analogous to those of 'real' physical spaces. These spheres are socially-constructed and can impose limits upon, and provide opportunities for, participation, whether in politics, social spheres, economic life and so on. That is, the ways that space is *imagined* have a crucial impact on the ways that the activities of individuals and organizations are understood and interpreted. This is particularly important in the case of analysis of international affairs, as the deep entrenchment of a state-spatial imaging of politics tends to frame the ways all other actors are positioned.

This chapter analyses how spatial ontologies have been constructed in IR and examines how these affect analysis of international politics. It also examines how and why the spatial assumptions which inform the vocabulary of IR limit its effectiveness in describing politics at inter-state level, and between state and non-state actors. Later chapters analyse the use of the Internet by transnational NGOs and other activists to provide examples of how the spatial theories outlined here can be applied. The use of spatial theories invokes less embedded – that is, more relational – spatial perspectives, highlighting the inadequacy of current perceptions of space in IR for interpreting change in international political practices.

Having examined some of the most significant works on spatial theories, the chapter extracts key features from the work of Henri Lefebvre and Edward Soja by identifying three headings that can supply an alternative approach to political analysis. These headings – spatial practice, representations of space and spaces of representation – are addressed in detail and their relevance to analysis of international politics is highlighted. These headings will provide the interpretative framework for analysis of the use of the Internet as a tool for political activism undertaken in later chapters.

IR and spatiality

Perhaps of all the social sciences, IR has the most potent, and the least examined, conceptualizations of space. Walker, who has been discussing the spatial constraints of IR since the early 1990s, has argued that modern theories of IR depend upon a discourse 'that systematically reifies a historically specific spatial ontology' (1993: 5). His work is referred to frequently in the coming pages because, although his ideas on spatiality have been around for some time, he was among the first to discuss the spatialization of IR and many of the issues he has raised remain relevant to the study of political space in the discipline. Despite many changes in the international system in the past decade, IR has not yet established a clear sense of how to deal with the multi-dimensionality of contemporary political practices and it is in critique of this shortcoming that Walker's work is most effective. Doreen Massey's work – originating in the discipline of geography but having a much broader application – is also used in this chapter, as she has been the key proponent of viewing relationality as central to understanding complex situations and circumstances.

Walker's theme of the reification of state-spatial interpretations of politics has been pursued more recently by many other scholars in IR. Agnew, for example, argues that 'political power is overwhelmingly associated with the quintessential modern state: it is envisioned as pooled up in equivalent units of territorial sovereignty ... that exercise power through their territories and vie with one another to acquire more power beyond their current boundaries' (1999: 499). The discourse of IR continues to re-affirm the spatial logic of territoriality and assumptions of territorial primacy prevail, despite the many challenges posed to this perspective. Despite the nuances of analysis of international politics today, conceptions of political legitimacy – of 'real' politics – start with states and work down from there. States, as the 'possessors' of territory, continue to be seen as the defining political unit. Whether the state is the most important or powerful actor is not the issue here. What is significant is the way the positioning of one actor as dominant establishes the categorization and perceived relevance of others.

Research and analysis in the field of international politics have consistently, albeit generally implicitly, assumed space to be two-dimensional, pre-supposing fixed and visible sites of politics which can be mapped accordingly. 'The state', as the embodiment of power in IR, is probably the most obvious and least sophisticated example of this. In recent years, scholars in the social sciences have been arguing for a move beyond these simplified, two-dimensional interpretations of space. Gillian Rose argued that space should be seen to be 'multi-dimensional, shifting and contingent' and suggested that 'spaces that would be mutually exclusive if charted on a two-dimensional map – centre and margin, inside and outside – are occupied simultaneously' (1993: 140). Massey made a similar point when emphasizing social constructions of space:

> Such a way of conceptualising the spatial ... inherently implies the existence in the lived world of a simultaneous multiplicity of spaces: cross-cutting, intersecting, aligning with one another, or existing in relations of paradox or antagonism.
>
> (1994: 3)

This type of spatial understanding, the idea that space may be interpreted in different ways, and moreover may have different meanings in different circumstances for different participants, has profound implications for the study of international politics. At the heart of these ideas about space is the notion that relations *between* actors are as significant as the structures within which they operate. At the same time, of course, these structures are created, maintained and altered by relationships between actors. In this sense, structure and agency – concepts that have been the subject of much debate in IR – are indivisible.

States are not pockets of territory but are created by a range of relations between peoples and places. Massey makes this point most clearly:

> Usually, perhaps, we think of 'countries' (for example) in relation to space-time, as areas on a flat map. Yet think of Hungary, or Montenegro, or the USA. They are not areas on maps. They are socially-constructed and labelled envelopes of space-time, which once did not exist (there was no such bounding and labelling), ... , which have always existed in *relation* to elsewhere ... and which maybe one day will cease to exist. The nation-state (like any society or culture) is a *spatio-temporal* event.
>
> (1999: 42, emphasis in original)

Although the range of scholarly endeavour in IR is wide and diffuse, the hegemony of the state in its discourse continues to inform analysis at all levels of research. The reification of territory as the legitimate centre of politics has its roots in state practice, of course. As Murphy has noted:

> The spatial organization of society in west-central Europe after the Peace of Westphalia fostered a world view in which discrete, quasi-independent territorial units were seen as the principal building blocks for social and political life.
>
> (1996: 82)

Murphy also points out, however, that the dominant theories of IR which treat the world's states as taken-for-granted analytical units provide an inadequate framework for interpretation of the complexities of contemporary politics (ibid.: 103). For those who conduct research into issues once invisible to IR, such as social movements or sex tourism, such claims of state centrism may seem invalid today. Deibert's view on this matter is, though, fairly incisive: 'For all the talk of the "end of Westphalia" in practice, the paradigm does have deeply entrenched supports and not an insignificant coterie of fashionable reaction in the IR field' (2001: 3).

In response to the apparent shortcomings of the state-centric discourse (see Linklater 1998; Murphy 1996; Walker 1993), approaches that explore non-state spaces of politics have gained currency in recent years, and critical reflections on the ways embedded spatial conceptions shape meanings and definitions in the discipline are evolving. Many of these analyses of non-state spaces have been undertaken by feminist theorists, seeking to explore how gender relations are structured both in practice and discursively (see Enloe 1989, 1993; Pettman 1996; Zalewsi and Enloe 1995).[3] Others have challenged the state centrism of IR by examining how power relations operate at multiple levels, suggesting that states and other actors are involved in mutually causative relations (see Linklater 1998; Rosenau 1997).

Agnew and Corbridge have claimed that the geographical division of the world into mutually exclusive territorial states has served to define the field of study in IR by providing clear demarcations of space that represent centres of power (1995: 78). Elsewhere, Agnew has used the work of Kenneth Waltz and Robert Keohane as examples of realist and liberal 'extremes' [his inverted commas], which both nonetheless use a pervasive state-spatial framework (1998: 52). Claims like these suggest that territorial conceptions of space in IR represent a signature in the discipline, shaping the terrain of analysis, and an analytical given, which assumes that diverse political practices can be analysed through a single, largely unacknowledged, spatial formulation.

Assuming that states have devised, created and maintained the spaces of politics is problematic in two other important respects. First, it situates the territorial state as essentially a fixed variable in political analysis, which implies that it is a critical component of analysis in all instances. Situating the state as a discursive constant confers upon it the role of hegemon in defining the roles and significance of other actors. Second, and as a consequence of the assumption of state primacy, political interactions and activities are understood primarily by how they affect, appear to affect or are affected by state practices. Activities that do not appear to influence states in some way have a fairly low profile in the study of international politics. This reification of the state has increasingly been highlighted as an ontological limitation in IR (see Linklater 1998; Agnew 1999) and the need to expand discursive parameters to allow non-state political practices to be interpreted as influential *in their own right* is apparent.

For many people, boundaries other than those identified in IR shape their conceptions of politics. Membership of a non-governmental organization, for example, or regional dependence on income generated by a multi-national corporation may map the social and political parameters of individual or collective existence more accurately than state-national structures do. That is, political activism depends on the ability to effect change, and movement actors will design their activities to seek influence over those who are most likely, in any given situation, to facilitate this.

This should be a key concern of analysts of international politics, particularly as the expansion of communications technologies and international trade means that there is now an unprecedented intensity to transnational interactions. Activities such as the use of the Internet by an individual political activist or a loose collective of movement actors cannot be adequately interpreted through the lens of the state structures or the cipher of international organizations. Nor, of course, can the activities of a multi-faceted, multinational corporation be understood simply by applying a super-structural analytical framework of 'global capital'. As the case studies in later chapters demonstrate, social movement actors see a multi-layering to global political, cultural and economic activities. Analysis of these complexities requires more flexible interpretative frameworks that can be adapted to reflect the circumstances of particular practices, processes and interactions.

To challenge the centrality of the state in spatial conceptions is not to deny the significance of territory or location, nor to dispute the importance of state practices in many aspects of global politics. However, it is evident that the ways space is represented in the discourse of IR do not adequately reflect contemporary political practices, either of non-state actors or of states themselves. The territorial imagination, though often inadvertently applied, is a spatialized imagination which imposes (problematic) conceptual boundaries.

Discussing the spatialization of politics is not based on the notion of ignoring or denying the power of states, armies and gross national product. Territory does matter, of course. Warring factions have always sought to seize territory and resources from opponents, and the mapping of states as geographical entities is important in maintaining control of borders, resources, people and so on. In addition, an important element of political identity relates to the creation of national identity through association with a particular territory (see McDowell and Sharp 1997; Yuval-Davis 1996). Territory remains an important element of interpretation in IR, but its primacy as the central pillar of IR's spatial conceptions is subject to challenge. In particular, its representational abstraction, the state, provides an inadequate context for analysis of other spaces of international affairs; inter alia, spaces of migration, of economic growth and decline, of communication, of access to or denial of political choice and so on.

Overwhelming attention has been paid to state governments at the expense of other political actors (Murphy 1996: 103) and it is in an attempt to produce a more realistic reflection of contemporary political practices that spatial theorists have challenged the state-centric bias.

There has been a general acknowledgement among scholars in IR in recent years that the range and scope of political activity extends far beyond the real and metaphoric confines of the territorial state. Impressions of space as multi-dimensional which have gained credence in social theory, however, require some translation to the political. Increased communications, in terms of both the growth of telecommunications infrastructures and of individual interactions, the transnationalization or globalization of some aspects of commercial activity, the expansion of the NGO sector and the development of some co-operative international political regimes, among other factors, suggest that it is no longer possible, if it ever were, to maintain an analytical distinction between social, economic and political spheres. While there are practices unique to each, the impact of global economic activity on national politics, or social movements on economic actors and so on cannot be ignored in the theories we use for analysis.

Walker notes that the state system constructed in early modern Europe has dominated both recent experience and collective memory (1995: 308). In this regard, spatial theorists in IR are challenging culturally embedded understandings of political space, as well as disciplinary assumptions. Thus:

> Modern accounts of the political are still framed spatially: here and there, inside and outside, First World and Third World. It is within that framing that modern conceptions of temporality, of progressive history and development, have found their political purchase. Without that framing, it is difficult to make sense of politics at all.
>
> (Walker 1993: 314)

This framing of politics reflects a geographical imagination which, Rose argues, assumes that space can always be known and mapped, that it is infinitely knowable and is devoid of impenetrable obscure areas (1993: 70). Hence, even in disciplines which are essentially 'non-geographic', such as politics, sociology and economics, a geographical understanding of space as a given has generally been implicitly assumed. Anything, or perhaps more importantly anyone, not conforming to the mainstream 'geography' of inclusion – including non-elites, women, sex workers, people of colour and political activists and so on and so on – have tended to be positioned as marginal to IR's core concerns.

The state-centric discourse has, of course, been widely criticized, if not entirely debunked, by scholars operating from a vast range of differing perspectives. On the one hand, postmodern, post-colonial, critical, gender theorists and others have offered insights into the exclusions and elisions of 'traditional' IR. As a result, we have seen an increase in the range of actors and practices included in the discipline's field of vision. At the same time, though, we have seen the discourse of globalization gather all of these, and many other, actors and practices within its ambit. While there is certainly evidence of globalizing phenomena, Massey makes an important point when she suggests that economic globalization (through which all other forms are largely filtered) 'comes to have almost the inevitability of a grand narrative' (1999: 34). This can be neatly related back to a point made earlier in this chapter, that the ways we imagine space have an important impact on the ways we understand it. Thus, for Massey: 'the material and the discursive interlock: the way we imagine globalization will affect the form that it takes' (ibid.: 35) In this sense, although the globalization thesis brings more actors and issues to IR, it retains the exclusionary character of the state-spatial discourse.

Post-positivist debates and interdisciplinary research have extended the range of IR and challenged this reductionist tendency in recent years. Smith identified critical theory, feminism, historical sociology and postmodernism as the central pillars of contemporary challenges to the Realist assumptions that underpin the paradigmatic structure of the discipline (1995). Despite the diverse nature and complexity of these literatures, he suggests that they have in common 'a rejection of the simplistic philosophy of science that underlines most positivist scholarship in international theory' (ibid.: 26). The positivist foundations of IR reflected in its spatial ontology, most notably through the promotion of the state as an independent unit operating in a system of comparable entities, objectify the spaces of politics and emphasize a division from social phenomena. Post-positivist approaches have frequently, though often implicitly, challenged the spatial ontologies of IR, by viewing the social as intrinsically linked to the political, and by denying the validity of the state as the defining site of political engagement. Power, too, has been argued to operate at multiple levels, with states and other actors seen to be involved in mutually causative relations (see Linklater 1998).

Thus a respatializing of the discourse of IR has been in progress for several years, although the language of spatial theory has not always been applied. Much contemporary theory in IR has served to erode the concept of the state as central actor, and in particular has challenged the notion of the state as the embodiment of political community (see Linklater 1998; Rodgers 1999). Given dynamic changes to the nature of international affairs as a field of study, and related adjustments to the ontological assumptions and epistemological approaches of IR, Walker's warning that 'we should not be surprised if we are forced to revise our understanding of the relationships between universality and particularity, Them and Us, or space and time' (1990: 23) now seems prescient.

Historical framings of space

In recent years, scholars from a range of disciplines have suggested that conceptions of space based on geographical determinants – that is, as contained and containable – are analytically limiting. Suggestions that space should be seen as multi-dimensional, variable, contingent and constructed by human behaviour are now fairly commonplace among social science theorists. Spatial arrangements as diverse as the global economy, perceptions of the human body, and the built environments of modern cities have become relatively familiar areas of research. Analysis of such arrangements often reveals how perceptions of space define epistemological parameters and consequently determine how key concepts such as power, agency and authority are understood.

Relating this literature to IR, it becomes evident that state-centric spatial ontologies limit the potential to analyse metaphoric spaces within the discipline. That is, the positioning of the state as the signifier of political legitimacy constructs ontological boundaries which influence perceptions of both what political activity is, and how it can be analysed. In essence, state-centric ontologies limit the ways in which political participation can be understood; the ontological framing of issues and actors serves to pre-determine their significance.

Framing conceptions of *political* space are more general, historically-embedded interpretations of space. The dominant spatial image for most people probably emanates from the dominant Western image of geographic space; that is, the spaces related to and determined by physical characteristics, such as landscape and terrain. This cartographic imagination perceives space to be mensurable and finite. Space in this conception is understood to be complete, pre-existing and potentially quantifiable, essentially mathematical (Lefebvre 1991: 1). Agnew has argued that 'turning time into space' (1999: 32) in this way is a fundamental characteristic of modern geopolitical thought (ibid.)

Soja describes how, in the late nineteenth century, the three major realms of socialist, idealist and empiricist thought came to view the placing of phenomena in temporal sequence as more revealing than putting them side by side in spatial configuration (1996: 168). Thus the established interpretative framework for human and social development placed time – associated with dynamic characteristics like evolution, modernization and change – in the foreground. Space became what Soja describes as an 'extra-social environment', or a stage upon which history takes place (see ibid.).

The norm, therefore, has been to view time as the dominant partner in the time-space relationship. In discursive practices, the standard, generally subconscious, approach, is to define a space (a territory, region, 'the international', and so on) and to observe 'history happen' upon or within it. Soja refers to this privileging of time over space as the 'alluring logic of historicism' (1989: 14), where 'an already made geography sets the stage, while the wilful making of history dictates the action and the storyline' (ibid.). In effect, time *does*, while space merely *is*.

For Agnew and Corbridge, 'space is regarded as an unchanging "essence" that constantly produces the same effects' (1995: xi). This taken-for-granted impression of space is increasingly subject to question and a conceptualization of socially-constructed spaces, which are understood to be multi-faceted and relational, has been developed. Socially-constructed spaces have multiple meanings and are interpreted differently by different actors. Consequently, it is not sufficient to imagine a particular space as a stage on which history may happen; political activity is neither linear nor constant, and the priorities and concerns of actors vary according to circumstance. Although many scholars are now highlighting the limitations of conventional interpretations of political space for investigating contemporary practices, developing spatial frameworks appropriate to analysis of the nuances of contemporary politics has, to date, proved problematic. Whether we take a state-centric model or a globalization thesis or civil society framework, the relationality – Massey's 'mixity' (1999: 34) – of actors, processes and practices is difficult to interpret.

In other work, Massey uses the example of a factory to illustrate the concept of relationality well. The location and physical construction of a factory embody a form of physical space. The factory, however, is a productive unit, which employs and grades people, operates within an economic system, participates in trade, is subject to legislation from domestic and international institutions, and so on. The relations between these various phenomena contribute to the construction of social, economic, cultural and political spaces which have only a limited relationship with the geographical location of the factory – the place where it is situated (see Massey 1995: Chapter 1). It is evident that we need to find ways to interpret these multi-way relations and understand the power constructions within them.

Space is not given but constructed, and is not pre-determined but relational and variable. For Massey:

> To say space is relational means both that it should not be conceptualised as some absolute (that is to say, pre-existing) dimension and also that it is actually constructed out of, is a product of, the relations between social phenomena.
>
> (ibid.: 1)

These perceptions, which identify space as dynamic and mutable, contradict the geographical imagination that implies space to be both static and finite. In assuming that spatial relations incorporate human activity as well as geographical considerations, space can be understood to be intrinsically connected to social relations, involved in multi-dimensional associations of both cause and effect.

As McDowell and Sharp note, 'physical and social boundaries reinforce each other and spatial relations act to socialise people into the acceptance of power relations – they reinforce power, privilege and oppression' (1997: 3). Social relations are not simply the product of interpersonal interaction, but are produced and reproduced across myriad levels of human activity. In respect of this, in applying conceptions of the social to images of space it is possible for Massey to argue that:

> The 'spatial' ... can be seen as constructed out of the multiplicity of social relations across all spatial scales, from the global reach of finance and telecommunications, through the geography of the tentacles of national political power, to the social relations within the town, the settlement and the workplace.
>
> (Massey 1994: 5)

The challenge of these conceptions of space to territorial interpretations obviously has important resonance for IR. Such conceptions acknowledge the significance of place but also highlight metaphoric and material boundaries that structure social relations.

The issue of place *is* important; the significant terrain for any given analysis *may* be the state. It may equally, though, be a region, a city, a nation, a diasporic connection and so on. Plotting analysis against a given spatial frame of reference will position actors and practices accordingly and will, as a result, place limitations on what we can expect to learn. Analysing political activity by using spatial theories, however, brings us to the issues from a different direction, allowing us to directly address relations and interactions between actors and practices. The implications of this multi-dimensional approach are significant for IR, as the spheres of activity which impinge upon the political – social, economic and cultural activity – need to find a natural home within the discipline (apologies for the spatial metaphor). At present, the fairly limited landscape of the political plotted in IR restricts its potential to pursue multi-dimensional interpretations of politics effectively.

Developments in spatial ontologies

Lefebvre published a wide-ranging critique of spatial assumptions in historical and social theories and introduced new conceptions of the relevance of space for social analysis (1991, 1996). Largely in response to this work, most academic disciplines have now been subject to some revision of their often hidden spatial assumptions, with many scholars arguing for more inclusive, interdisciplinary approaches to understandings of space. Geographers started it all, of course (see Massey 1994, 1995; Rose 1993). Sociologists followed (see Crang *et al.* 1999; Featherstone *et al.* 1995; Lash and Urry 1994; Smith and Katz 1993) and IR, IPE and political theorists began working with similar themes (see Agnew 1999; Agnew and Corbridge 1995; Murphy 1996; Niemman 2001; Rosow *et al.* 1994; Walker 1990, 1991, 1993; and Youngs 1996b). All have argued for the inclusion of social interpretations of space in academic discourse. One argument frequently put forward by these scholars is that although spatial metaphors are used frequently in everyday language, their impact on our ways of thinking is rarely acknowledged.

For Agnew, representations of space in everyday life are so familiar as to be largely unquestioned (1994: 87), and Soja suggests that we need to think differently about the meanings and significance of space and related concepts which comprise the inherent spatiality of human life: place, location, territory, environment, region and so on (1996: 1). Terms such as in/out, national/global and so on, while apparently innocuous, invoke perceptions of inclusion, exclusion and situation that delineate debate and discussion (see Walker 1993). For Agnew and Corbridge, although these terms are usually implicit rather than overtly contemplated, they are 'deeply symbolic of how we define what is right and wrong and whom we identify with and against' (1995: 79). Discursive representations of space 'define and limit ... conceptions of social and political discourse' (ibid.) Given the growth in migration and international trade, the use of telecommunications systems and links between the 'real' and 'virtual' worlds, it is evident that new ways of conceiving of space which permit analysis of these multiple constructions and interpretations, and which avoid the constraints of pre-defined roles are required.

Despite the general accord among scholars of spatiality about the need to incorporate space into academic discourse and social and political praxis, there has been little consensus on how this might best be achieved. Three reasons for the absence of a clear spatial methodology are evident. First, the interdisciplinary nature of spatial theorizing transcends and challenges the ontological assumptions of individual fields of study. Indeed Lefebvre suggested that spatiality, along with historicality and sociality, is too important to be confined within the narrow specializations of academia (cited in Soja 1996: 6). In this respect, spatial theorizing challenges the disciplinary distinctions upon which academic exercise is premised.

Second, the notion of socially-constructed space precludes the possibility of a common scheme of categorization. The phrases most frequently arising in spatial theory, which posit space as relational, as fluid and as contingent, negate the possibility of a single theoretical approach. Third, with particular reference to concepts of political space, this area of study is relatively new and there are few, if any, theoretical givens. Although work on spatiality in the broader social sciences is now relatively extensive, pinning down how to use spatial theories has proved elusive so far.

It is possible, though, to identify spatial theories that can provide a framework for analysis of political activity. The prevalent strands of spatial theory most pertinent to developing new approaches to political analysis are those which provide an interpretative framework for examining links across social and political spheres, an aspect of analysis on which IR is currently weak. It is this dimension of spatial theory – which emphasizes the impact of social practices on political activity – that is applied to the use of the Internet by political activists in later chapters. How these, the social and political dimensions of activism, are separated is, of course, a product of the broader ontological constructions of a discipline that creates an exclusionary discourse that imposes fairly rigid limits on both what politics is and what it can be.

A useful starting point for interpreting spatial ontologies is Lefebvre's suggestion that 'space is nothing but the inscription of time in the world, spaces are the realizations, inscriptions in the simultaneity of the external world of a series of times' (1996: 16). Lefebvre elucidated some key notions about space, arguing that the ways we perceive space are neither accidental nor incidental. One analysis of his work suggests that 'the spatialization of society and history are ideological; [it] belongs to the realm of conceived and not lived space' (see Lefebvre 1996: 48). That is, our conceptions of space define and situate agents and actions conceived to be of significance, underplaying or ignoring the relevance of others.

Space can be understood both as the ways the world is organized, and the ways in which these forms of organization are understood and interpreted. Using Lefebvre's ideas on inscriptions of time, it is possible to argue that the world *as it has been* is not necessarily the world *as it is now*. Agnew has suggested that a state-centred spatial interpretation of the world made perfect sense in the nineteenth century:

> trajectories of economic and social change [were] increasingly characterised in terms of the experiences of the bits of space delimited by the geographical boundaries of states. Businesses and trade unions, representative politics, and social life were increasingly organized on a state-by-state basis.
>
> (1999: 49)

He goes on to note, though, that we now:

> live in an epoch in which the declining military viability of even the largest states, growing global markets, expanding transnational capitalism, and modes of governance alternative to that of the territorial state ... have begun to undermine the possibility of seeing power as solely a spatial monopoly exercised by states.
>
> (ibid.: 50)

In this respect, the historical inscriptions upon which understanding is based are supplemented, reaffirmed, altered and sometimes erased over time, adjusting the foundations upon which understanding depends. Consequently, both the assumptions of what knowledge is, and how it can be interpreted, change over time. It is possible to see, therefore, why it is necessary for the discourse of IR to change to reflect the nature of contemporary political practices. The reification of the state or of the power of global capital or of grassroots political actors inscribes a bounded political landscape inadequate for analysis of the complexities of contemporary politics.

Lefebvre outlined a tripartite conceptualization of space: spatial practice; representations of space; and the spaces of representation, which offer an alternative framework for analysis (see ibid.; Soja 1989, 1996).[4] These three elements of spatial process are closely inter-related: though distinguishable from each other in form, the nature of each critically influences the others. Though Lefebvre's categories do not form an unassailable foundation for spatial analysis, they do provide a loose structure through which some of the more complex characteristics of contemporary politics can be interrogated.

Spatial practice relates to the ways in which societies are organized, both by the material environment, and through the social behaviours of people within them. Soja suggests that 'spatial practice, as the process of producing the material form of social spatiality, is ... presented as both medium and outcome of human activity' (ibid.: 66). Spatial practice encompasses the relations between people, their environment, their modes of interaction, and the nature of the work, leisure, social and political opportunities and so on available to them. These are, for Lefebvre, the *perceived* spaces of human existence. As a consequence, spatial practices differ from society to society, and to greater or lesser degrees from person to person.

Representations of space relate to conceptualized spaces which, for Lefebvre, constitute control over knowledge, signs and codes. The ways societies represent space are articulated in dominant discourses and theories, through the lexicons of academic disciplines, through accepted codes of social behaviour and so on. Representations of space effectively define our perceptions of ourselves and the world(s) we inhabit and are, for Lefebvre, 'the dominant space in any society' (cited Soja 1996: 67). For Soja they constitute 'a storehouse of epistemological power' (ibid.) For these reasons, representations of space are obviously an important tool of hegemony, authority and control and refer to the ontologies and epistemologies of academia, and to the structuring codes of social and political praxis. Representations of space define the accepted limits of social and political activity within societies, and are viewed by Lefebvre to be the *conceived* spaces of human existence.

Spaces of representation, on the other hand, equate most closely with concepts of agency and particularly with social practices of resistance, of struggle and of opposition to dominant values. The suggestion here is that spaces of representation are the *lived* spaces of human action, both distinct from the other two spaces and encompassing them (ibid.) In essence, individuals exist within and through spatial practice, and are constrained within representations of space. The social and political choices made in relation to these real and metaphoric demarcations constitute the spaces of representation of each individual. These lived spaces of representation function as 'the terrain for a generation of "counterspaces", spaces of resistance to the dominant order arising precisely from their subordinate, peripheral or marginalized position' (ibid.: 68). Although struggles against power and authority are highlighted within interpretations of this aspect of social life, in many senses all social and political action involves negotiating individual spaces of representation.

Soja has used Lefebvre's tripartite structure as the foundation for his more recently developed theoretical approach to analysis of space in contemporary existence. Arguing that 'the spatial dimension of our lives has never been of greater practical and political relevance than it is today' (ibid.: 1), Soja has produced a theoretical framework which both illuminates some of the key critiques of traditional spatial ontologies and extends Lefebvre's tripartite approach. In particular, he outlines how spatial theories can be used to challenge the dominance of the dualisms of social and political analysis discussed earlier in this chapter. He labels this approach as 'critical thirding' and proposes a theory where the original binary choice is subjected to a process of *restructuring* that draws selectively and strategically from the two opposing categories to open new alternatives (ibid.: 5). This approach challenges the historical bias in social and political analysis but does not attempt to deny the significance of the temporal dimensions of human existence.

Applying the idea of restructuring discursive parameters, Soja introduces the concepts of Firstspace, Secondspace and Thirdspace. Firstspace refers to the concrete materiality of spatial forms, on things that can be empirically mapped and measured. Secondspace relates to conceived ideas about space, to mental and cognitive representations of human spatiality. For Soja, these two spaces roughly coincide with Lefebvre's ideas on spatial practices and representations of space. Perhaps Soja's major contribution to debates on spatiality, though, is to illustrate how these categories reflect the binary logic of traditional discourses. Thus, Firstspace (effectively equivalent to spatial practices) represents the 'real' spaces of human existence and Secondspace the spaces 'imagined' in the dominant discourse.

With Thirdspace, Soja calls for 'the creation of another mode of thinking about space that draws upon the material and mental spaces of the traditional dualism but extends well beyond them in scope, substance and meaning' (ibid.: 11). Thirdspace acknowledges the influence of material circumstance and the structuring influence of dominant codes of representation and practice. It also, however, suggests that there are other ways of operating within and analysing the shapes and structures of societies, which may produce more revealing insights into the nature of contemporary life than dualistic interpretations can offer.

Another scholar, bell hooks, has also made a significant contribution to debates on the nature of spatial politics. The aspect of her work most relevant to the arguments of this book lies in her discussions of choosing the margin as a site of resistance (1984, 1991). As a black, female, feminist scholar, hooks argues that it is possible to reside in both the centre and the margin, and to have an insight into and awareness of both. hooks says of herself and others who lived in the community she grew up in: 'we looked both from the outside in and from the inside out. We focused our attention on the center as well as on the margin. We understood both' (1984: preface). Both hooks and Soja emphasize that this alternative space – Thirdspace or the margin – is a site of radical politics and resistance. It is perhaps this area that has most relevance to the development of spatial theories in IR. If, as later chapters explore, the use of the Internet by activists has some impact on the ways politics can be *understood*, then it may be assumed that the methods of resistance to dominant political structures may also be affected. While the material and conceptual framing of political practices may be relatively easy to assess, it is in combination with this third area – opportunities for resistance – that a more complete picture of the political practices of non-state actors may best be acquired.

The social and political activities of non-state and non-elite actors are often undertaken without specific reference to the dominant discourse, nor even necessarily to the material situation of individual actors. This is most easily illustrated by looking at the multiple relations of normative political practices. For example, membership of Amnesty International only rarely reflects the immediate geographical environment of a political activist, and equally rarely do the agendas of the organization correlate with those of state agencies. Few members of Amnesty International are actually political prisoners and few governments directly equate Amnesty's aims with their own. This situation is paralleled at all levels and in all kinds of politics, producing a situation where any given issue is interpreted and acted upon in a wide range of different ways. To address these issues adequately we need, as Massey puts it, to 'hold open the possibility of the existence of alternative narratives' (1999: 43).

In this sense, all non-state actors are situated at the margins of international politics as perceived in IR, though the activities they engage in reflect upon both their own spaces of politics and upon the dominant structures of political interpretation. Consequently, many non-state actors are acting from the margins of international political theory and practice, but are aware of and informed about activities at the centre in the manner described by hooks. Moreover, communications technologies play an increasingly important role in allowing non-state actors to occupy these different spaces simultaneously.

The three literatures considered above are drawn together here and in later chapters to allow the development of a clear system for spatial interpretation. Soja's ideas on the necessity of viewing spatial theorizing as a restructuring rather than a wholesale rejection of traditional modes of analysis underpin the methodological approach of the book. hooks' claims on marginality are also taken into account, and the notion that the political activities of non-state actors represent a method of engagement inadequately understood by the dominant discourse of IR also inform the ways the analysis of spatiality is undertaken here.

It is the tripartite conceptualization outlined by Lefebvre that is used as the basis for interpretation of the use of the Internet by activists in later chapters, however. The notions of spatial practices, representations of space and of spaces of representation offer an alternative to the dominant discourse in IR by providing analytical criteria which can reflect changes in the political practices of non-state actors more effectively than existing approaches. Case studies in later chapters examine how a range of different organizations and actors use the Internet to promote their respective causes. The tripartite model is then used to assess how each of the different dimensions of space identified is affected by the presence or absence of networked communications technologies.

Conclusion

The dominant state-centric discourse has had a critical impact on the structuring of space in IR. This ontological foundation is pervasive in interpretation and analysis of politics in the discipline and has dominated analysis for decades. For some, of course, it still does. However, new actors, practices and ways of conceptualizing IR have been evolving and the field of study is now wide and diverse. One problem prevails, though, and this is the tendency to map analyses against pre-given templates, whether these be state centrism, globalization or some other 'picture' of how the world is or should be. As a consequence, the spatial limits of politics remain largely intact in the discipline.

The rise in transnational activism, the growth in number of supranational organizations, increased travel and migration, the increase in scale of global business operation and so on contribute to the complicating of the international political arena. Many books have been written about this, of course, but what they often ignore is the difficulties of addressing the relationships between these various facets adequately. Spatial theories which provide a mechanism for analysing change in various different aspects of political practice may offer a way of overcoming this epistemological impasse. For example, spatial theories provide a framework for analysing what happens to the ways an organization interacts with other political entities when the Internet is introduced, how it represents itself, what political opportunities the use of this technology opens up and so on. The same framework can be applied to other actors at the same time, helping us to build those complex, multi-faceted images of politics that IR has been struggling with in recent years.

2 Feminists and space

Introduction

Like spatial theorists, feminists have been arguing for some time that certain images and interpretative frameworks have dominated our understanding of the political arena. Indeed, feminists have been posing these challenges to IR for considerably longer than any other group of scholars. Much of this work has tended to be positioned at the margins of the discipline[1] but it has made important contributions to debates on the ways politics are constructed in IR. This chapter examines some of the issues raised by feminist theorists about the ways international politics are spatialized in both theory and practice. More relational, inclusive modes of interpretation have been promoted by feminists and the key claims behind these ideas are explored. Feminist scholarship on this subject is not posited here as oppositional to other forms of spatial analysis (indeed, as you read further it will become clear how inappropriate such a dichotomization would be). The feminist work referred to here both contributes to and compliments other forms of spatial analysis, though one would sometimes have to conclude that many other spatial analysts haven't noticed this yet.

Feminist theorists have done some of the most important work in 'respatializing' our conceptualizations of the social and political spheres. By challenging the legitimacy of accepted discursive hierarchies, feminists have forced scholars to question assumptions of legitimacy and power embedded in political institutions, and in academic analysis of them. This is not to suggest that all feminist analysis is 'right' – feminist work demonstrates the same strengths and weaknesses as any other area of research. Nor does this suggest that feminist respatializing represents the hitherto hidden truth of political relations. The suggestion is, rather, that feminist work on spatiality has asked some of the most interesting and enlightening questions on how the world of politics is imagined and constructed. Feminists have pushed the issue of exclusionary political praxis onto research agendas by highlighting the ways certain groups of actors and some forms of political engagement are ignored in mainstream analysis. In doing this, they have pushed the boundaries of political analysis by promoting more inclusive conceptualizations of politics. This, in conjunction with the 'post moves', as Peterson has called them (1992b: 19), of postmodernism, post-positivism and post-structuralism has had the effect of expanding the field of analysis by extending the range of actors and practices seen to be affected by, and influential in, the political realm. Moreover, though many feminists often feel that their work goes unrecognized, their role in extending the scope of IR has gained recognition in the mainstream of the discipline, although it has to be said that there is often a sense of tokenism in acknowledgement of its merits.

As a foundation for analysis of international politics, the dominant discourse of IR displays some significant limitations. The most obvious of these – state-spatial, territorial and geographical assumptions about legitimate political activity – was examined in Chapter 1. Feminist scholarship reveals three further, perhaps equally restrictive, shortcomings in mainstream analysis of international politics. First (though there is no real hierarchy here), 'the state' in IR is criticized for being an abstract concept, embodying an entity where interpersonal power relations are elided. Gender relations in particular are rendered invisible in this image of the international state, though other forms of individual and institutional interactions are obscured too.

Second, political power and legitimacy is presumed to reside within 'official' public spaces. This effectively delegitimizes 'non-official' politics by creating a sense that activities outside of the corridors of power do not constitute 'real' politics.[2] In separating official spaces from social and cultural realms, analysis of international politics obscures the impact of gender relations and creates an impression of gender-neutral praxis. As Peterson points out, though, 'gender is a pervasive feature of social life: ungendered identities, epistemologies, states and markets are not to be found' (1996b: 22). Social and political realms are neither separable – analytically or otherwise – nor gender-neutral. NGOs and other non-state actors are also affected by this separation of social and political realms, as the normative concerns of many fall outside of the 'official' label. How this affects these organizations and other non-state actors will be considered in later chapters.

Third, there is inherent in IR, as in other social science disciplines, a 'dichotomous dualism' (Massey 1994: 256) that obscures the many nuances of political interactions. Noted in Chapter 1, through the notions of inclusion/exclusion, order/anarchy, state/non-state, these dichotomies also contribute to a gendering of IR by promoting 'man' and masculine characteristics as representative of political legitimacy (see Enloe 1989; Yuval-Davis 1997). Feminist scholarship 'is centrally concerned with breaking down or deconstructing this hierachical dualism of masculinity/ femininity, which constitutes an ordering system that determines what is deemed to be of value and what is not' (Marchand and Runyan 2000b: 13). This dualism sees politics as 'rational', 'objective' and 'logical' (see Peterson and Runyan 1999: 40), characteristics associated with the Enlightenment male. As a consequence of these gender-blind assumptions, analysis of political practices, and understandings of concepts such as agency and power, are filtered not only through a state-centric interpretative framework but also through a gendered conceptualization of politics. It is the impact that these gendered discursive limitations place on the ability to interpret political activity within IR effectively that are explored in this chapter.

Of course, feminist scholarship is a diverse and complex area. This brief summary of feminist work on spatiality makes no claims to distil this vast body of work into a neat bundle of ideas. Instead, it draws out some of the key feminist themes that have extended notions of the political, by raising the issue of how the field of international politics is interpreted. Zalewski's suggestion that there is not a feminist view, only the interpretations of feminists (1995: 340) is useful in this context. Feminist scholarship is not a homogeneous body; claims regarding 'feminist thinking' and 'feminist scholarship' made here identify trends rather than doctrines.

Concern about the dynamics of gender/power relations led feminist theorists towards analysis of the ways notions of legitimacy can be imbued within structures, practices and interpretations of politics. In addressing the ways the 'meanings' of politics are conveyed, feminists have identified some of the most powerful but often unquestioned constructions of political discourse. This is important in the context of analysis of transnational political activity, as it is becoming increasingly necessary to consider precisely who political actors are assumed to be and how their activities can be understood. Feminist work on identifying the role of the discourse of political analysis in legitimizing some activities and de-legitimizing or disregarding others has made an important contribution to debates in this area. Feminist respatializations of IR demonstrate how constrictive its traditional discourse has been and how it is possible to move beyond this.

Gendered spaces in IR

IR is not simply constituted by the transfer of discussion from the domestic to the international arena. In the translation of political discourse from the micro to the macro level, the state essentially becomes a self-contained unit, which forms the fundamental and hegemonic unit of analysis in IR. Though we have been 'warned not to exaggerate either its unity or coherence' (Peterson 1992a: 3), it remains clear that the bodies that comprise the population of IR are not people but states (see Linklater 1998 for discussion of the creation of the 'community' of states). Conceptions of interdependence and relative power are consequently located in and through state practices, rather than in and through the lives of people, and societal constructions are subsumed within dominant-actor suppositions about where power resides. These 'top-down' interpretations of politics obscure reflexive, interactive relationships between states, organizations and individuals, and substantiate the claim of feminist scholars that more relational forms of analysis are also required. In essence, the framing of international politics as a 'top-down' enterprise provides only one, fairly limited, approach to analysis of complex political practices.

Peterson has called attention to 'the Janus-faced nature of states' (1992a: 3) in IR, where there is a separation of their internal dynamics and their external relations (ibid.) This has the effect of depoliticizing the state 'as a political space within which power struggles take place' (Youngs 2000: 46). That is, the state is envisioned to a large extent as removed from governmental processes and from interactions between citizens/subjects and political institutions. Discussion of, for example, human rights violations or drugs trafficking in IR often functions at a level of abstraction that inadequately reflects the real experiences of either governments or populations, creating a barrier separating individuals as political *actors* from political *processes* in the discipline.

It has taken feminists some time to gain a handle on how to bring *people* in to analysis of international politics (see Enloe 1989, 2000), as the assumption of gender neutrality and the level of abstraction implied in IR's conceptualization of political relationships has made it difficult to demonstrate the ways gender – and other aspects of interpersonal and structural – politics are played out. There has been, to a certain extent, a two-pronged attack on the perceived 'common sense' (see Youngs 2000: 46) of this abstract approach. Both dimensions contrast with the dichotomous approach to political analysis by promoting relationality in political discourse, creating links between issues and actors, rather than installing exclusions.

One key approach has been to place domestic politics and economic relations in international contexts, bringing the private realm into international political discourse. The other is to contextualize international politics at local and regional levels, effectively identifying how public policies can affect private practices across national borders. The primacy given to the state as political space provides a metaphoric demarcation in the discourse of IR, and situates concepts of affiliation as an essentially unrelated dimension of political engagement. For Stavropoulos:

> International relations has made its own the relations between states and has been principally pre-occupied with the systemic or the structural. Questions related to the personal or to cultural particularity, or the relations within and between societies as distinct from states, have fallen outside of its purview.
>
> (1997: 197)

This, of course, renders analysis of multi-faceted relations between states and non-state actors difficult, as terms such as agency and co-operation are constrained by state-centric interpretations.

States as individual entities are also, of course, considered a legitimate target for feminist critique in IR, but the key focus of criticism is the discourse which fails to adequately recognize other actors and institutions. The disembodiment of government, through its conversion to the abstract entity of the state, creates problems in giving tangible form to gender relations. This is because the causal role of gender constructions is frequently obscured by the masculinist assumptions underpinning the language of diplomacy, statecraft, nationalism and so on which are central to analysis of international politics. The hegemonic discourse of IR reifies and frequently justifies the state as the primary site of political authority and it effectively becomes, in this approach, a de-gendered space.

It was initially difficult to demonstrate the relevance of gender to the conduct and discursive constructions of international politics. For example, in feminist analyses of *domestic* politics, issues such as authority and agency can be addressed from a perspective which views the state as pro-active or complicit in promoting, denying or disregarding the rights, responsibilities and needs of women. The state often functions, in this vision, as an embodiment of patriarchal values, and consequently as a legitimate target for feminist critique. This type of analysis can readily identify how and why a particular governmental decision affects the lives of individuals, as the material practices of governments have both a tangible presence and visible effects. It has become easier over time for feminists to demonstrate how the actions of international actors (including powerful states, MNCs and supranational institutions) can have an impact on gender relations at local, international and regional levels.

Feminist theorists have deconstructed this notion and demonstrated how internal power relationships affect and are influenced by factors across and beyond state borders. Feminists have insisted that the state should be seen 'not as a "thing" but as an ongoing process' (Peterson 1992a: 4). Cynthia Enloe has become the mistress, as it were, of this reframing of state-societal relations through her analysis of gendered, militarized international relations, by demonstrating the multi-layering of effects of military decisions and actions (1988, 1989, 2000). Given its focus on military practices, Enloe's work is perhaps among the most obviously 'IR' of feminist research in this area (though the male academe is unlikely to concur on this: indeed, she may disagree herself).

Many others have taken a similar approach by insisting on seeing political relations as embedded in broader social and cultural landscapes and by refusing to adopt an abstract and decontextualized framework of interpretation. As Marchand and Runyan put it, 'feminist scholars have repeatedly shown that gender operates at various levels at which it intersects with class, ethnicity, race, nationality and sexuality' (2000b: 8). This insight has allowed feminists to demonstrate how the language of 'classical' IR obscures gender relations and thus how diplomacy, statecraft, nationalism and so on can and should be approached in different ways.

It also means that forms of political agency that the classical cannon ignores have been introduced onto the landscape of the discipline. The introduction of these new characters and practices has important implications for the ways the discipline can deal with the kinds of complex transnational, individual and collective political action which are considered in later chapters.

Gendered political realms

In relation to claims about the separation of political and social spaces, and of structure and agency, feminists have also argued that there is a gendered division between the 'public' political arena and 'private' domestic spaces. This division situates politics as a field related to the public sphere, rendering the domestic arena an a- or non-political space. As a consequence, women, who often spend more of their time in this 'private' space than men, can be conceived of as somehow non-political actors unless they are active in the public arena. This form of public/private separation is based on the Aristotelian conceptualization of public sphere politics, a profoundly masculine vision of political space. That women are under-represented in public-sphere politics is a truism in almost all societies. As Connell has noted:

> Public politics on almost any definition is men's politics. Men predominate in cabinets, general staffs, the senior civil service, political parties and pressure groups as well as in the executive levels of corporations.
>
> (1996: 204)

This is problematic for most feminists and many have sought to influence policy to redress the gender balance in political institutions.[3] At the same time as they have sought to alter political structures and practices, though, feminists have endeavoured to influence the discourses of politics; to challenge what politics are and can be conceived to consist of. In this, they have been pushing the boundaries of political discourse by arguing that the field cannot be divided into public and private spaces, as these spheres are inextricably related.

Because of the public/private division, the areas of politics in which many women are engaged are often under-explored in IR. For example, though few women are represented in the higher echelons of 'official' political institutions,[4] many are involved in forms of activism (human rights, community, environmental and so on) which the public/private division does not adequately acknowledge. Thus there are the 'real' politics of diplomacy, inter-institutional interactions and so on, and there are the social movement politics that women are often engaged in. Feminists have argued that all of these activities are legitimately 'political' and that the significance of political actions cannot be assessed purely by their impact on states and governments.

Even where alternative political practices have been acknowledged, though, the gendering of practices within them and the theories used in their interpretation has been noted:

> Feminist scholars ... have been disheartened by the binary opposi-
> tions in social movements theory – for example, the distinction
> between expressive and instrumental politics, identity and strategic
> activism, cultural and structural change, and rational and emotional
> action.
>
> (Taylor and Whittier 1999: 5)

In the newer theories that are having an impact on analysis of international politics, a lack of gender awareness – not all-pervasive but certainly influential on the development of the discourse – is evident. This is largely because the gendering of the political realm operates not only at the level of practice but also, and more insidiously, at the level of discourse. The ways politics are represented to us, and the analytical frameworks we apply to the field, position us as actors – in the manner described in Lefebvre's theories – and, for feminists, it is as important to question exclusionary discourse as it is to challenge discriminatory practices.

The public/private division means that many of the social and political activities that affect women have not been conceived within the dominant discourse of IR to belong within the political realm. Awareness of the global sex trade, militarization and masculinization, rape as a war crime and so on, have come to affect how politics is interpreted, largely because feminists have shown how the lives of individual women and men can be affected by institutional practices, and have identified how the public sphere is linked to the private. In this sense, feminist scholars have sought to respatialize analysis of international politics by challenging assumptions about authority, agency and political legitimacy – indeed the very constitution of politics – that underpin the discipline of IR.

The privileging of the public over the private presents two dimensions of gendered discourse. Because women are not prominent as institutional actors in large numbers, their political relevance is not always evident within the masculinist discourse of IR; as a consequence, the forms of action they do engage in are frequently obscured by the emphasis placed on recorded, public activities in political theorizing. Gendered power relations are hidden because much 'female' activity is not considered to be politically significant and, as a consequence, is unrecorded and becomes ephemeral. 'Private' spaces were historically contrived within patriarchal constructs as the domain of women for the convenience of a masculinist political structure, and have been manipulated over time according to governmental priorities. Policies to persuade women to enter the workforce in times of economic need and to force them out again when they are no longer required are common. As Peterson and Runyan note:

> Depending on what the situation calls for, gender ideology may promote women as physically strong and capable of backbreaking work (e.g., slave women, frontier women), as competent to do men's work (e.g., Rosie the Riveter in World War II), as dexterous and immune to boredom (e.g., electronics assembly industries), or as full-time housewives and devoted mothers (e.g., post-war demands that women vacate jobs in favor of returning soldiers and repopulate the nation.
>
> (1999: 42)

This type of practice continues today (see Rodgers 1999 and 2001b on similar practices in Bosnia, Serbia and Kosovo).

As well as manipulating women for political and economic purposes, such policies obscure the fact that for many women the domestic space is a workplace. In many instances the domestic environment is also one focus of women's social and political interests, whether around their personal relationships or in networking beyond the home. In this respect, the circumscription of the private realm, and the characterization of non-public sites as devoid of political content, is manifestly inappropriate. Domestic power relations, questions of economics, divisions of labour and so on, are not contained within the artificial distinction of private and public spaces, and there is an overspill from each and all of these issues which serves to shape and is shaped by gender relations across multiple spaces. Feminist scholars have done much to demonstrate how these spatial divisions limit research by failing to recognize the significance of relationships between and across different areas of social and political life.

In addition, the apparent ephemerality – and therefore limited significance – of the political actions of women in many circumstances is compounded in IR because the public spaces of politics the discipline emphasizes are equated with historicity. 'Political' events in the discipline are those that are visible and recorded, and are thus perceived to be essentially meaningful. Private spaces, by contrast, are devoid of such consequence. The marginalization of the private realm, and particularly the low profile of women on the landscape of political theory, has been well-documented. Insights by scholars like Elshtain (1987, 1991), Peterson and Runyan (1999), Rinehart (1992), and Sunstein (1990) have now entered the body of literature which challenges this public/private dichotomy and serves to demonstrate the complexity of contemporary political relations.

The marginalization of women is increased, in discursive terms, by the seemingly transitory nature of private-space existence. Public political activities, which are recorded and re-visited for historical analysis, have a temporal resonance which private spaces lack. In this sense, private spaces are doubly de-legitimized, first by being considered a-political and then by a conceptualization of their apparently inherent ephemerality. That is, the discourse of IR underplays gender issues by perceiving private spaces to lack a political dimension. It also implicitly assumes that activities that have not traditionally been recorded by the institutions of the state (in which we could include today, in many instances, the mass media) should not be conceived of as 'political' in any meaningful sense.

Feminists respatializing IR

At the heart of much feminist critique is Massey's 'dichotomous dualism' (1994: 256), noted earlier in this chapter. The production of these oppositional categories, which validate one subject position by negating another, is still characteristic of much scholarship in IR. For example, the discipline's approach to ideology and the choice offered between realist and idealist perspectives illustrates the dichotomous approach much criticized by feminists. For Elshtain, this attitude pits idealists (those who are not realists) against realists (those who are) (1995a: 265), and allows little room for seeing politics as a more complex picture. The categories of realist and idealist, which persist in the teaching of IR today, are discrete and mutually exclusive, with the subject position of one defined by its opposition to the other. The lexicon of IR is riddled with examples of this dualistic approach. It is enshrined in the order/anarchy conceptions of the international system, in structure/agency debates and in notions of inside/outside associated with sovereign statehood (see Walker 1993). Non-feminists have also noted the problems associated with the dualistic discourse, (see Agnew 1998, 1999; Linklater 1998; Smith *et al.* 1997) but most give little or no credit to the contribution of feminists to this debate. Dualism remains a discursive undercurrent in IR, as it is still difficult to define actors as political subjects in their own right, rather than through their relationship with (or opposition to) something else.

Feminists have adopted a variety of approaches in their attempts to bring other forms of political practice into the discipline and to demonstrate the relationships between different actors, spheres and issues; in effect, to respatialize IR. There has been some work concentrated on case studies, for example, adapting one of the characteristic approaches of social science research in IR to feminist priorities (see, for example: Alternatives 1993; Rodgers 1998a). These have focused on examination of how states and international institutions treat women in particular circumstances, or seek to include women in analyses where they have traditionally been absent or invisible, for example through analysis of gendered patterns of labour or migration. This method illustrates how women are hidden in the conventional discourse of IR, simply by showing what research that does include them looks like. There have also been some reinterpretations of conventional histories by feminist scholars, examining masculinist bias in the historiography of IR, particularly in texts seen as classical in IR (see

Elshtain 1987, 1991; Tickner 1992). This work, highlighting the gender bias in IR literature, broadens the base of the discipline and gives scholars wishing to develop research in this area some foundational structure to develop upon.

This is important because, as Rose noted, 'dominant subject position(s) see difference only in relation to themselves' (1993: 137). Consequently challenges to the authority of dominant subject positions are rendered incoherent if they seek to apply a non-dualistic approach and it has been necessary for feminists to challenge the authority of the dominant discourse by attempting to broaden the horizons of IR. The hidden power of the dominant discourse can be seen through a simple example: a woman who participates in a demonstration against World Bank policies is not male, is non-state and is anti-capitalist to the dualistic mind. None of these characteristics bears *positive* connotations and none of the subtleties underlying her reasons for involvement in campaigning are identifiable from the labels applied to her.

Feminist theorists, as noted, have generally rejected dualism and proposed relational and inclusive, rather than oppositional and exclusive. Challenging the social/political, public/private divisions and other examples of this 'either/or' vision of politics presents a problem, however. In failing to provide a dualistic alternative to the dominant model feminist theorizing provides no tangible response to the discipline's existing terms, *within* those terms. To some extent, the call for context and the rejection of dualism inherent in feminist theory paradoxically consolidates the discipline's usual approach. In not accepting the 'either/or' perspective but seeking to understand also 'how, why and in relation to what?' feminist thinking may inevitably position itself outside of discursive norms.

For feminist theorists, the conceptualization of space as physical and static is a reflection and continuation of masculine subjectivities that depend upon presence and absence to convey meaning and which depend upon a superior versus inferior ranking (Walker 1993; Youngs 1996b). So, though time, space and matter are seen as inextricably connected in the history and philosophy of Western science (Soja 1989: 79), time is consistently perceived as dominant. Or, as Massey suggests: 'Over and over again, time is defined by such things as change, movement, history, dynamism; while space, rather lamely by comparison, is simply the absence of these things' (Massey 1994: 256). Grosz argues that reconceptualization of gender relations entails reconceptualization of representations of space and time because 'the ways in which space has been historically conceived have always functioned to contain women or to obliterate them' (1995: 55). The time/space dichotomy in IR matters because the *only* space given any real credence in its discourse is the state and, as we have seen, this space hides the impact of gender dynamics.

Feminist scholars in this field see the positioning of time as dominant over space as something that contributes to the gendering of political discourse. The dynamic realm of public office – time, historic, recorded – associated with the male-dominated sphere of politics hides the political actions of many women and many forms of non-elite political practices. Massey suggests that 'this pervasive and influential view of the relationship between space and time sees them as dichotomous and as dichotomous in a particular way. It is a formulation in which time is the privileged signifier in a distinction of the type A/not-A' (1994: 6). The temporal, associated with progress and development and the masculine field of public politics, dominates political analysis. The spatial realm – or, rather, a particular non-state, non-official, private spatial realm – is consequently marginalized and analysis of its significance has, until recently, been very limited.

Another point of note is that the creation of conceptual boundaries imbues some issues with legitimacy at the expense of others. Massey notes that 'all attempts to institute horizons, to establish boundaries, to secure identity of places, ... can ... be seen as *attempts to stabilise the meanings of particular envelopes of space-time*' (1994: 5, emphasis in original). The privileging of time over space constitutes a form of control over the perceived legitimacy of some actors and issues. This again relates closely to Lefebvre's concept of representations of space – how the world is represented to us influences our opportunities for action within it. Moreover, these boundaries are created by dualisms – in/out, us/them, etc. The particular dominant space-time envelopes of the past few decades (certainly for the latter half of the twentieth century) have been articulated in IR through the neo/Realist hegemony, which established the dominance of the state as the signifier of political validity, underplaying the role of non-state actors. This relates the debate on gendered assumptions about space back to Lefebvre and his point, noted in Chapter 1, regarding space and particular 'inscriptions of time' (Lefebvre 1996: 16) – the world as it is is not necessarily the world as it has been, but interpretative frameworks do not always shift quickly enough to reflect this. Feminist scholars and other spatial theorists have in common their criticism of restrictive discourses that spatialize social and political activity in particular ways that limit understanding of complex interactions.

Feminist contributions

All of the issues raised by feminists about the nature of spatialization in the dominant discourse of IR inevitably lead to questions about the impact of these challenges on discourse and practice. What influence has feminist thinking had on the ways politics is understood in IR? Is it all about women or does it have broader applications? How does it relate to the wider questions addressed in this book regarding transnational activism and the use of the Internet?

In challenging key assumptions of the discipline, feminists have sought to extend some non-traditional, de-masculinized ways of interpreting international politics and to move beyond the limitations of more traditional assumptions about international politics. Feminists focus not only upon women as a category, but also upon gendered constructions of IR theory and practice. This challenges IR on many levels, by endowing women not only with international political agency, despite their often non-traditional roles, but also by acknowledging a wide range of other actors and practices too. The growth in feminist scholarship in this area has coincided with the spread of transnational activism – not just of women's movements but also of non-state politics more generally – and the relationality espoused in this work has much to offer the interpretation of non-elite political practices.

Despite these moves to create alternative interpretations of international politics, the ontologies of IR reflect and sustain an artificial impression of political practices. Youngs has argued that only rudimentary attention has been paid to questions of spatiality in IR and that there is a 'danger of a *gender-neutral sense of spatiality* persisting even in new critical work in this area' (1996b: 2, emphasis in original), a challenge that could still be levelled today. Given the danger of a pervasive assumption of gender-neutrality, it is necessary to analyse gender and space in IR as intrinsically linked, rather than to create or sustain a synthetic division between them.

Feminist work generally *starts* with women or gender but its applications are evidently much wider than this. Analysis of the social construction of gender relations compels us to think about the ways in which all social relations are constructed (see Whitworth 1994/1997: 56). In linking the social with the political, feminist approaches can offer a greater insight into the nature of contemporary international affairs, where many of the key players, such as NGOs and MNCs, are evidently socio-political, rather than exclusively political actors, in the traditional IR sense. For example, taking out a membership subscription to Greenpeace, deciding not to purchase genetically modified foods or signing an e-petition against a government policy are all clearly political acts which may have an impact on other political actors and their agendas. Within traditional state-centred notions of politics, however, these acts would be barely visible. Feminist scholarship pushes these and other issues onto the field of IR by suggesting that actors, institutions, structures and practices are engaged in mutually causative actions – back to the now familiar term again; they are relational and cannot be understood otherwise.

Beyond re-imagining the constituents of politics by demonstrating the range of actors and practices involved, a key contribution of feminist scholars to debates on spatiality has been to highlight and explore the dichotomous logic which underpins all academic disciplines but which has been particularly influential in IR. The feminist critique of public/private divisions and of the dualistic approach that this reflects is based on a significant body of work that seeks to produce multi-dimensional interpretations of political practice. Overcoming this dualism is important as the nature of political practice becomes more complex. If we look at the many layers of contemporary politics, it becomes clear that the 'either/or' dualism is untenable and that the relationality proposed by spatial theorists and feminists is perhaps not only useful but is necessary in understanding how twenty-first century politics operates.

Imagine, for example, any eighteen-year-old, anywhere in the world. S/he will have very little political power or influence in any traditional sense of the word. The richer and more educated s/he is, the more likely this power is to increase over time. The more networks s/he has access to, the more likely it is that political information will become available. If s/he has access to the Internet, the opportunities for engaging in political actions of some kind will also be enhanced. This is not to suggest that s/he will *become* political just because networks are available – none of the evidence to date suggests this to be the case (see Gauntlett and Rodgers 2002). It does suggest, however, that the dualism that would see this person as lacking political agency would be untenable. There are many ways that this person and the many millions like her/him could influence 'official' political actors, economic policies and practices and non-state and international organizations, both directly through political participation and indirectly through the social structures within which they reside.

Conclusion

Given the apparent convergence of many social and political phenomena, which both transcend geographical boundaries and contribute to the construction of new metaphoric spaces (see Peterson 1996b), it is necessary to explore how IR may address the nature of political, or more correctly socio-political, activities which do not fall either within given spatial parameters, or within its pre-existing definitions of what constitutes the political. Spatial ontologies that view definitions of the political as neither necessarily based on state agendas, nor as defined in and through these, thus form a significant challenge to the authority of existing norms in IR.

Looking at the challenges posed by feminists, it is possible to see a number of discursive limitations that prevail in the discipline of IR, based largely on its patterns of inclusion and exclusion. The first, as noted earlier, is that the state is situated as the definitional space of political authority in the discipline, which renders effective analysis of other sites and spaces problematic. The second is that masculinist constructions of meaning are seen as inherent to definitions of political legitimacy in IR, which positions gender as a subordinate category of analysis. The third is seen in the combination of these two elements: political power, endowed and pursued through 'official' channels, is associated with the public spaces emphasized in the discourse of IR. Consequently, non-state actors and non-official activities are under-represented and under-explored in analysis of international affairs.

The fourth discursive limitation lies in the tendency to emphasize the historical over the spatial in the discipline, which means that the state has come to embody conceptions of political community. As a result, transborder, transnational, regional or globally-defined organizations and communities are analysed within the context of a state-oriented interpretative framework which is ill-suited to the task (see Rodgers 1999). The evident impact of transnational actors and activities on patterns of political engagement consequently requires an analytical schema better able to accommodate the complexities of contemporary politics.

Moreover, with the spread of interactive communications technologies and the growth of normative politics, the dualisms of state/non-state, internal/external, even national/international and so on appear to be increasingly unsustainable. Although there are obvious issues about power and decision-making relating to state governments, these can rarely be analysed in isolation from broader global economic and institutional circumstances. Feminists were among the first political analysts to argue that societal constructs do not begin and end at state boundaries. For feminists, these questions initially focused upon issues such as power and patriarchy but they have shown that both institutional practices and discursive constructs – the systemic dimensions of politics – have an impact both at individual and societal levels.

These observations are important in the analysis of complex political practices, as they allow different actors and practices to be seen in context and in relation to one another. This represents a significant advance on the traditional discourse of IR: it is not necessary to assess how the actions of, say, political activists in Guatemala affect the US government, or indeed even the Guatemalan government, to know that they have significance and may be of international consequence. There is no such thing today (if there ever was) as pure and simple politics. The complexities of the political realm seemingly become more evident every day and it is becoming necessary to find ways of acknowledging, accepting and attempting to address this. Feminist theories suggest that we need to see politics as multidimensional and, because of this, find ways of researching the relationality of actors and practices. Spatial theorists, similarly, have suggested that a failure to acknowledge how we structure the discourse of politics limits our abilities to understand and interpret its intricacies. This notion of relationality, along with Lefebvre's tripartite vision of different types of spatial analysis, will be useful in the coming chapters, where the activities and range of actors, using varying practices and media to engage in different forms of politics are analysed.

3 The politics of the Internet

Introduction

Given their synergetic relations with economic, social and political spheres, communications technologies can, as most societies have experienced, have quite profound effects on human interactions. Their impact is not always readily identifiable or quantifiable, though. Pool argued, for example, that it would have been possible to conclude ten years after the invention of the printing press that the device was of little significance, as change was in large measure incremental and qualitative (1990: 4). The availability of the printing press permitted only the mass production of texts; the social conditions for mass literacy were not in place contemporaneously. This phenomena was termed a 'cultural lag' by Ogburn (cited Fischer 1992: 8), defined as 'a period of dislocation when changes in social practice have not yet accommodated the new material culture' (ibid.) These social conditions were themselves affected by the wider availability of printed material, reflecting the inter-relationship between invention and social change.

This is useful to remember when analysing the impact of the Internet. The relentless utopian arguments about how earth-shatteringly wonderful it is, and the countering comments about inequity and uneven access tell us only part of the story. As far as its role in politics is concerned, it may be more useful to look at the characteristics of the technology and the nature, aims and objectives of the movements using it.

The Internet does not necessarily bring 'new' actors into the political arena, though it can build upon existing networks. We cannot assume either that connections made between activists and institutions constitute 'new' forms of political practice. By simplifying the process of transmitting and exchanging information, the Internet undoubtedly internationalizes the connections between movement activists to such a degree that their relevance to analysis of political communication can no longer be ignored. The Internet is not *only* internationalizing political activity, though; it is being used in different ways and these uses need to be considered in context. In particular, the aims and objectives behind the application of communications technologies by different actors needs to be addressed.

The main difficulty in analysing the Internet and its effects lies in the dramatic pace of change and the increasing overlaps not only between social and political spheres, but also between real and virtual worlds. At this juncture – where these real and virtual worlds meet, where broad- and narrow-casting can reach the same audiences in different ways, and where traditional patterns of political communication are fractured – the analytical dilemmas of addressing the Internet become evident. When addressing Internet use it is evident that the complex interweaving of its technological capabilities with social and political structures forces us to re-examine many of the core assumptions underpinning academic disciplines. Some of these assumptions have been unpacked in the previous two chapters. Others, relating to the role of communications in political processes, will be considered here.

Access to network technologies is becoming an increasingly important factor in social and political activity, with the presence or absence of this form of communication relevant to both the ways politics are organized and to the opportunities for participation in political activity. This chapter moves away from emphasis on spatial theories towards an examination of some of the *practical* implications of the use of communications technologies in the political arena. It starts by providing an overview of the development of networked communications systems, examining how Internet technologies evolved, how they function and how the forms of interaction they offer differ from other media. The analysis of these technologies undertaken here examines what they are, how they differ from previous forms of communication, particularly the mass media, and why their development and growth are of particular relevance to the study of international affairs.

The Internet infrastructure

This section will perhaps be a little dull for those who are not of a techie persuasion. It is useful to analysis of the Internet as a political tool, though, since it illustrates (as briefly as possible) how the networks of which it is comprised evolved. It is not crucial to know these things to understand the Internet as a political tool but it helps. There is some dispute among scholars regarding precise dates in the development of particular key aspects of the Internet. This can be attributed partly to secrecy surrounding the origins of some aspects of the Internet in military and defence research in the USA, and partly to the fact that the Internet evolved through a series of actors and institutions, rather than from a single source. No one has yet managed to provide a definitive chronology. There are, instead, lots of overviews, and the brief details given below draw upon some of these.

More comprehensive outlines, each with slight variations on relevant dates, are given in Slevin (2000), Walch (1999) and Warkentin (2001). It should be noted, too, that though it is now generally accepted that American scientists played the leading role in developing Internet technologies, there is a growing revisionist school which argues that the contributory role of European scientists has been underplayed in most accounts (see Wyatt 2000: online). Both the contentions over Internet origins and the range of actors involved in its development indicate that the technology has never followed a linear trajectory. In this sense, this form of communication has always transcended public/private distinctions, or imagined political boundaries, with no single group, whether military or political, private or public sector, having a monopoly on its evolution.

According to most accounts, the potential for communication between computers was first realized by the United States Defense Department's Advanced Research Projects Agency (ARPA, now DARPA) in the 1960s. The aim at this stage was, it is often suggested, to produce a computer system that could resist nuclear attack. No single computer would act as host to vital information; any networked machine could supply and retrieve data; so destruction of one part of the system could not disrupt the function of the remainder. From this basic idea, the now-familiar model of networked computers with no single central host evolved. This received wisdom on the motives behind the development of the Internet is not without its detractors. Lipson and Gayton have argued that ARPA's work required a national security rationale to justify research spending (1998: 3), thus establishing the official line on the context of the agency's operations. Kitchin argues that the desire to foster interagency collaboration was another key objective for scientists (1998: 29). Whether by design or default, the result was an inherently decentralized communications technology which could be used to establish direct and indirect links between individuals and institutions.

The Internet evolved against a background of public and private sector collaboration, with a symbiotic partnership of government research and trade interests in operation. Bell Laboratories, its parent company AT&T, and Harvard, Stanford and Berkeley universities were all involved in the development of networked computing in the 1950s and 1960s (see Castells 1996). As is now well known, the first computer network, dubbed ARPANET, went online in 1969, and was available for the use of research scientists working with or for US defence agencies. At this point the network model still operated as an effectively closed computer community; random access was available to all users, but the community of users was highly restricted. Technological advances in electronics and communications fields made during the preceding decades, however, had broad effects, and were experienced in two significant ways. First, a computer culture that was not linked to commercial or state interests was developing and, second, other mainstream actors were keen to make use of the Internet. As a consequence, the Internet developed through a combination of interests, based in both public and private realms, and through the interests of both individuals and government.

The modem was invented in 1978 by two Chicago students who developed a computer protocol that allowed computers to transfer files directly, without going through any form of centralized host (ibid: 353). They perhaps also helped to establish the spirit of anarchy that later came to characterize the Internet by diffusing the technology without charge. Individuals and groups were now able to make use of similar technologies and were coming close to developing compatibility with the larger, 'legitimate' network.

There were some parallel and related developments taking place. Bell had developed Unix, an operating system enabling access from computer to computer in 1969. In 1979, another group of US students created a modified version of the Unix protocol which allowed computer links over ordinary telephone lines. Then, in 1983, research funded by DARPA, this time at Berkeley, led to the development of TCP/IP (Transmission Control Protocol/Internet Protocol), the language which computers connected to networks use. TCP/IP provides the common standard for communication between different computer systems (Dutton *et al.* 1996: 392), allowing the exchange of data between computers of differing capacities and software.

The form of the Internet originally envisaged by the US government and related agencies was intended to serve bureaucratic needs such as faster and more direct communication between departments. Those with access to the Internet networks used them for other purposes as well, though, and it became as much a social as an administrative tool. The introduction of TCP/IP made the networks easier, quicker, and therefore cheaper to use. The potential size and composition of the audience was also increased, as people outside 'official' systems were able to use the technologies from home, and use of this form of communication began to diffuse.

ARPANET was separated into two networks in 1983, one retaining that name and being designated for scientific purposes, the other named MILNET and used for military communications. Several other networks were created in the early 1980s, most notably by the US National Science Foundation (NSF). The increasing numbers of users, and their applications of the available technologies, led to the development of the electronic mail, file transfer and remote login facilities which are now standard features of network computing. Applying the TCP/IP protocol, all of the new networks linked in with ARPANET and eventually mutated into the system now known as the Internet, which is effectively a vast number of intersecting networks.

Perhaps the final key development, in terms of establishing the Internet infrastructure, came with the development of Hypertext Transport Protocol (http), developed in 1992 at the CERN laboratories in Switzerland. This uses the hypertext language now current on the web. This allows the creation of web-pages by users and provides the links between online documents. One further important feature of the Internet technology is the device known as packet switching. This allows 'packets' of binarized data to be routed by flexible computer-based switches, reaching their destination in the form in which they were sent (ibid.) A confluence of many of these technological developments – networking facilities, modems, transfer protocols and so on – with the growth in the use of home computers led, possibly inevitably, to the development of wide-scale interactive computing systems. As Abbate suggests, public access meant that people 'could grasp the possibilities for information gathering, social interaction, entertainment, and self-expression' (1999: 181) the Internet had to offer.

The development of wireless technologies should also be noted, as this is likely to become an important avenue for access in areas where hardwiring of telecommunications networks is limited. The cost of hardwiring is enormous and the use of wireless Internet technologies, like the growth of mobile telephony, is perceived by some to be a potential route to development through the 'leapfrogging' of the built communications infrastructure (see Singh 1999). Where wireless technologies are used, laptop computers can also make use of combined information and communications technologies, and it is not necessary to have access to a telephone point to link into networks. The type of line to which a computer is linked, or whether use is made of wireless (that is, satellite) connections, makes a difference only to the speed of information transfer, and does not prevent the use of the Internet (see Hogan 1997).

This brief overview of the development of the Internet provides background information on how the technologies involved in this new form of communication evolved, and illustrates the conjunction of inter-agency and non-institutional activity in its development. The Internet today has a global reach and there has been much debate about the real number of users, partly because of its decentralized nature and partly because of the sheer scale of the technologies of which it is comprised. There have been claims that the Internet now reaches ten per cent of the world's population, though only one per cent of its users are in each of the Middle East and Africa (O'Sullivan 2002: online). Many such figures are bandied about and their reliability, given the complexity of the networks and the many different systems used to provide access, will always be open to question. As the telecommunications arm of the United Nations, the International Telecommunications Union (ITU) probably supplies the most reliable estimates; Wolcott *et al.*, conducting a major research project under the auspices of the organization, suggest that there were probably some three hundred million users by the end of the 1990s (2001: online). They also note that 'the Internet typology is constantly changing and [it] is a delivery mechanism for a constantly evolving array of software applications and information' (ibid.) As the case studies in later chapters will show, the context and objectives of Internet use are important factors in determining how the technology is applied. In essence, my Internet is not the same as yours, so pinning down 'the Internet' is an impossible task.

Technological innovation is not isolated from social factors and the ways in which the Internet first diffused from state agencies into the social realm, and subsequently extended to a global stage, is relevant to its uses and applications today. As Dutton points out, users shape the design and impacts of technological change (1996: 7) – that is, the Internet is socially constructed. Even if we can measure how many people have access to the Internet – Wolcott *et al.* suggest we probably cannot (2001: online) – we still need to place their use of it in context. The Internet is as much a social as a technological development. There is no technological determinism inherent in the introduction of a new form of information exchange. Fischer suggests that 'mechanical properties do not predestine the development and employment of an innovation. Instead struggles and negotiations among interested parties shape that history' (1992: 16).

Technologies do not exist outside of social context; commercial interests, regulatory systems, consumer demand and so on all influence the ways in which a particular technology may be adopted or applied (see Cockburn and Ormrod 1993). Or, as Warkentin puts it, the development of the Internet is not just about technological advances:

> It is also a story of people and groups interacting with each other, under varying social and political conditions, at particular points in history, using technology to respond to and help shape the world in which we live.
>
> (2001: 27)

The social construction of the Internet is evident in the ways users apply it to their own needs and interests. It would be naïve to assume, though, that externalities like political and economic factors do not play a major role in determining the options available to people using the networks. It is true that the Internet has spread rapidly. It would not be true to suggest that it has grown organically. There are many factors – not least regulatory control, corporate investments and the channelling of access through Internet Service Providers – that hinder or promote Internet development and use in different ways in different areas. The dynamic relationships between user and technology constitute an important element of spatial interpretation: how technologies are made available and how their possible uses are interpreted evidently influences the opportunities that they afford.

Internet communications

In order to assess the role of the Internet in changing political practices, we need to look at how and why the type of communication it offers differs from other media, giving some insight into why it is considered to be such an important political tool for non-state actors. Why, for example, is it seen as more valuable than television, radio or video technologies? Is it more effective than hard-copy mail-shots, press releases or mass media advertisements? Does it not simply provide more advanced versions of letter-writing, broadcasting or data exchange facilities? There are a number of features which are unique to this type of technology, and which may contribute to its usefulness for political actors. Despite occasional arguments to the contrary, there is no sense that nothing is changing with the Internet; there are features of this technology – not least its intersection with others – that create conditions for political activism which differ from those previously available. Not necessarily new communities, not new actors, but certainly – for some – new conditions. Asking how and why this is the case tells us a lot about the nature of contemporary political activism and consequently how politics can be spatialized. In some senses, the Internet is a mechanism for both interpersonal and broadcast communications, and the technical capabilities that facilitate these forms of interaction and data transmission are examined below.

Historically, developments in communications technologies have taken two forms: either to increase the amount of information transmitted or to increase the number of possible recipients. The convergence of computing and telecommunications technologies in the form of the Internet conflates these capabilities, permitting (theoretically) the simultaneous transmission of potentially infinite quantities of data around the globe. That is, the Internet has a capacity to deliver vast amounts of information to widely dispersed audiences, using complex networks and data-exchange mechanisms unavailable through any other media. Many scholars are sceptical about the globalizing tendencies of the Internet, of course, arguing that its spread mirrors the interests of already powerful actors (see McChesney 1997b). Certainly, plenty of evidence has been produced to suggest that the Internet is not having a uniformly beneficial impact on the disenfranchised, and it has been suggested that this is 'the historic preserve of an elite stratum within advanced industrial societies that is, for the most part, white, male and professional' (Lekhi 2000: 78). Silver notes that class, race, age and education are all significant factors affecting access to online communications (2000: 27). Countering this are the claims that normally marginalized groups are using the Internet to 'establish self-defined, self-determined' spaces online in ways they are unable to in the 'real' world (ibid.: 28).

If we consider simply the *potential* to reach global audiences it is clear that the technical barriers to this are now minimal. The size of the potential audience means little on its own, of course. The ability to reach several billion people does not translate into the ability to influence them or prompt them into some form of action. Indeed, Internet use is often targeted at specific groups, rather than directed to a mass audience, with its broadcasting potential often of greater appeal to existing mass media organizations than to political actors. While Internet communications *can* reach millions, the vast majority of emails and websites don't, and often are not intended to.

The types of communication the Internet permits offer an important dimension to its influence in the political arena. Traditionally, communications theorists distinguished three types of interaction in which humans engage: 'face-to-face', 'mediated interaction' and 'mediated quasi-interaction' (Thompson 1994). The meaning of 'face-to-face' interaction is fairly self-evident, being premised on the shared presence of participants, where the spoken word and physical signifiers – 'body language' – aid the transmission and reception of information. 'Mediated interaction' is of the type characterized by the use of telephones, letter-writing and so on, where a technical medium is used to convey information to a party not sharing the same spatio-temporal frame of reference.

The third form of communication, 'mediated quasi-interaction' is also dependent upon a time-space differential between communicating parties, but refers to the monological – one-way – flow of information from sender to receiver. This is exemplified by mass communication media, such as newspapers, radio and television broadcasting. The spatio-temporal framework for this form of communication is largely determined by the sender: programmes are scheduled according to broadcasters' priorities, newspapers are published daily or weekly, and so on. Digitization is changing all this in some ways, as the sender–receiver relationship is adjusted across space and time, particularly with the introduction of interactive broadcasting.

The Internet has some similarities to other media but also offers some new communicative possibilities. For Pool, advanced electronic facilities differ radically from mass media modes of communication, with the key difference lying in the ways in which audiences access information, and in how information is made available. For Pool, the newness of this form of communication lay in the nature of reception:

> The mass media revolution is being reversed; instead of identical messages being disseminated to millions of people, electronic technology permits the adaptation of electronic messages to the specialized or unique needs of individuals.
>
> (1990: 8)

The Internet doesn't replace mass media, or any other mode of communication, though some technologies may be superseded. As the spoken word, and written text have endured, and have been supplemented by telephones, faxes and so on, it appears probable that the Internet will continue, for now at least, to constitute an additional, rather than a replacement, technological development.

Youngs suggests that 'use of the Internet is transforming established narrow parameters of mediation, and encouraging diverse forms of interactivity' (2001: 222) highlighting how different it can be from other communications technologies. The Internet offers modes of communication that differ significantly from those we have traditionally understood in some important ways. Unlike other communications technologies, communication through the Internet can be both mono- and dialogical in character. It can be monological in one-to-one emails and through the use of web pages which do not receive user-responses. As the technologies, and users understanding of them, become more sophisticated, this latter is a feature that is rarely used, not least because interactivity is one of the Internet's most compelling features. Interactive links have now become the norm on the web but the possibility for one-way communication does still exist.

Indeed, the notion that the provision of links removes barriers to communication needs to be called into question, as the appearance of interactivity sometimes belies the reality of relatively closed access to information online. Many hyperlinks on web pages provide access to further information but often preclude the potential for communication. Although most websites appear to be highly interactive they are, in some respects, often based on largely monological forms of communication. Websites provide only limited access to organizations, institutions and other information providers. We can't respond to everything on a website, only to what the information provider wants us to respond to. Many corporate and government websites provide perfect examples of this, often giving a sense of transparency while offering no real possibility for any meaningful form of communication.

This challenges the myth that the Internet is an open, free-for-all space. Its restrictions as a tool for promoting free exchange between political institutions and the public can be seen to take two forms. First, as noted earlier, 'the Internet' is not '*the* Internet' so it cannot be seen as something which has the same meaning, uses or value for everyone with access to it. As Miller and Slater note 'the Internet is not a monolithic or placeless "cyberspace"; rather, it is numerous new technologies, used by diverse people, in diverse real-world locations' (cited Wolcott *et al.* 2001: online). It would thus be wrong to assume that we can identify a model of online activity – political or otherwise – that can be broadly applied. The contexts of use, the availability of particular soft- or hardware, the networks of people accessing any particular online resource and so on all affect its potential to promote or precipitate political change. There are certainly patterns of use, and information providers will aim to direct users to particular resources, but models are a long way off yet.

Second, we cannot assume that just because governments provide websites actually communicating with decision-makers has become more straightforward. Access to organizations and information providers through the Internet is structured in much the same way as in the 'real' world. Thus, although websites are used as a portal to institutions, their gateways are managed like any other entrance might be. That is, metaphorically speaking, we still need to make it past the receptionist to get to where we really want to be. While access to official documents is becoming much more straightforward, access to decision-makers and power-brokers is not necessarily easier than it has been in the past. Elites are able to install online protective layers shielding them from non-elites just as they do offline. At the same time, political institutions are struggling to come to terms with their increased accessibility (however specious) to the general public. The volume of email traffic on top of 'real' world demands is something that politicians are still trying to come to terms with. Following the release of the Starr Report on the Clinton–Lewinski affair, for example, one senator received 6 700 emails in four days (Stromer-Galley 2000: 49), a fairly unmanageable number by anyone's standards. Ferdinand highlights the problems this information overload can cause for decision-makers and representative politicians: 'the more they are contacted by individual citizens, the more difficult they will find it to respond in a reflective way to the particular concerns of each citizen' (2000b: 176).

With email, of course, documents and images can be transmitted to the receiver almost instantaneously. In terms of organizational efficiency, this provides a mechanism for acquiring rapid response to campaigns, promotions, sales and so on. This use of the Internet is therefore becoming increasingly common with both commercial and political organizations (see Walch 1999). This rapid response capability has its drawbacks, though. On the one hand, it serves commercial organizations well to know how many customers are interested in a particular offer or how rapid a response a particular promotion generates. NGOs too value a high return rate on online campaigns such as e-petitions. On the other, however, many politicians are deeply suspicious of the apparent ease of access to political processes that the Internet affords and feel that the luxury of 'armchair activism' lacks the commitment of real politics. It has been argued by others, though, that the 'real' politics of voting participation places equally few demands on people's time and energies (see Inglehart and Norris 2003). In this sense, Internet participation is perhaps no more or less lacking in commitment.

Perhaps the most significant feature of the Internet in respect of political space, is its capacity for multi-logicality. As Dahlgren notes, it offers extensions of the one-to-many form of mass media and introduces many-to-many facilities for the first time (2001b: 46). To put it another way, it encompasses the features of traditional media and adds new ones. The multi-logical communication of the Internet operates through email and web pages, and permits interaction between multiple users through newsgroups, mailing lists and discussion groups. Interactive groups may form around a specific social or political issue and individuals can engage in debate and discussion with a wide range of actors in varying roles and locations. This multi-logicality is crucial to the use of the Internet as a political tool, as it provides a 'voice' that no other medium can supply. Mass media, whether press or broadcast, have very little room for what are seen to be minority interests; the concerns of death penalty abolitionists, anti-war campaigners and environmental activists, for example, are rarely covered on prime-time television but these issues are major and fairly high-profile concerns for many NGOs and other activists. Even when such issues are addressed in the mass media, there is usually little opportunity for debate or direct engagement with the people putting across a particular case.

The Internet's capacity for interactivity and multi-logicality can thus be seen as the most obvious, and probably the most important way the Internet differs from other forms of communication, in terms of providing a facility for political interaction. Youngs suggests that:

> It contains the established 'few to many' mass media model, where major public service (for example, the BBC) and commercial (for example, CNN) players play a particularly influential role, but it extends that environment to include a 'many to many' model that enables more individual entities, be they governments, NGOs, companies, voluntary groups or individuals, to communicate *directly* with international audiences.
>
> (2001: 222, emphasis in original)

Again, though, this is not entirely straightforward. The Internet is still – despite the fuss about its possible impact – largely an invisible network. Although information available on the Internet *can* reach a mass audience, it only does so if an audience seeks it out. There is, as yet, no evidence that more people are becoming engaged in politics just because more information is available to them. Indeed, as Dahlgren points out, we should note that the use of the Internet for serious information searches or for political engagement appears to be a minor sideline for most people (2001a: 75). There is nothing yet to suggest that we become 'more political' just because more political information is available to us (see Gauntlett and Rodgers 2002).

The Internet audience

The construction of audiences is an important but often ignored feature of the Internet relevant to analysis of its role in politics. The term 'audience' is used here to indicate a group with access to the same information, rather than to suggest the defined and targeted body of recipients which the output of broadcast media presupposes. Internet users can send, receive or participate in the production of information in ways that are not available through other communications media. Users of the Internet have a significant degree of choice when applying its facilities, and a wide range of options regarding receipt and exchange of information. As noted, though, this information isn't beamed directly to them – they have to seek it out, be drawn to it or chance upon it. This becomes important when we consider how the Internet is used in political practices. What strategies are used to persuade people to 'act politically' online? Are these based on offline persuasive techniques? What barriers or stepping stones to political participation does the Internet present? And so on.

One of the key issues relating to our assumptions about the relevance of the Internet as a political tool centres upon the ways we understand audiences and sources of information. The notion of 'an audience' as essentially passive and contained, typical of early mass media analysis, has been largely discredited and it is now assumed that we interpret media texts according to our own experiences, both shared and individual (see McQuail 2000: 360–82; Mattelart and Mattelart 1995/8). That we do not simply act as sponges soaking up media messages is now widely accepted. Very little work on who comprises the Internet audience and how they interact with the texts they receive is being undertaken, however. This is odd because, as Lacey says, 'audiences are the Holy Grail of virtually all media texts; after all, if no one experiences the text then it might as well never have been created' (2002: 181).

Although some of the standard assumptions regarding the active audience can be applied to the Internet – indeed, surely this is the most active audience ever – the particularities of this form of communication render the construction of audiences (and consequently the techniques used to generate and maintain their interest) quite complex. The dominant discourse of mass media may influence how we use the Internet, what we find there and what meanings it may impart to us. The Internet, as both a narrow- and a broadcast technology, and as an intensive data-exchange network, can be simultaneously a structured communications mechanism and the apparently anarchic space that early analysts of cyberspace anticipated. These features operate alongside the mass media to affect the discourses available to us. We are, one could say, an influenced and an active audience at one and the same time.

Thompson has argued that the development of new forms of communication affects the domain of institutionalized power by altering the relationship between what is public and visible, and what is private and essentially closed to public view (1994: 29). This point provides an interesting twist on the public/private debate considered in Chapter 2, where public politics have gained legitimacy over activities in the private realm. The mass media do, of course, reinforce the apparent importance of governments and elite actors, not least through their dependence on state institutions for information (see Boyd-Barrett and Rantanen 1998; Thussu 2000). How government/media relationships, as well as media/audience interactions, are affected by the Internet must also be explored. There have been some relatively high profile and well-documented cases of wide-scale Internet networking which has been seen to have an impact on policy. Cases like that of the Chiapas uprising (see Ferdinand 2000a; Walch 1999) and the Multilateral Agreement on Investments backlash (see Kobrin 1998) have received wide coverage in Internet research circles and it is usually argued that these demonstrate the power of the Internet as a political tool. This is probably true enough but whether awareness of these campaigns has filtered through to a broader audience is open to question.

Ang has argued that, through the use of audience measurement techniques, broadcasters operate under the implicit and erroneous assumption that an 'audience' can be understood as a finite totality, 'made up of subdivisions or segments which can be synchronically or diachronically "fixed"' (1991: 204). For Ang, a precise construction of audience is a necessary fiction for broadcasters, who seek to define a compact public, the audience, which does not reflect the social practices of viewers and listeners (ibid.) Attempts to define or measure the mass media audience have been complicated by changes in the social practices which accompany media reception, such as different working patterns and viewing habits of people sharing households, the locating of television sets and radios in public places, use of video recorders, the introduction of satellite and cable channels, and so on. The Internet pushes the dislocation of the notion of a definable and measurable audience still further, by allowing the user to s/elect from multiple sources, opt into particular discussion groups, act as an information provider, and so on. We have always been members of many different audiences; with the Internet we join more of them and they are often more diffuse, increasing the complexity of our social and political interactions and the opportunities of analysts to understand them.

Although broadcasters are undoubtedly aware of the audiences' active role in mediation of their output, the defined and deliberate targeting of an assumed homogeneous group has been the norm for decades. As with other aspects of the user/media relationship, this is changing with the spread of interactive technologies. Though broadcasters still tend to see their audiences in 'broad' terms – that is, as a mass – there are moves towards multi-platform delivery, making use of a range of technologies to deliver the same programme/product in a variety of different ways through a range of media. The most successful of these to date has been the 'Big Brother' television format, sold on a global scale and making using of the Internet and mobile telephony to increase audience participation (see Gauntlett and Rodgers 2002). It is interesting to note here how the Internet becomes a tool in the armoury of mass media organizations. This is important for activists, as the major media players have an important presence on the Internet. Public (and therefore visible) discourse is still dominated by mass media output and not by Internet content.

The Internet provides a 's/elective' form of communication, a term that encapsulates the element of choice available to Internet users. Internet technologies are 'elective' in that, as discussed in the preceding paragraphs, users opt in to most forms of interaction via the Internet. They are 'selective' because users also have a significant degree of control over the type of material they access and the networks in which they participate. The relatively high level of control Internet users have over the information communities within which they function, when compared to the use of information from other sources, is significant to its analysis. What we need to consider, then, is how the dominant everyday discourses that we as a general audience accept, refute and are part of are framed for us in the Internet age.

Examination of the impact of the Internet has become crucial to understanding changing political practices, and how contemporary political communities are maintained and established. Street suggests that at one level 'technology is the embodiment of certain interests and possibilities' but at another 'it is the bearer of effects: it changes what we can imagine and what we want, it alters our politics' (1997: 35). For these reasons, it is useful to look at some of the ways new communications technologies affect our assumptions about the nature of information provision and exchange. The ways the mass media, in particular, frame political issues is important to interpreting Internet use by activists, since our opportunities for s/electivity with offline information sources are perhaps more limited than with those online. We need to ask, therefore, whether the ways politics are framed in the mass media have an impact on how online users interpret the issues and lead them to feel compelled to 'act politically' (or not).

Mass media and framing

Referring to the development of mass communications technologies, Thompson argues that:

> the publicness (or visibility) of actions or events is no longer linked to the sharing of a common locale, and hence actions and events can acquire a publicness which is independent of their capacity to be seen or heard directly by a plurality of co-present individuals.
>
> (1994: 39)

That is, it is not necessary to be in a given location to bear witness to events taking place there, nor does the public that receives information remain constant, as it possible to be a member of multiple publics. This has always been the case, with stories told and filtered from person to person and the use of various technologies as mediating tools. Reception of media discourses is experiential and multi-faceted. The growth of mass media has vastly increased the volume and reach of information spread, though, creating for Thompson a kind of 'mediated publicness ... which differs in fundamental respects from the traditional publicness of co-presence' (ibid.) Most people are not actively involved in the current affairs outlined by the mass media. Many, though, feel affected by them and, occasionally, compelled to act on them. As Phillips says:

> distant events are now integrated into frameworks of personal experience rendering the phenomenal world global and making people

just as aware of, and emotionally attached to, objects of which they have only mediated experience.

(2000: 172)

Media coverage in the form of press, radio or television reports makes public details of socially and politically significant events, such as some humanitarian crises, war, foreign policy decisions and inter-governmental conferences. These are the public events which are deemed to be of significance to a general audience by media organizations. In most cases, however, media coverage is decided in a fairly arbitrary fashion (Hopkinson 1995: 10). The priorities regarding the output of print and broadcast media organizations tend to be event-driven but are rarely determined purely by reference to the general, long-term or local impact of an event.

As a further limitation, media organizations tend to use pre-determined criteria to manage output. Generalized news values – the editorial conventions which follow a fairly uniform pattern across the media as a whole – also have the effect of foreclosing reportage of many events (see Boyd-Barrett 1998; Allan 1999). Although a particular event may be unusual, and therefore newsworthy, the way it is covered will conform to a pretty rigid pattern. News values reflect priorities such as dramatic impact, ease of access to location, cost to the broadcaster or publisher, quality of available text or footage, and judgements about likely levels of interest among the receiving public (see Hopkinson 1995). In this sense, the media again acts as a gatekeeper, channelling and filtering information before it enters the public domain.

Identifying two senses of 'public', Thompson argues that both are challenged by the wide range of media organizations and output, and by the problems inherent in controlling their operations (1994: 34). This has become particularly relevant with the increased availability of transborder transmissions, satellite communications and widespread deregulation of media activities since the 1980s. The first sense of public identified by Thompson is the equation of public with institutionalized political power, contrasting with private, non-state activities. This is the public element of the public–private divide which gender theorists find so problematic, as it relegates non-institutional actors to the discursive realm of the private, as discussed in detail in Chapter 2. To a significant degree, the news values and scheduling requirements of media organizations – which require a rapid flow of information and easy access to sources, both of which governments readily provide – promote the image of public politics as the 'real thing'. Through this the sense of 'otherness' and illegitimacy often associated with non-state political practices is perpetuated.

It is the second sense of public space identified by Thompson that is of particular relevance to this chapter, however. He argues that another way of interpreting 'public' is to view it as that which is open or available to the general public, signifying visibility or openness (1994: 38), and suggests that:

it is no longer possible to circumscribe the management of visibility ... Moreover, the messages transmitted by the media may be received and understood in ways that cannot be directly monitored and controlled by communicators.

(ibid.: 40)

The rise of spin-doctoring and information management is testament to the difficulties now faced in conveying the desired political messages in an age of information saturation.

With the use of broadcast communications, and increasingly with the use of the Internet, public political activity is intrinsically linked to the private realm; the mediated discourse of mass media is, potentially, open to scrutiny through an information-rich, interactive medium. The s/elective nature of Internet interactions means that information available in the public domain can perhaps be more easily verified or refuted. The lack of control powerful actors have over media framings which has been slowly developing in recent decades is extended by the arrival of technologies which allow individuals to bypass those framings.

This is not to suggest the utopia of free and open information exchange over the ether. Though there is plenty to talk about out there, there still needs to be some sort of catalyst to promote interest in, and possible action on any given issue. This is largely because, although 'the Net's development and spread over the past few years is having an enormous impact on media structures and patterns of use' (Dahlgren 2001b: 47), Internet users 'are often probing deeper into something they have seen in the traditional mass media; they are getting more, but largely not very different information' (ibid.: 48). Moreover, we tend to favour specialized news providers (ibid.), which are linked to the major media organizations.

There is clearly a need for those seeking to promote political activism online to be aware of, responsive to, and make attempts to influence, mass media coverage of certain issues. *Potential* activists are not necessarily aware of the specialist discourse accessed by the committed activist (see Gamson 1995: 85) and it is still necessary to have some impact on the *general* discourse if one is to promote activism beyond the already-interested, specialist community. For Gamson, 'only general-audience media provide a potentially shared public discourse' (ibid.). This is not to claim shared meanings – as noted earlier, we are not passive sponges for information – but 'one can draw on this public discourse to frame an issue with some assurance that potential challengers will understand the references and allusions' (ibid.: 86). The general audience media, in the shape of the mainstream press and prime-time television programming, reach a broad public and provide fairly basic information; it has, we could say, breadth but not depth. The Internet, at this stage in its evolution at least, offers the opposite – detail for those who seek it but little in the way of blanket coverage. The capacity to do this exists but the technology is not, at the moment, used in this way.

While it may be true that 'governments and traditional mass media have lost their control over information and publicity' (Smythe and Smith 2001: 17), movements need to find ways of influencing mass media output to reflect their own interests and priorities – to find ways of making sure that general audience media contain at least some specialist messages. The problem of overcoming the standardized general news values and broadcasting priorities of major media organizations has already been noted. Tarrow has argued that social movements find it more difficult to 'make' news than in the past, given 'the permanent fair of news and entertainment that suffuses the airwaves today' (1994: 119). Even where they do find a place on news bulletins and documentaries, in newspapers and so on, he argues that their capacity to use the media for their own purposes is limited (ibid.: 128), in part because the 'otherness' of political activism is often represented through violence, militancy and a failure to fully explain the context of actions. So, for Tarrow:

> The media – which can shift rapidly from one newsworthy item to another – do not depend on movement activities for news. Movements briefly, provisionally and often dramatically 'make news'; but they cannot make the media publish news the way they want it to be made.
>
> (ibid.: 129)

It becomes apparent when considering this why the Internet has been adopted with such enthusiasm by some activists.

Another stumbling block for activists in trying to convey their understanding of politics is the spatialization of media framing:

> Media are an integral part of public sphere functioning and traditional media of the broadcast and print variety have been predominantly mapped along national lines, whether we are thinking in terms of entities designated as public service or commercial.
>
> (Youngs 2001: 219)

Despite the hegemony of a few major global media players, their output is often g/localized to reflect the demands of different markets: same format, same company, slightly different content. Even in the global media market, there is much about both programming and print that is nationally framed. Not only are activists and movements less useful to media organizations in providing information than governments are, and not only are they discursively positioned, and consequently delegitimized, by a non-public political perspective: they are also often promoting normative, *international* concepts of politics that contradict the state-centric norms of media representations of the field.

The Internet is in some ways an extension of this form of mass media, through online versions of television programmes, radio stations and news services (Dahlgren 2001b: 46). Within the same technology, though, the alternative readings, framings and discourses of politics that social movements espouse can be promoted. There isn't a place to 'do' politics on the Internet: as Noveck says, there isn't really a 'public architecture' of the Internet, designed for 'conversation, interaction, deliberation, education and engagement' (2000: 31). The facilities to do all of these things are there but they are provided and used in a fairly random fashion, on an *ad hoc* basis, with no obvious open forum for debate. People seeking political information have to find it (in which case, you need to know what you're looking for and have the technical skills to track it down) or be shown it (which necessitates knowing someone else who can). In this sense, the patterns of political engagement on the Internet reflect real-world interactions to some degree – politics don't just appear out of nowhere but are constructed from existing and evolving relationships and experiences.

Conclusion

Changes in the way information is transmitted and received are obviously relevant to the way political activity is carried out, indeed to what actually constitutes the realm of politics. In the contemporary system, it is evident that states now have less opportunity than in the past to control either the reach or content of representations of their actions. The mass media, for reasons noted above, still tend to represent politics in a state-centric manner, separating national from global politics and working in tandem with governments – for all sorts of logistical reasons – in their framing of politics. The Internet gives activists the potential to challenge this spatialization of politics, and to contribute to the ongoing reconfigurations of political practices which have been taking place for decades now. It becomes quite clear when assessing the characteristics of this technology that its role in contemporary political practices was bound to be central, as it can apparently serve governments, institutions and other political actors equally well, if in different ways.

Although brief and by no means definitive, the outline of the development of the Internet given in this chapter indicates that these technologies evolved across both public and private sectors, through the efforts of both state and non-state agencies and individuals. Users play an active role in determining modes of engagement and so the traditional tools of gate-keeping and information control, whether overt or unconscious, which characterize broadcast media are less evident in the use of the Internet. This would suggest that processes of political communication are becoming increasingly diffuse, though it can't be assumed that governments have forgone attempts to maintain control over the information available to their citizens. As the next chapter will show, both social movements and the Internet have been subject to some fairly draconian responses from governments in attempts to limit their possible influence.

The ways NGOs and other actors in social movements – the formal and informal elements of activism, we could say – use the Internet indicates that this technology is being used across the political spectrum, both 'up' and 'down' the range of political actors, with the potential to affect political practices at all levels. It is clear from the discussions above that the Internet has the potential to change politics somehow. We need to ask next, then, who these movements are and who their audiences are. Are they trying to attract new people or influence and motivate the old ones? How do people join movements, how is their interest maintained and where does the Internet fit into these processes? These questions are addressed next, providing a foundation for analysis of some specific practices, and the application of spatial theories to these, which is undertaken in the concluding chapters.

4 Activism and the Internet

Introduction

This chapter is mainly concerned with determining how activist networks develop, which will help to make sense of the role of the Internet in political protest. At the same time, it will help us to see why not all activists need or want to make this technology a key tool in their campaigning. The relationships between on- and off-line activism – indeed, the intrinsic links between them for many activists – need to be explored. To assume 'Internet activism' is perhaps to ignore the contexts of both the activism itself and the applications of the technology. This chapter looks at what activism *is* – the 'real' world, offline motivations and practices of movement actors. It also explores the phenomenon of online activism – where and how the latter fits with the former.

Three main issues are addressed. The first and most important of these is to consider how social movement networks evolve. The rise of the NGO movement, the heightened profile of international political activism and the apparent shift towards normative political thinking are considered by many analysts to have dramatically altered the landscape of politics in recent decades. How movements evolve and how they determine their strategies for action will be explored, albeit briefly, here. The other issues examined in this chapter lead on from this, to begin to explore in more detail the relationships between activists and the tools they use to achieve their objectives.

The second issue addressed is the notion that change is being effected in the political behaviour of the non-state actors who make use of these technologies. An insight into what some of these changes are is given, something which will be expanded upon in greater detail in the case studies in later chapters. Finally, there is an examination of the idea that the changes wrought by the introduction of the Internet have the potential to transform the nature of political activity, for activists and, as a consequence, for other actors. Much of the literature on the Internet as a political tool separates actors and politics into generic types, still tending to spatialize the field through dichotomies – national/international, state/non-state, and so on. This underplays the levels of potential connectivity the technologies provide and means that images of the changing face of politics (if such there is) are often separated. The impression given is that the practices of states change, as do those of international organizations, and of NGOs and activists, and of individual actors; the bigger picture of how these changes impact upon each other is often unseen in these interpretations, though.

Social movement networks

There is a vast range of non-state political practices and it is rather problematic to attempt to gather them all together under one all-embracing banner. There is a mountain of literature on social movements and how they form, develop and die, and libraries full of theories on how they function, flourish or fail. This section draws on some of the most popular themes and on the work of some the best-known of the social movement theorists. Because social movements are complex composites, the emphasis is on attempting to identify some of their key features, those which are most relevant to the respatializing of the political landscape and to the use of communications technologies in this process.

Following the brief analysis of the nature of social movements, NGOs and what we could call unaffiliated activists are considered separately, as this will be useful in determining where the Internet fits into different types of activism. The distinction between 'formal' and 'informal' activists is, of course, a little misleading, as there are many overlaps between the practices of the two. NGOs are usually, to greater or lesser degrees, activist organizations. Individual activists are often linked in some way to NGOs or to looser collectives. It *is* helpful, though, to compare the more obviously structured activities of NGOs – particularly large international organizations – with those of their unaffiliated peers. There are, as this and later chapters will demonstrate, many different ways the Internet can be used by non-state actors. By identifying some of the key practices of social movements – or, more specifically, two slightly different kinds of network activism – we can later explore how the introduction of the Internet has affected how they operate. While different kinds of movement actor often have similar objectives, their strategies for achieving their goals are not necessarily the same.

It is not possible to produce standard models of NGO and activist behaviour. Many are a partial product of broader social movements, with membership and support based on normative interpretations of politics, focusing on issues such as human rights, gender and/or racial awareness, environmental protection, economic development and dependency, and so on. Moreover, many of these concerns are seen as indivisible, from each other, and from broader political issues and structures. For example, Amnesty International, which campaigns on behalf of political prisoners, views gender as a central issue, arguing that there are many, often hidden, gender-related causes and consequences in cases of human rights abuse. Similarly, Oxfam, whose prime concern is the alleviation of poverty, links this, as a human rights issue, to political processes relating to trade and development. Despite these kinds of normative links across organizations and issues, it is impossible to produce a generic model encompassing even NGOs and activists who campaign around comparable projects. It is more enlightening to consider the movements in which activists participate, as these provide a framework for understanding some of the dynamics of political activism. So what are social movements and where do 'formal' organizations like NGOs and 'informal' actors, such as some anti-globalization protesters, fit into them?

All sorts of different terms are now used to talk about social movements: new social movements (NSMs) is one,[1] social movement organizations (SMOs) another, transnational social movement organizations (TSMOs) (see Smith *et al.* (eds) 1997) and advocacy networks (see Keck and Sikkink 1998a) and others still. The terms encompass 'formal' and 'informal' actors and are often subject to lengthy debate about who is and who is not involved and what they actually do (see McAdam *et al.* 2001; Smith *et al.* (eds) 1997). As Tarrow pointed out, 'people associate with movements for a wide spectrum of reasons: from the desire for personal advantage, to group solidarity, to principled commitment to a cause, to the desire to be part of a group' (1994: 15). There isn't a 'classic' social movement actor.

Della Porta and Diani make a clear distinction between social movement *organizations* and social movements, arguing that 'membership of movements ... consists ... of a series of differentiated acts, which, taken together, reinforce the feeling of belonging and identity' (1999: 18). Social movements are fluid and have participants rather than members (ibid.: 16). I can be a member of Amnesty International and a participant in a social movement that supports political prisoners and is against human rights abuses. These two things can be coterminous but they are not the same:

> Social movements are not organizations, not even of a particular kind ... They are networks of interaction between different actors which may either include formal organizations or not, depending on shifting circumstances.
>
> (ibid.)

It makes sense, then, to look first at what social movements are and then to consider the differences between the two types of actor which are the subjects of the case studies in Chapters 5 and 6. The 'formal'/'informal' split may seem an awkward dichotomy (particularly given everything that was said in earlier chapters about this kind of division) but making this distinction opens up the concept of Internet activism as a nuanced, multi-faceted form of political engagement, by identifying the many structures and different forms of agency involved in and influencing them.

Social movements cover all shades of the political spectrum, and actors within them come from all kinds of different economic, educational, ethnic and class backgrounds. This is not to suggest that all movements are happily harmonious, all-inclusive affairs; many, nationalist movements in particular, are based on their opposition to certain social groups (see Carnegie 2000: online). To further complicate matters, individuals play a number of different roles within any movement: 'Any particular person often plays parts within more than one political actor, sometimes participating as worker, sometimes as a member of a religious congregation and so on' (McAdam *et al.* 2001: 12).[2]

The terms we use to describe movements do not always offer clarity:

> Movements, identities, governments, revolutions, classes, and similar collective nouns do not represent hard, fixed, sharply bounded objects, but observers' abstractions from continuously negotiated interactions among persons and sets of persons.
>
> (McAdam *et al.* 2001: 12)

What is common to all social movements is the desire to find a voice for the un- or under-represented. They come about:

> When networks of actors relatively excluded from routine decision-making processes engage in collective attempts to change 'some elements of the social structure and/or reward distribution of society'.
>
> (Smith *et al.* 1997, citing McCarthy and Zald 1977: 59)

These voices don't just appear from nowhere, of course, and a sense of collective identity is not innate. Opportunities to engage in political action occur or are created and, when this happens, the familiar terms from social movement literature start to appear:

> Movements are created when political opportunities open up for social actors who usually lack them. They draw people into collective action through known repertoires of contention and by creating innovations around their margins. At their base are the social networks and cultural symbols through which social relations are organized.
>
> (Tarrow 1994: 1)

For a social movement to exist, then, several factors need to come into play. The vast amount of research on social movements has taken many different directions and identified many different facets to collective action. There are at root, though, a number of common features to social movements. For Kuumba:

Their definitive features include organization, consciousness, non-institutionalized strategies, and prolonged duration. In contrast to riots, fads, and crowd behavior, social movements commonly exhibit some degree of structure and organization; a consciousness that links social discontent and grievances with a rationale or logic; noninstitutionalized action strategies; and a relatively long duration.

(2001: 4)

McAdam *et al.* position these characteristics in a tighter conceptual framework in suggesting that, despite the many theoretical traditions now emerging, three broad sets of factors feature in most analyses:

These three factors are (1) the structure of political opportunities and constraints confronting the movement; (2) the forms of organization (informal as well as formal), available to insurgents; and (3) the collective processes of interpretation, attribution and social construction that mediate between opportunity and action.

(1996: 2)

These opportunity structures are 'factors that facilitate or constrain social change efforts' (Smith *et al.* 1997: 66). Factors such as tolerance of rights to political expression, laws which affect fundraising possibilities and the existence of the right to free association all influence the opportunity structures available to movement actors (see ibid.) Perhaps most importantly for analysis of Internet activism is what Tarrow sees as the major activating factor for social movements which 'consists of the changes in political opportunities that give rise to new waves of movements and shape their unfolding' (1994: 7).

The political opportunity structures available to actors and their value for activists are issue-specific and can vary depending on the national and international focus of the movement. The number of transnational movements has grown as national structures fail to provide a satisfactory forum for dealing with an increasing number of issues. Smith suggests that movements dealing with excluded groups are 'among the top transnational movement industries' (1997: 57) but peace and world order issues and now also environmental issues have moved to the global stage as national governments lose their ability to deal with them unilaterally (see ibid.)

The forms of organization available to actors depend on both the resources available to them and the structures within which they are operating. The resources referred to here can be material, such as access to the funds and equipment required to undertake political action. They are more specifically, though, what social movement theorists term 'mobilization resources', that is, the skills and tools available to activists to persuade others to participate. As transnational activism has risen, both NGOs and grassroots activists have had to develop new ways of generating and sustaining public interest in their concerns. They have also had to find new ways of making their claims heard, while pitching their rhetoric to both policy-makers and a general audience.

In order to achieve this, social movements establish patterns of action – 'repertoires of contention', according to the phrase coined by Charles Tilly (1986: 2). These repertoires of contention refer to 'the whole set of means [a group] has for making claims of different individuals or groups' (Tarrow 1994: 31); they are based on established practices and relate to 'not only what people *do* when they are engaged in conflict with others; it is what they know *how to do* and what others *expect* them to do' (ibid.: 32). Different repertoires work for different types of protest and some – such as boycotting, mass petitioning and barricades – were used in particular struggles before being copied and adapted by, or diffused to, other movements (Keck and Sikkink 1998a: 43). Repertoires of contention evolve over time but the pace of change can be glacial (see Tarrow 1994: 32).[3] When looking at Internet activism, we should consider whether this technology is (a) introducing something new to the repertoires of contention available to social movements and (b) if it is having an impact on the opportunity structures available to activists by providing new routes to political information, new ways of networking and different forums for sharing information.

The framing of issues by activists is also an important element of their armoury of persuasion. Often activists are framing issues in a way that goes against the grain of governmental or mainstream political thought. It has been argued that 'one of the main tasks that social movements undertake ... is to make possible the previously unimaginable, by framing problems in such a way that their solution comes to appear inevitable' (ibid.: 41). As noted in Chapter 3, though, the opportunities for activists to create the dominant framing discourse are limited by their relatively low levels of access to mass media outlets. Indeed, there is something of a tussle between two groups of actors here. Mainstream mass media organizations, as noted in Chapter 3, operate closely with governments and tend to frame non-state actors as other to 'real' politics. They also tend to frame politics along national lines, while social movements often see politics as operating at multiple levels. While influencing policy at national level *can* be one of their goals, it is by no means their only one. In many cases, it is not an objective at all.

NGOs as political actors

The difficulties of classifying NGO activity have been subject to much academic scrutiny, with scholars from a range of disciplines attempting to clarify their position within contemporary social and political systems. Vakil has noted that the absence of a framework for classifying NGOs may have seriously impeded an understanding of the sector (1997: 2057). The term 'non-governmental organization' was first used in 1950 to refer to 'officially recognized organizations with no governmental affiliation that had consultative status within the United Nations' (ibid.: 2068). The term has stuck. Despite a huge rise in NGO numbers in recent decades, and the increased politicization of many, they retain the negative non-governmental/non-state – and, by inference, not *really* political – definition. It is now generally acknowledged, though, that non-state political communities have an important impact on state practices, and that NGOs play a key role in the formation of such communities by providing an organizational framework around which political action may be structured or mediated (see Rodgers 1999). There has been incredible growth in the sector in recent years, a change characterized as 'nothing short of phenomenal' by some (see Smythe and Smith 2001: 11).

Given the breadth, scale and diversity of the NGO movement, it is perhaps prudent to consider their forms of political agency, rather than to attempt to generalize about their objectives and their means of achieving them. NGO activity may be large-scale; some perceive themselves to be global actors and have offices worldwide. Many others are highly localized, focusing their operations on specific regions. Such a local focus, however, does not necessarily limit their activities to within state borders (see Frederick 1997).

Charlton *et al.* suggested that 'NGO' should be viewed as a conceptually distinct but empirically imprecise organizational category (1995: 19). Their key characteristics are that they are independent of state control, in terms of decision-making processes, and that they are institutions, in that they structure social behaviours around a particular set of goals. Independence from state control does not suggest that they are necessarily averse to accepting funding from governments. Some, such as Amnesty International and Greenpeace, fiercely defend their fiscal autonomy, while others, such as Oxfam, are happy to accept funds from governments and from international organizations. OneWorld, one of the major Internet NGOs, accepts a large grant from DFID, the UK government's Department for International Development, and has also taken funds from the EU, the UK's National Lottery Charities Board and the British Council (Warkentin 2001: 164). The sources of funding are the subject of much contention in the NGO sector. Funding from governments is often considered to come with too many strings attached, corporate support is seen by some as a double-edged sword, while funding from individual donations is subject to the vagaries of public opinion (see Pharoah 2002: online).

For Willetts, 'NGOs become theoretically important when it is appreciated that they are agents of social change, projected to the level of global politics' (1996: 57). As agents of social change, NGOs cover a diverse range of interests, areas and objectives; there is, therefore, no such thing as a typical NGO and their organizational structures tend to arise as social movements grow (ibid.) Given the normative, issue-based perceptions of politics which NGOs generally endorse, it is evident that the potential to transcend territory and forge links through and across organizational boundaries, both those internal to NGOs and in the wider political realm, is a facet of the Internet which closely reflects the objectives of international organizations. In this sense, the Internet reflects the relatively diffuse organizational structures of many NGOs.

NGO undertakings are characterized by a diffusion of activities across a range of actors, often with a wide-ranging geographical reach. International NGOs – for obvious reasons – invariably have transborder and/or transnational concerns. Keck and Sikkink note that opportunities for networking across borders have increased over the past couple of decades:

> In addition to the efforts of pioneers, a proliferation of international conferences has provided foci for connections. Cheaper air travel and new electronic communications technologies speed information flows and simplify personal contact among activists.
>
> (1998a: 14)

It isn't necessarily particularly difficult to engage in transnational activism these days and, given both the ease of engagement and the nature of normative political interactions, there is often a tendency towards transnationalization of even some highly localized campaigns. There are two main reasons for this. One is that transnational movements 'will form around issues for which national opportunity structures are relatively closed, or for which purely national solutions are inappropriate' (ibid.: 57). The other is that:

> In order to be able to speak of social movements it is necessary that single episodes are perceived as components of a longer-lasting action, rather than discrete events; and that those who are engaged feel linked by ties of solidarity of ideal communion with protagonists of other analogous mobilizations.
>
> (Della Porta and Diana 1999: 19)

These two factors are often closely related, as the relative openness or otherwise of national structures can be a catalyst for extending perceptions of what political claims should be and how they can be achieved. In addition, campaigns about particular issues, such as human rights in Burma, draw upon broader frameworks of understanding, both about what human rights should be and how other movement actors have sought to achieve them. The sense of solidarity is, for many movement actors, inherently transcendental, as it is based on issues rather than places.

An NGO concerned about a transborder issue may respond to this by lobbying governments and/or regional authorities and/or the local population where a problem originates or occurs. For this reason, NGO interaction with governments will often be based upon how much impact a given government can actually have on an issue: NGOs, like other activists, do not necessarily assume a government to be the primary actor when seeking to elicit social or political change. In any given instance a multinational corporation, a regional authority, an international organization, a community group or individual, or a combination thereof, may be better able to effect change than a state agency. Hence, to some degree, politics as understood by NGOs as non-state actors differs from that outlined and applied by governments. The spaces that activists perceive to be of political relevance are often dependent upon the territorial assumptions of states, but frequently extend beyond the public parameters outlined in the dominant discourse. Indeed, Smith argues that transnational social movements, in which NGOs play an important role, tend to form around issues for which purely national solutions are inappropriate (1997: 57).[4]

As a consequence of the broader definitions of politics under which they operate, NGOs are generally less closely bound than states to the agendas of high politics. They may act in co-operation with government agencies, international organizations and so on, but are often responsible for introducing new items to standard political agendas, in line with their particular area of interest or operation. Kriesberg talks of TSMOs (of which NGOs are a part) helping to:

> Transmit information by providing a network of relations for the diffusion of ideas and practices, thereby facilitating mobilization for movement goals. They also help diffuse norms and values about participation in policymaking and execution and serve as constituencies for other NGOs and for IGOs.

> (1997: 14)

On the whole, they tend to conform to the characteristics identified by Charlton *et al.* These suggest that NGOs are generally distinguished by pursuit of collective action on the basis of 'voluntaristic mechanisms', based on processes of bargaining, accommodation, discussion and persuasion which are conceptually distinct from the hierarchical operational principles of either states or profit-driven market institutions (1995: 26). The work of some NGOs is widely credited with introducing issues such as human rights, environmental change and gender discrimination to international political agendas. Analysis of regime formation also often acknowledges the normative role activists play in the evolution of co-operative practices in international politics.

NGOs can't be categorized as acting either specifically in 'public' or 'private' spheres. As international actors, they may be engaged in research and political activities aimed at altering governmental policy with respect to the environment, to international aid policies and so on. Also as international actors, however, they draw upon the membership and support of private individuals, that is, of members of the general public. The interests of these individuals may have a basis in social rather than overtly political concerns. Membership of Friends of the Earth, for example, could be prompted by a localized issue, such as river pollution in a member's hometown area, or a more general interest, such as a concern for the global environment. In neither case can membership be assumed to be intentionally 'political'. In this sense, the metaphoric spaces of access to political structures are extended to individuals through membership of NGOs in that social and political fields overlap within their operations.

The growth in number and type of NGOs in recent decades has had the effect of politicizing many issues previously considered to be of social, or private, concern. They can provide indirect access to 'official' political structures for otherwise marginalized actors, through their coalescence of the social and political realms. They also work with, have contact with and/or provide connections to other movement actors, including the following:

(1) international and domestic nongovernmental research and advocacy networks; (2) local social movements; (3) foundations; (4) the media; (5) churches, trade unions, consumer organizations, and intellectuals; (6) parts of regional and international intergovernmental organizations; and (7) parts of the executive and / or parliamentary branches of government.

(Keck and Sikkink 1998a: 9)

All of this contributes to the process of rendering 'the political' an increasingly imprecise category. For example, the manner in which abortion has become a politicized issue of international concern, related to gender, human rights, national and international norms and to development agendas demonstrates this blurring of categories.

In some cases NGOs can act as a bridge between individuals and governmental actors. Through membership of NGOs, individuals move closer to the political arena by engaging by proxy with other political actors. Concerns of individuals or groups may be more easily represented through NGOs than through the direct engagement of individuals with state agencies, as most political structures, representative or otherwise, militate against the direct involvement of the public in affairs of the state. The World Bank holds the view that NGOs often act as social and political intermediaries who 'can create links both upward and downward in society' (Charlton *et al.* 1995: 24). Moreover, in lobbying both governments and international governmental organizations, NGOs can be both part of broader social movements, and effective organizations in their own right (Willetts 1996: 61). NGOs tend to emphasize the importance of partnership between themselves, governmental agencies, international governmental organizations and 'ordinary people'. Thus, while remaining outside the realm of official institutions of politics, they often 'seek to establish the interests and rights of those generally excluded from discussion' (Devetak and Higgott 1999: 491). The value of effective communications systems in this respect, both in terms of technological provision and access to information, across a range of actors, is apparent.

NGOs are able to adopt less pragmatic positions than governments and have less need to satisfy competing domestic interest groups (Smith 1995: 306). Some of the many features of twenty-first century life which serve to undermine the state as the primary site of political legitimacy, such as increasingly globalized markets and economies, and the spread of new communications technologies, may often be advantageous to NGOs, given that they are unrestrained by the bureaucratic mechanisms associated with the management of territory. Hurrell suggested that NGOs in the environmental movement possess four strengths, which make them important players in their own right. First, activists have the ability to develop and disseminate knowledge. Such knowledge will generally be issue-specific, transcending both discursive barriers and national borders. Second, NGOs often articulate a powerful set of human values and, third, their actions may harness a growing sense of moral awareness. These last two are related, in that the actions of NGOs are often based on a concern to develop more equitable social and political systems than exist at present. As the growth of the NGO movement testifies, this type of concern has widespread support. Finally, NGOs respond to the multiple weaknesses of the state system, both at global and local levels (see Hurrell 1995). The characteristics attributed to environmental activists may readily be transferred to activists which focus on other concerns.

The characteristics highlighted by Hurrell illustrate the key strengths of NGOs as political actors, and reflect the relevance to such organizations of the Internet. The development and dissemination of information across barriers and borders, the articulation of human values, the harnessing of a growing common awareness and responding to the weaknesses of the state system are all features which the Internet has the potential to consolidate, in terms of both extending audiences and influencing discourse. Wartenkin (2001) highlights dynamism, exhibited through flexibility and adaptability; inclusiveness, seen in networking and participation; and cognisance, shown through 'informed activism' as the key features which distinguish NGOs from other political actors. Again, in theory, the Internet could perfectly complement these features.

Research suggests that the influence of NGOs is not experienced only at the level of policy-making (see Bailie and Winseck 1997; Keck and Sikkink 1998a), but is manifested in three other important ways. First, they tend to be inherently de-centralizing, working across multiple spaces, both geographical and metaphoric. As noted earlier, NGOs will, in pursuit of their objectives, lobby and/or work with any actor who may influence changes, with questions of geography and status relevant only to a specific goal. This means that 'the rational, centralized administrative state, along with other bureaucratic institutions in society, is losing monopoly over key sources of power, information and the capacity of surveillance' (Smythe and Smith 2001: 13). Such changes are embedded in others, of course, with globalizing processes at structure, agency and all other levels in between having an impact on the state's capacity to control, and the ability of NGOs to challenge this control.

Second, these organizations may often be structurally less prone to gender imbalance than are state agencies. Though women are barely represented at the 'top' of politics, they are widely active as members of local, national and international organizations (Peterson and Runyan 1999: 149).[5] For Inglehart and Norris, 'the evidence that women have commonly participated less than men in conventional state-oriented forms of political expression, organization and mobilization is well-established' (2003). This is not to suggest that gender bias does not exist in NGOs; as social institutions they are potentially just as likely to have discriminatory structures and practices as any other organization. The forms of politics undertaken by NGOs do, however, seem to offer opportunities for women often denied to them by 'official' political institutions, at least in the developed world: 'The patterns ... suggest that overall men continue to predominate as members and activists in less prosperous developing societies, but the gender gap in civic activism has diminished substantially, or possibly even reversed, in more affluent nations' (ibid.)

Third, although often operating in co-operation with governments, the emphasis of many NGOs on normative issues, rather than on conventional agendas, extends the scale and scope of politics, thus providing alternative spatial constructions. To a certain degree, NGOs act as one mechanism for facilitating the increasing links between areas previously considered to be separate areas: public politics and the private lives of individuals. Clarke has suggested that as the links between public affairs and the private realm increase:

> The conception of what falls under the public domain might be widened so that more of what we do, regardless of the domain in which it formally falls, is treated as political.
>
> (1996: 89)

The alternative conceptualizations of politics with which many NGOs operate has led many scholars to situate their activity under the rubric of 'global civil society'. Those promoting the concept of global civil society suggest that non-governmental actors, and in particular activists, are developing forms of interaction which create social and political links across societies, often with little recourse to formal institutions of governance. Indeed, Stavenhagen suggests that civil society challenges existing paradigms of governance and relates to objectives that entail alternative forms of economic development, political control and social organization (1997: 34).

The concept of global civil society promotes individuals, activists and less formal collectives as political agents and has had a demonstrable impact on the ways politics are now being understood in IR. For Lipschutz, global civil society is characterized by the 'emergence of a parallel arrangement of political interaction ... focused on the self-conscious construction of networks of knowledge and action, by decentred, local actors' (1992: 390). This parallel arrangement challenges, albeit often implicitly, the concept of the state as central to political practice, and acknowledges the significance of non-territorial forms of political association more fully than the dominant discourse of IR does.

Proponents (for example Cox 1997; Rosenau 1997) and detractors (such as Baker 1999) alike acknowledge a transnationalization of political activity in recent years, with a related shift in the significance of activists as actors and of communications technologies as a driving mechanism. In this respect, the concept of a global civil society is of enormous relevance to analysis of changing political spaces and, in particular, of activists and their use of communications technologies. Cox has argued that civil society has become a crucial battleground for recovering citizen control of public life (1999: 27) and in this respect its relevance to analysis of the links across social and political spheres is evident.

As key players in connecting governments, institutions and individuals to the political process both NGOs and the Internet represent challenges to state-centric norms of political analysis. In this sense, in common with feminist theorists, those analysing global civil society have been 're-visioning' politics as a more diffuse, decentralized enterprise. For Devetak and Higgott, activists represent an important alternative voice aspiring to the development of a 'justice-based' dialogue beyond the level of the sovereign state (1999: 485) and, as a consequence, they push the conceptual boundaries of political analysis beyond state-related definitions of the political. There is little doubt that some form of global civil society now exists, in that a diffusion of political interests across state boundaries among non-state actors is evident. Mahon, however, is highly critical of the concept and suggests it is part of a broader neo-liberal project which legitimates a shift in power from states to the world market (1996: 299). Baker, too, sees the conflation of civil society with market ideals and suggests that the theory of global civil society has effectively been demobilized by this orientation (1999: 24).

As Walker has argued, however, the concept of civil society provides another spatial container (1995: 312) which can be viewed as comparable to state-centric norms in its discursive closure. The concept of global civil society, while taking analysis in IR an important step away from state centrism, effectively posits another, potentially equally limiting, version of politics, in terms of the interpretative possibilities it permits. Thus for Walker:

> For all the sophistications of the literature on social movements ... ,
> it still seems bound by conceptions of political possibility that preclude
> debates about what it would mean to put established conceptions of
> political community and identity into question.
>
> (ibid.)

Although it has been argued that politics can now be seen as a triangular
configuration of state, market and civil society (Devetak and Higgott 1999:
490), this still positions political analysis under a fairly rigid set of
assumptions regarding how such analysis can take place. Looking back to
Lefebvre and the concept of representations of space, we can see that the
rubric of global civil society codifies relations between actors in much the
same manner as state centrism does. This is not to suggest that the global
civil society literature is not valuable: its contribution to the 're-visioning'
of IR has been extremely important. As a framework for analysis, though, it
suffers from the same limitations as any other structure-led ontology. In
particular, there is the emphasis on global interactions that obscures a range
of activities and actors.

'Informal' activists

The notion of 'informal' activism is a bit of an uncomfortable one, implying
lack of gravitas and commitment. That isn't what is intended here. The idea
is to make a distinction between those social movement members who seek
institutional representation and those who do not. We are not talking about
individual activists with no form of connection to other movement actors;
the people referred to as 'informal activists' are those who may be linked to
any number of networks but who do not necessarily view NGOs or formal
organizational frameworks as representative of their normative vision of
politics in the global arena.

Many of the points made about formal movement actors also apply to
these informal actors. We need to ask, then, why some people engage in
'informal' activism rather than take a more structural perspective. When
people are concerned about environmental degradation, for example, why
do some people join Greenpeace and Friends of the Earth, while others
build tunnels or chain themselves to trees to prevent road-building projects?
Even if a concerned individual does join an NGO, this does not limit his/her
interest to membership of that organization, nor does it mean that the
agendas and framings of political issues by the organization will be
uncritically accepted. S/he may decide to pay his/her subscription and let an
NGO do the campaigning on his/her behalf. On the other hand, s/he may
become involved in other networks too but this campaigning will often be
less visible than that undertaken by a major international NGO. Are these
forms of campaigning part of a continuum, or do they represent different
kinds of politics altogether?

Although they are labelled 'informal' activists here to indicate a contrast with the formal structures of NGOs, the two sets of actors share some similarities: their vision of politics is usually based on normative concerns; they often see their concerns as shifting between global, local, and other arenas; and their image of politics is not necessarily focussed on states or governments. However, 'since NGOs are sectoral in their interests there is a clear limit to their ability to claim general representativity – compared with political parties, for example, their scope is narrower even if their membership is often far greater' (Warleigh 2001: 623). For many activists, this is perceived as a problem for the NGO movement: while their remit – as a rule of thumb, social change of some form or another – is wide, their focus is often, of necessity, narrow. This frequently means that, although they are often praised for their innovation in campaigning, their strategies for promoting political change are viewed as restrictive by some activists. This criticism is levelled particularly at large, transnational NGOs, whose bureaucratic networks are extensive. In addition, the apparently close relationship between some of the major NGOs and governments is viewed with suspicion by some activists.

Inglehart and Norris divide political activism into three categories: traditional, civic and protest activism (2003). Traditional activism includes voting participation and party and/or union membership; civic activism includes work within voluntary organizations, community associations and other social movement organizations; and protest activism involves activities such as demonstrations, boycotts and petitioning (see ibid.) As we can see, there is a considerable overlap today between what might be considered 'formal' activism and less formal kinds; organizations co-ordinate boycotts, demonstrations and petitions, while people participating in them may or may not have an institutional affiliation.

As Smythe and Smith say, 'rarely is there an international issue that does not attract a transnational network of NGOs, TSMOs, and informal associations organizing and mobilizing to express their point of view' (2001: 2). Often the issues are considered to be the same, or substantially similar, by movement actors at different levels. That is not to say that actors in different areas of movements are *intrinsically* linked, but that the likelihood is that they will be in some ways. There can be 'frame alignment' (see Keck and Sikkink 1998a: 17), where NGOs and unaffiliated actors assume a shared set of meanings. Often, though, while there is agreement on the central concerns – say, ending human rights abuses or preventing global warming – there may be disagreements on the causes, culprits, curses and cures which the umbrella of shared interests is unable to cover adequately. That said, while people engaged in protest activism will not always agree with a 'formal' movement's framing of an issue, they will often make use of their expertise and the information provided by them. The same applies in reverse; the often dynamic and innovative strategies of informal activists may be replicated, in modified forms, by mainstream organizations.

NGOs are not able to represent all of the views of all of the people, as it were, and cannot hope to represent a broad spectrum of political views. While one of the perceived strengths of the NGO movement is considered to be its focus on single-issue politics, it can also be regarded as a weakness where a broader range of issues can be considered to be relevant. Gamson suggested that 'however much we identify with a movement, we have other sub-identities built around other social roles. Inevitably, we may face conflicts between how we as movement members feel called upon to act and the actions called for by these other role identities' (1991: 45). In building their 'brand identity', large NGOs focus clearly on some issues to the exclusion of others. At the same time, they use tried and tested – some would suggest quasi-corporate – strategies to achieve their objectives. For many anti-capitalist protesters in particular, becoming involved with global bureaucracies – however much each side empathizes with the other's core principles – is unacceptable.

Tarrow has said that people band together in movements 'to mount common claims against opponents, authorities or elites' (1994: 4). For some people, in some circumstances, mounting such claims is best effected through institutional structures. For others, making claims is something that works best without formal frameworks. In some cases this is for purely pragmatic reasons:

> Time, energy and initiative is needed to work in voluntary organizations and community associations, such as attending local meetings, organizing community groups or editing newsletters.
>
> (Inglehart and Norris 2003)

Informal association with social movements does not necessarily mean that activists will not be engaging in these kinds of activities. In the absence of institutional affiliation, though, there is a greater potential to control the level of participation required. This control over access, coupled with the perceived impact of any engagement in activism, can influence decisions to become involved in political campaigns. This seems to be particularly true for women. Kuumba's research has shown that women may establish influence and control in social movements through informal and community-based networks (2001: 54). In such cases, the gender relations of activist practices are highlighted. As noted in Chapter 2, these are generally underplayed in the literature on social movements.

Occasionally, informal activism can be a stepping stone to closer engagement with political movements, sometimes through NGOs or other, more formal structures. Existing social networks are a key feature of activist movements:

> We know ... how important social networks are for recruiting people and drawing them into political action with their friends. People

sometimes act first and only through participating develop the political
consciousness that supports the action.

(Gamson 1995: 89)

If our friends and family talk about politics, there is a strong likelihood that
we will also do so. And if they are drawn to a particular cause, we may well
become involved in it too (see Pickerill 2000: online). In this respect, the
personal costs of engaging with a political movement (see Tarrow 1994: 18)
are lowered, as an inclusive network of support is already in existence.

Introducing the Internet into politics

NGOs and other activists are not the only political actors making use of the
Internet and the dynamics of political change through its use are by no
means limited to social movements. Warkentin puts this well when he offers
a 'things change' caveat in his book on NGOs and the Internet (2001: xiii).
In effect, he suggests that the Internet, the actors using it and the structures
within which they operate are all dynamically related, and changes in any
or all of these areas result in changes in others. The numbers of NGO and
activist networks has been growing for decades, their relationships with
political institutions are constantly evolving, the nature of activist practices
continues to develop and so on. The Internet is only part of this, though the
more complex and globalized technologies and values appear to become,
the more difficult it is to determine which, if any, factors can be identified as
catalysts for change.

Activist use of the Internet relates, of course, to the broader structural
change fostered by the diffusion of telecommunications technologies across
real and metaphoric boundaries. Information, as both commodity and
resource, can affect all political actors, with changes in the behaviour of one
group influencing the behaviour of others. In this sense, activist use of the
Internet links to a wider adjustment of power and control relations wrought
by the 'information age'. It is possible to argue that if activists change *their*
behaviour, then governments and other political institutions inevitably do
likewise. The ability to gather, potentially at least, a constituency of
millions into any political network makes the Internet domino effect in
politics seem more of a real possibility. Does this pose a challenge to the
power of states regarding censorship, propaganda and national interest?
And if Amnesty International, say, can gather ten thousand click-signatures
on an online petition, does this constitute a new form of power-in-numbers
politics, or does it represent little more than lazy, uncommitted 'armchair
activism' of the kind noted earlier.

Patterns of activist behaviour are, superficially at least, reflected by the
spatial forms of network communications. These are essentially decen-
tralizing 'in the sense that they democratize information flow, break down
hierarchies of power, and make communication from the top and bottom

just as easy as from horizon to horizon' (Frederick 1997: 256). Although complex, there are identifiable patterns of construction and use of the Internet which provide tangible communications infrastructures for political activity. The form of these infrastructures contrasts with the geographical structures upon which IR has traditionally based its ontologies, in that they are socially constructed and intrinsically mutable (see Libicki 1995, 1996). Although activists are not immune to dispute and dissent, co-operation is something of a byword in the NGO approach to politics: as a consequence, 'Organizationally, networking is seen ... as the NGO's trump card' (Charlton *et al.* 1995: 27). In this sense, the use of the Internet appears to compliment their *modus operandi.*

Network technologies appear to provide a digital continuum of the existing mode of operation of activists, whether formally attached to organizational structures or not. The mutability and multi-dimensionality of the Internet does not preclude analysis of their forms and effects. There are many aspects of the use of the Internet which are subject to design and which conform to regulated organizational patterns, particularly on the part of information providers. For example, contact with an NGO may frequently be random on the part of an individual using the Internet. 'Surfing', fairly casual exploration of the Internet, means that chance encounters with NGO and activist sites are likely.

As information providers, however, activists – formal or otherwise – structure information both through access mechanisms and website design. Online access mechanisms, particularly search engines, are used by activists in the same way as corporations would apply them. Key words on search engines give organizations one opportunity to try to position their information high on search results lists. Some organizations – such as Human Rights Watch – have taken this strategy a step further by forging links with ISPs to ensure that their information comes to the top of the list on general searches. Activists use the Internet as a tool with which to extend their audience and promote their causes. Any contact with these organizations through the use of the Internet, therefore, is structured at least in part by the decisions on communications infrastructures made by the original information provider.

Similarly, the design of web pages can influence the types of information Internet users can access. As the case studies in the following chapters show, the Internet is being used as one feature of multi-dimensional political campaigning. It is also, at the same time, being used to promote links beyond activist networks. Many organizations provide links to, for example, governments and international organizations. While this information could be found elsewhere, there is a definite sense that the perceived boundaries of politics are stretching. The use of such structuring devices is significant; perceptions that Internet use is fairly random are erroneous. The structuring of links and access are important in creating a sense of investment in an activity on the part of the Internet user:

There are, in effect, two levels of structuring to internet use: the choices of individuals in what they search for and the persuasive strategies of the sites they visit, designed to encourage networking, participation, spending and so on.

(Gauntlett and Rodgers 2002: online)

The strategies that activists use to encourage participation online fit in, in part, with social movement theories, by extending pre-existing networks. An environmental activist, for example, can gain access to a new range of already-existing networks.

These strategies are based upon the forging of contacts between and across interested, affected and influential groups and individuals. The technical capabilities of the Internet, that is the communications possibilities they offer, can enhance the existing operational methods of activists. In this sense, use of the Internet expands the repertoires of contention available to political activists, by providing new avenues for engagement. The real test lies in whether these repertoires are added to the range of possibilities open to activists. If so, and we do see new repertoires of contention evolving, we can conclude that the Internet is indeed a revolutionary technology in terms of its impact on political practices. This is because repertoires 'once used and understood, ... [can] ... be diffused elsewhere and employed on behalf of wider coalitions' (Tarrow 1994: 40).

New communications technologies appear to be making a considerable difference to the ways in which activists can approach their activities. Electronic communications networks are partially responsible for

producing forms of social organization – social networks, communications networks, and especially the emergence of multi-organizational networks – that allow people and groups to play an increasingly significant role in international relations as governmental and market hierarchies are eroded by the diffusion of power to smaller groups.

(Frederick 1997: 256)

This view is supported by Hurrell, who has argued that an increased level of economic globalization provides an infrastructure for enhanced social communication. Hence the communications networks which have evolved in tandem with economic structures are a mechanism for 'facilitating the flow of values, knowledge and ideas and in allowing like-minded groups to organize across national boundaries' (Hurrell 1995: 144).

One paradox of the spread of the Internet as a tool of political activism is that states are necessarily both drivers of the technology and among those who have most interest in controlling certain aspects of its development. Many governments have been actively promoting the Internet for use by their citizens, under rubrics such as the 'Global Information Infrastructure' in the US, and the 'information superhighway' in the UK. For Castells, all states are, and will become increasingly, informational societies:

> in the sense that the core processes of knowledge production, economic productivity, political/military power and media communication are already deeply transformed by the informational paradigm, and are connected to global networks of wealth, power, and symbols working under such a logic.
>
> (1996: 21)

These networks are diffused across multiple levels and layers of societies, and states are necessarily both contending against and participating in their development.

Conclusion

The intrinsic transcendence of boundaries which the Internet implies suggests to many that it is an inherently globalizing medium. Much of the research on this type of technology adopts this premise and identifies this as the Internet's primary characteristic. Although the Internet is made up of theoretically 'global' technologies, networks are essentially formed by their use, rather than by their reach or availability. Thus, the Internet is equally likely to be used to reinforce local connections through, for example, their use by community or environmental groups (see Pickerill 2000). Analysis of activist use of the Internet in the international arena does not therefore imply that some form of 'global society' or 'world community' is likely to develop as the result of the spread of this technology. Indeed, Carothers *et al.* point out that the web is used to advance nefarious as well as worthy ends (1999: online) and for this reason the Internet cannot be considered to be an inherently unifying technology. It can be used to extend political networks, though, both 'good' and 'bad' ones.

Although different kinds of activists may have different objectives, their use of the Internet is designed both to provide information and to promote political engagement. In some cases the kind of engagement encouraged may be direct action (in the 'real' world), in others it may be to simply persuade people to click on an e-petition or send an e-card to a government minister. In both cases, there is a strong sense that political engagement through the Internet is considered by both formal and informal activists to have a legitimacy comparable with that of offline political engagement. This is interesting because, as noted in Chapter 3, many governments have not caught up with this conceptualization of politics yet. In the case studies in the following chapters, we can see examples of how activists have been using the Internet to steal a march on the more slow-moving bureaucracies of governments.

5 Activism case studies
Structural challenges

Introduction

Some forms of contemporary political protest – particularly nationalist struggles – can still be partially, perhaps largely, explained with reference to traditional models of politics and political communication that are based on territorial assumptions. Four case studies – two in this and two in the next chapter – are used to demonstrate some of the factors influencing the methods used in social movement politics today, particularly the forms of transnational protest which make use of the Internet as a tool for information provision and networking. They show how political activists are using the Internet in ways that defy traditional spatial assumptions, making the need for new theoretical tools evident.

The case studies are designed to show some of the many different ways the Internet is used by non-state actors in political processes. This helps to contextualize 'Internet activism' as a variable and contingent practice. The application of the Internet as a political tool takes many forms and operates in many different contexts and the case studies used here give examples of how the Internet is being used in contemporary protest politics. Each demonstrates differing applications of the Internet both as a technology (that is, how it can be used), and as a strategic tool (that is, how it can be applied to meet specific objectives). In later chapters, spatial theories are applied to the case studies to illustrate how they provide new ways of looking at the complex forms of political activity.

The case studies outline different issues and actors and examine how the Internet has been used to meet the objectives of activists in each case. Given the normative basis of much political protest, there are overlaps between the issues activists consider to be at stake in some cases. Some of these will be drawn together in later chapters. The case studies are separated under two banners. This chapter looks at what could be termed structural issues. These relate to the use of the Internet as a tool of persuasion, directed as a challenge to existing political and economic structures. The first looks at global NGOs – two 'traditional' international organizations, Amnesty International and Friends of the Earth, and two Internet-based, OneWorld and APC (the Association for Progressive Communications). This case describes some of the ways the Internet is used in promoting the activities of NGOs on the international stage. The second addresses the growth of independent media on the Internet, looking particularly at the activities of Squall, an online activist newspaper. The transition from offline to online press is examined and the role of the Internet in challenging mass media representations and respatializing the media arena is considered.

The case studies in Chapter 6 focus on issue-specific politics, namely the genetic modification of foods and the Missile Defense programme. These are also transnational issues, subject to transnational protest networking. They also pose structural challenges. The case studies focus, though, on how interest in their particular areas of concern is generated and maintained (or otherwise) by movement activists. The first case looks at the issue of genetically modified foods and the widescale protest against their introduction to the food chain outside of the United States. In this case, the role of the Internet in challenging international actors such as multinational corporations and regulatory institutions such as the WTO is particularly significant. The movement against GM foods is wide-scale and has been described as 'the most vibrant' of the movements 'explicitly organized around limiting corporate power' (Starr 2000: 65). The second case study is on the US government's missile defence project, known variously as NMD (National Missile Defense), BMD (Ballistic Missile Defense) and 'Son of Star Wars'. Here, the role of the Internet in protest against both national governments and perceived US hegemony is explored; that is, how the Internet is applied by protesters at the intersection of foreign policy and domestic politics is considered.

Case Study 5.1: Transnational NGOs

The growth of normative movements around human rights, environmental and peace issues has been having a slow and steady impact on the landscape of international politics in recent years. The rise in the number of NGOs who deal with these transcendental issues has been dramatic. Warkentin suggests that the number of active NGOs rose from less than two hundred in the early twentieth century to more than forty thousand by the late 1990s (2001: 4). The introduction of the Internet has added another layer of engagement to these existing forms of issue-based politics, apparently providing a mechanism for expanding and extending transnational forms of collective association.

The Internet appears to provide a valuable tool for NGOs in two key aspects of their activities. First, it further disrupts state-determined definitions of politics – already weakened by the rise in normative approaches – by providing a platform for promotion of grassroots, issue-based and 'bottom-up' (as opposed to 'top-down') politics. Second, Internet technology can be used to provide a voice for marginalized and disenfranchised groups whose concerns are not generally prioritized on state or mass media agendas (Axford and Huggins 2001; Rodgers 2001a). In these two respects, both the structures of politics and the range of actors involved in it are considered to be adjusted by the introduction of the Internet into the political arena. For many academics, practitioners and policy-makers the Internet 'brings new opportunities for direct access to politically relevant information, for unmediated communication between political organizations and potential members, and for interactive discourse among citizens themselves' (Moog and Sluyter-Beltrao 2001: 56).

This case study draws on interviews with activists from four trans-national NGOs: Amnesty International (AI), Friends of the Earth (FOE), the Association of Progressive Communications (APC) and OneWorld.[1] AI and FOE are widely recognized 'brands' in international political campaigning, the former on human rights, the latter on environmental issues. APC and OneWorld are both 'umbrella' organizations who provide online networks for NGOs. In respect of APC, this case study focuses on its Women's Network Support Programme (WNSP), which has been a key element of APC's strategy to improve access to Internet technologies for women. The case study looks at some of the strategies used and dilemmas faced in the drive to develop Internet services suitable to the needs of their respective organizations. These organizations have all been extremely pro-active in the promotion of the Internet, seeing in it a mechanism for creating and extending networks between a range of political actors.

The Internet and advocacy networks

NGOs operating across national borders may seek to influence a broad range of actors, some engaged in 'high' politics, some in 'low' and others – such as multinational corporations – who ostensibly operate outside of the political arena. The NGOs in this case study all represent formalized elements of transnational social networks, in that they provide structures for information exchange, lobbying and mobilization. Keck and Sikkink's suggestion that transnational advocacy networks are communicative structures for political exchange (1998a: 214) highlights how evidence on NGO use of the Internet becomes crucial to understanding the impact of this technology in the field of politics.

Large advocacy networks are structured not only by the principles behind their practices, but also by organizational needs and constraints. Actors, interactions, and the effects of specific practices alter according to circumstance, and between organizations. The use of the Internet by NGOs, therefore, has different effects from case to case and thus the problem of pinning its impact down is compounded. For this reason, no case study evidence on NGO practices can be applied as a standard model across the board. Smith makes this point well, noting that 'the advantage of transnational mobilization certainly varies according to issue. Whereas human rights and some environmental activists find natural and necessary connections to multilateral processes, other areas ... require more local and national emphases' (2001: 9). On top of this, the effectiveness of individual campaigns may be case-specific, as the application of a technology to long- and short-term goals inevitably has differing manifestations.

Despite the difficulties in pinning down obvious points of reference, there are some clear connections between what the organizations are aiming to do and what the technology can offer. Internet technology reflects the diversity of many NGO activities and provides an ideal medium of communication for many. It is generally more useful than the mass media in providing a voice for NGO interests, particularly where debate or detailed information is required. NGO voices in the mass media are often heard only in reaction to the actions of governments, despite the widely acknowledged expertise of some on major normative political issues. In this respect, NGOs, as portrayed by the mass media, are not politically relevant in their own right, but tend to represent an anti-establishment position. The APC WNSP note, for example, that mass media coverage of their work at the Beijing conference focused on stereotypes and spectacle, rather than on the aims or achievements of the networking project (APC WNSP 2001: interview).[2] The gatekeeping functions and commercial ethos (including, increasingly, in public service broadcasting) of mass media, offers little air time to the concerns of most NGOs. The Internet provides organizations with an opportunity to publish material which may not otherwise receive an airing.

The range of communicative possibilities offered by the Internet is another of its virtues for many NGOs. The one-to-one, many-to-many, many-to-few variables inherent to the technology are ideally suited to the conducting of multiple campaigns simultaneously, as they provide mechanisms for targeting different publics. As access issues continue to trouble information providers, the range of actors reachable in cyberspace is undoubtedly limited to a minority. Dahlgren points out, though, that the small numbers of politically engaged people in cyberspace are 'to a degree offset by the sociological profile of the group: affluence and high education are important variables in the shaping of opinion and political climates' (2001a: 75). One thing that has not yet been established is whether the level of political engagement among the affluent educated is increasing, or whether mass media coverage of high-profile protests such as those in Davos and Gothenburg in 2001, and at the Earth Summit in Johannesburg in 2002, is simply making some elements of this elite more visible.

Assessing the success of online campaigning

There is an implicit assumption in much of the literature on the use of the Internet for political purposes that, because the technology is potentially *globalizing,* it must therefore be *globalized.* That is, there is a tendency to equate the range of the technology with the size of the potential audience. In most cases, though, the power of the web relates not to the number of people it can reach but to its impact on specific audiences. For the NGOs considered here the plural – 'audiences' – carries a particular significance, as a wide range of actors, including politicians, other lobbyist organizations, specialists such as legal professionals, a broad general public and so on may need to be targeted simultaneously using the same technology. Transnational NGOs with normative values thus need to develop quite sophisticated techniques to apply Internet technologies to appeal to local, national and international audiences, to specialist users and to a broad general public.

Many NGOs have, of necessity, become much more adept at targeting their web-based information and at using strategic applications of Internet technology. The gold-rush to simply have a presence on the Internet is over and many organizations are now using the technology much more strategically, designing online campaigns around specific goals. In this respect, there has been a move away from viewing the Internet as an inherently globalizing technology and a shift towards using it specifically to suit the needs of the organizations themselves. Rather than aiming to reach as many people as possible, there is now an assumption that reaching the *right* people – i.e., those who will respond, protest and campaign – should be the aim of providing information on the Internet. For many large NGOs, use of websites and email is based not only on the volume of information which can be transmitted but also on finding appropriate means of targeting their communications to reach specific audiences. The cost of Internet provision relative to the amount of information it can convey is negligible. AI and FOE both suggest that the aim of publications in any medium is to raise public awareness and to provide reliable information to campaigners who can make use of it. In the case of AI, for example, some publications are intended for use by legal professionals working with refugees or medics working with victims of torture. Targeting this type of publication at a limited, specialized but global audience is extremely difficult to do in the 'real' world. Thus cost is not the only factor in whether online or offline publication is more appropriate; the relative ease of reaching some particular targets is also taken into account.

Even global NGOs operate tiny Internet co-ordination teams. This is, of course, one of the virtues of the technology. Although the initial outlay involved in introducing an Internet capability can be comparatively high, maintaining an online presence and reaching a wide audience can be extremely cost-effective. This becomes clear when ICT costs are compared to other forms of publication and campaigning, such as newspaper advertisements or direct lobbying of political representatives. Specialist publications aside, the facility to reach the widest possible audiences is one of the obvious benefits of the Internet and much of the information placed online by NGOs is designed to attract the interest of a broad public. That said, the volume of material these organizations deal with means that wholesale online publishing can make websites unwieldy and this is something that web designers in larger NGOs are now starting to address. With the impetus to publish as much information online as possible, web developers are faced with the challenge of ensuring that sites are structured in such a way that information is both accessible to multiple audiences and adaptable for use as a campaigning resource. Careful design of web pages, with search facilities and links rather than straight lists of contents, make the sites more user-friendly.

In addition, many regions where Internet access is poor have precisely the audiences some normative NGOs are trying to reach. Consequently, OneWorld, whose remit is to promote the use of ICTs, has acknowledged that hi-tech provision serves only some sectors and that lower tech measures – such as email lists rather than interactive websites – serve the purposes of information exchange better. All of the organizations who took part in this research also continue to conduct their campaigns both on- and off-line, so that those who cannot or do not wish to use the Internet can still participate in political actions under their auspices.

Relating the desired outcomes of specific actions to Internet use, it is evident that the 'success' of a campaign cannot be measured simply by counting the number of people who access a web page. Statistics can be, and are, produced by NGOs to gain some sense of the geographical range of their communications and the demographics thereof. However, these figures tell them – and us – little about the responses of audiences to the information contained in documents. In short, statistics tell us little about the effectiveness of Internet communications. Indeed, one of the anomalies that both academics and practitioners may have to accept is that the 'success' of the online activities of NGOs and social movements may frequently be unquantifiable. As all of the NGOs involved in this research pointed out, success is measured in relation to specific objectives and the number of people involved in an action – online or otherwise – is only one of the indicators used to assess the efficacy of a campaign.

Statistical data – particularly that drawn from user-profile surveys on the websites, which all of these organizations gather – is useful in helping to understand audience demographics and to find ways of best targeting them and serving their interests most effectively. Just as useful, though, is the less empirical and rather more anecdotal 'evidence' on the apparently causal role of Internet campaigns in influencing either policy or politicians. For example, FOE provide an inventory of pollution data on its Factory Watch site in the UK. This inventory can be interrogated by postcode, so that it is possible to gather information on local businesses which are the sources of pollutants. Visitors to the site are asked to email their local member of parliament (MP) to raise the issue and FOE have an archive of evidence which shows that MPs tend to respond favourably to constituent complaints of this kind. As well as indicating that well-planned online campaigns can trigger the desired response, this also indicates that the global–local dimensions of Internet use are not simply about its geographical reach. While Factory Watch is available to everyone online, its use by a small number of people, directed towards a small number of others, can carry significant weight (FOE 2001: interview). In addition, the Factory Watch campaign acts as a catalyst for engagement between MPs and the constituents to whom they are accountable. As a consequence, the level of engagement is not inter-organizational but agent/structure, and the campaign promotes interaction between politicians and the public, rather than between the NGO and the government.

The ways information is being structured to target politicians specifically are significant in another respect; much of the focus of analysis of transnational mobilization using the Internet has been upon global capital, with political representatives largely avoiding direct challenge from the electorate or from the mass media. That NGOs view governments as only one of a range of influential actors on the political stage is important in interpreting how they structure their Internet campaigns. Campaigns like Factory Watch demonstrate, however, that specific targeting of politicians remains one of the tools in the armoury of NGO activism.

Like FOE, AI suggest that sometimes it is better to have a smaller number of responses but from a more relevant geographical spread. For example, large numbers of emails from individuals in the USA to the government in Saudi Arabia are considered to carry very little weight, while just a few emails from other Middle Eastern countries can have an important impact. AI do point out, though, that there is a significant problem in determining the success of online campaigns, mainly because governments rarely admit that policy changes have been made on the basis of pressure from human rights campaigners (AI 2001: interview). Given the difficulty of interpreting the interface between lobbying and political decision-making, organizations are having to find other means of assessing the value of their Internet provision. At the most basic level, this involves analysis of who actually visits their websites. Research by all four organizations indicates that a significant majority – up to 80 per cent in one case – of visitors to their websites are not existing members. For organizations like these, where raising awareness is a key feature of their work, such statistics provide sufficient grounds for increasing investment in web provision.

Smith has suggested that the rapid expansion of transnational social movements (TSMOs) during the past fifty years has provided many activists with substantive knowledge of the political views of groups from different parts of the world, opportunities to gain skills and experience in international organizing work, expertise in international law and familiarity with multilateral negotiations (2001: 3). There is much in NGO use of the Internet to suggest that they are adapting the technology to extend their work in these areas. Umbrella organizations like OneWorld and APC were established specifically to facilitate links between activists, creating a forum for the exchange of information between groups and individuals on political issues. Membership of the APC WNSP requires 'a deep commitment to making new communication techniques available to movements working for social change' (Banks 2000: 2). Part of the rationale for these networks is to extend the opportunities to share knowledge and to gain skills in international organizing work which Smith suggests is an inherent part of the ecology of TSMOs.

The continuing growth of NGO web provision can, however, be problematic. APC WNSP highlight the problem of dealing with the organic growth of Internet use, in terms of managing change. APC WNSP has a very small professional team of ICT workers, backed up by legions of volunteers. This relates partly to cost issues but also reflects the desire of both activists and organizations to share available skills and interests. The APC WNSP African network is highly successful and has developed project work capabilities and a wide range of formal partnerships with government agencies, policy makers and other networks on a continental level. In the run-up to the Beijing 5+ conference, the network grew quickly from a fairly *ad hoc* arrangement to encompass the production of a daily news article, lobbying on gender and the Internet, providing training workshops onsite and running a consultation list prior to the event. According to the programme's co-ordinator 'as powerful as informal, fairly loose networks, based on principles of trust and honesty can be ... if you don't have the structures in place to deal with those processes [of change], there can be quite a lot of stress on the network' (APC WNSP 2001: interview).

One method used by NGOs to limit their growth within manageable proportions, particularly for umbrella networks, is to impose restrictions on membership. Through this mechanism, the network continues to grow but the pace is managed by the organization. OneWorld have partnership fees for joining the network, on a sliding scale based on the turnover of potential members. The network also has a set of criteria, or partnership principles, designed to help the network vet potential members. These criteria dictate that organizations which engage in violence are ineligible for partnership, for example, so there are no resistance movements linked to the network. Similarly organizations which are purely political or religious are not eligible to link to the site. Thus Christian Aid is linked to the network, because the organization is engaged in work beyond the promotion of a particular religion. Religious fundamentalist organizations, of whatever persuasion, would not, however, be accepted (OneWorld 2001: interview).

Use of the Internet by NGOs continues to grow apace and none of the organizations in this case study are short of members or potential members. As noted in Chapter 3, though, there has been much discussion about the minimal degree of commitment that is required of people using the Internet for political purposes (see Pickerill 2000). Signing e-petitions takes no more than a few seconds and, some suggest, is meaningless in terms of real political commitment. This is dealt with by the organizations addressed here in different ways. FOE, for example, operate a kind of cascading system, where people who participate in one online action are then provided with opportunities to become involved in others. In this way, it is hoped that individuals will move from being 'casually interested' to being 'concerned interested' to being actively involved, possibly as members as well as online activists (FOE 2001: interview).

The APC WNSP see the issue of commitment as being something which is more significant for the activist than for the organization. As the aim of the programme is to support women online, gender-based obstacles such as differing standards of childcare, training and education, particularly but not exclusively in developing countries, need to be taken into account. For this reason, the network strives to ensure that its members do not feel pressured into making regular commitments but feel able to opt into and out of the programme where necessary. Indeed, the programme's developer feels that this supportive environment actually increases rather than diminishes the level of engagement shown by members (APC WNSP 2001: interview).

One aspect of the structural impact of the Internet – its relationship with 'real' world infrastructures – is one which is often under-explored. AI highlight an interesting problem regarding the issue of engagement in online communities. As the organization is highly protective of its autonomy and refuses to accept funding from governments or international organizations, the funding base of the organization relies on membership fees and fund-raising activities by members. When some traditional political and geographical boundaries disappear, as they do with Internet use, the logistics of managing national and international funds become extremely complex. Moreover, the democratic constitution of the organization means that members of the virtual community have political rights within the organization, as would any other member. These include voting rights on organizational policies at national and international levels. As AI's web developer points out: 'That's a major infrastructural change ... and major changes [in a global organization] aren't easy' (AI 2001: interview).

Conclusion

The issue of infrastructural change is, to some extent, at the heart of debates about the role of the Internet in political processes. It is evident from this case study that the NGOs involved in this research are developing very clear strategies for making use of the Internet in the political arena. These organizations are not simply using the technology randomly: there have been important strategic decisions on how the Internet can be used to have the greatest impact at the lowest cost. In this respect, it can be argued that they are formalizing the use of the Internet on the political stage to some degree. The Internet is proving to be an extremely effective tool in international and local campaigning, despite the difficulties of quantifying its impact.

There is not, however, much evidence yet to suggest that anything other than a traditional political elite, albeit a twenty-first century version thereof, is operating online. Despite the dramatic rise in the numbers of organizations using the Internet as a tool for lobbying and campaigning, there is no hard (or indeed soft) evidence to suggest that the numbers of politically active individuals are growing. Despite this, large NGOs are finding in the Internet a valuable mechanism for extending their networks and reaching their target audiences. These audiences include new and existing members, and there are strong indicators from their campaigns that the Internet is making a useful contribution to their work. Whilst little of this evidence could be considered empirical, it certainly moves beyond the anecdotal and apocryphal indicators which both the organizations themselves and academics have often relied on to date.

The growing commercialization of the Internet is something which is not lost on the organizations who participated in this research. All are acutely aware that, although the number of people with Internet access grows daily, so too does the volume of information being transmitted. Maintaining political autonomy and at the same time making full use of the communicative potential the Internet offers is a delicate balancing act. OneWorld is sponsored in the UK by BT, one of the country's largest telecommunications companies, largely because this offers them an efficient network structure at the lowest possible cost (see also Warkentin 2001: Chapter 5). In this respect, the profit and non-profit sectors are finding ways of developing mutually-beneficial ways of working. OneWorld has also linked with Yahoo, a major Internet Service Provider (ISP), to provide information on its news pages, increasing the audience for its issues substantially. In the s/elective environment of the Internet, where people roam freely from site to site, it is likely that we will see the non-profit sector increasingly working symbiotically with commercial organizations through this type of innovation.

Internet campaigning takes a number of different forms and, among the NGOs analysed for this case study at least, is undertaken in a planned and targeted manner. The constituency for online campaigns is largely limited to a relatively affluent minority, though there is much work being undertaken, particularly in developing countries, to increase access to Internet technologies. Whether the use of email actions and petitions, and the provision of information through the Internet will fundamentally change the nature of political interactions between citizens, states and international organizations remains to be seen. That large scale NGOs carefully plan their Internet strategies to effect political change is, however, clear.

Case Study 5.2: Independent online media

Introduction

In recent years there has been an upsurge in the number of independent activist publications online. There are many practical reasons for this, some of which are explored in this case study. Underlying the rise in independent media is what many activists believe to be biased reporting and misrepresentations of their activities in mainstream media. Representations of demonstrations outside the summits of international institutions such as the World Trade Organization, IMF and the European Union in the mass media tend, activists argue, to portray political protest in a negative light. In addition, they claim, such coverage rarely offers insight into the reasons why people feel compelled to take to the streets. Independent media collectives like IndyMedia, Squall and AlterNet claim that both broadcast and print media fail to fully address the political principles of activists. In response to this, and making use of the Internet's publishing facilities, activists have sought to establish alternative information networks.

This case study looks at some of the reasons behind the establishment of these networks and examines the benefits working online offers to independent media organizations. The 'fairness' or 'accuracy' of mass media reports on political activism are not the concern of this case study, nor are the versions of these events outlined in the independent media. Of more interest is what might be missing from media reports of political protests and the implications this may have for the promotion, or otherwise, of political participation. If a strong public sphere is considered to be a crucial element of civil society (see Sassi 2001), does it matter that the mass media is often considered to serve only narrow political interests? Independent media organizations certainly think it does and claim that publishing online offers an opportunity to redress the balance in coverage of politics and political protest. The case study looks particularly at the ways mass media frame political protest and how the Internet provides a mechanism for overcoming this.

Mass media framing

Gitlin's early work on media framing remains significant and one simple sentence of his encapsulates the core area of mainstream/alternative media contention: 'media frames, largely unspoken and unacknowledged, organize the world both for journalists, who report it and, in some important degree, for us who rely on their reports' (1980: 7). Curran suggests that it is wrong to talk of the mass media as if they were a homogeneous group. He suggests, rather, that the freedom and diversity of the media are growing and that the active audience counteracts the effects of dominance of information provision by a few MNCs (2000: 11). Though accepting the nuances of this argument, research for this case study suggests that it is still possible to talk of 'mainstream' media which tend, for a variety of cultural, economic and historical reasons, to frame political issues in broadly similar ways.

There has been much debate about the notion of media bias – what it is, where it originates, how it is made manifest and so on (see Boyd-Barrett 1998; Street 2001). With the spread of technologies and the increasing integration of media industries, discussions about whether media content is biased to reflect the interests of one group of actors or another have become fairly complex. It is not sufficient to say that the 'governments' or 'corporations' control the media. It is possible to argue, however, that a tendency to portray particular kinds of information in particular kinds of ways can exclude information which may reasonably be expected to have a place in the public sphere. For Entman, '*bias* defines a tendency to frame different actors, events and issues in the same way, to select and highlight the same sort of selective realities, thus crafting a similar tale across a range of potential news stories' (1996: 78, emphasis in original). Accepting that audiences are 'not passively absorbent sponges but active 'negotiators' of meaning in media 'texts' (Carruthers 2001: 8), it is important to consider how partial representations of political protests influence audience interpretations of such events. Jim Carey of Squall, an independent online activist newspaper, counters this by arguing that, while we may be active negotiators of texts, 'in the deluge of information around us we are all sponges to some degree ... soaking up angles which get the most repetition in the media'.[3]

Like most other activities undertaken by non-elite non-state actors, political protests receive only limited coverage in the mass media. As considered in Chapter 4, where political activism does appear in the news, there is often a tendency to report protest in a negative light. Demonstrators are 'anarchists' and 'a challenge to the established order'. Many activists, of course, are the former and most are engaged in political processes precisely to achieve the latter. How these 'facts' are represented in news reports is for many activists, though, a cause for concern. In particular, the tendency to situate political protesters as 'other' to the democratic order, rather than as part of it, polarizes political debate. This is problematic because, as Mutz and Martin point out 'both in political theory and empirical work, there is near unanimous agreement that exposure to diverse political views is good for democracy and should be encouraged' (2001: 97).

There are three clearly identifiable areas where mass media coverage of activism could be considered to be problematic. First, the polarization of political opinions is characteristic of the construction of news as narrative. The 'good guy' versus 'bad guy' mode of representation fulfils the needs of news-makers to provide both drama and balance. The narrative construction of news often requires the presentation of conflict and activists as the dramatic 'other' to the stability and order of governments and international organizations. Tarrow suggests that the media 'are quick to give priority to violent or bizarre aspects of a protest – often focusing on the few violent members of a peaceful demonstration who are bent on disrupting it' (1994: 128). So ten thousand non-provocative marchers are not news, one rock-throwing student might be (see ibid.).

Second, for many social movement activists, the norm of 'objectivity' in news reporting reflects a form of framing which, whilst not necessarily always directed *against* activists, rarely operates in their favour. The notion of 'objectivity' in news reporting requires that 'the process of observing and reporting should ... not be contaminated by subjectivity, nor should it interfere with the reality being reported upon' (McQuail 2000: 172). Given this norm, all reporting should present a balanced version of events. Many activists believe, though, that a political protester, as 'other', will never be framed in the same way as a government minister or a captain of industry. As Tarrow put it, 'the media are far from neutral bystanders. ... While the media in capitalist democracies may not work directly for the ruling class, they certainly do not work for social movements' (1994: 127).

Beyond this, Boyd-Barrett has suggested that the notion of objectivity is at the heart of the commodification of news. News, as a saleable good, must offend the fewest possible people and must, therefore, be objectified to a point of uncontentiousness for the most (see Boyd-Barrett and Rantenan (eds) 1998). For Carruthers, 'news can never be "value-free", from "nobody's point of view", in the way its "manufacturers" like to claim' (2001: 17). This is not to suggest that the values that underpin news reporting are wrong, but to reiterate the tendency in reporting to close off certain tendentious subjects.

Finally, and rather more difficult to pin down, is the notion of structural bias in the global news arena. Does news reporting represent only elite opinion and government interests? The nebulous spectre of 'elite interests', both political and economic, is at the heart of much anti-capitalist[4] activism and, at the risk of over-simplifying the issues, it is possible to see a correlation between news reporting of activism and the interests of the neo-liberal econo-political order. In the political arena, Gamson argues that 'rebellious collective action can ... buttress the dominant world view by helping political elites in their construction of a stable enemy or threat that justifies their policies and provides a legitimation for political repression' (2001: 60). Problems, enemies and crises are constantly constructed and reconstructed to create a series of threats and reassurances (ibid.) Regardless of the validity or otherwise of the causes for their actions, activists often become the problem, the enemy *and* the crisis where the need to buttress the political order exists. The necessarily close relationships between governments and news providers – the one a vital information source to help fill schedules, the other providing distribution networks for policy pronouncements – is also a feature of this characterization of politics as dichotomy. It appears that 'real' politics for most mainstream media organizations still relates to foreign policy, diplomacy and the activities of politicians.

The positioning of the activist as 'other' is perhaps slightly easier to interpret in relation to the economic arena. As the majority of news providers are profit-making organizations, and many of them are part of major multinational corporations (see Herman and McChesney 1997; Variety 2002: online), there is an inherent need to avoid causing offence to their biggest source of income – not the audience but the advertisers. Carey argues that 'the bottom line is that every element of mainstream media relies on advertising: you can't get away from it. ... No magazine or newspaper survives on its cover price alone so if you do anything to upset that industry's acceptance of your organ as a suitable medium for advertising, you've got big problems' (2002: interview 1).[5] This claim is backed by Herman and McChesney:

> Owner and advertiser domination give the commercial media a dual bias threatening the public sphere: they tend to be politically conservative and hostile to criticism of the status quo in which they are the major beneficiaries; and they are concerned to provide a congenial media environment for advertising goods.
>
> (1997: 6)

This takes us neatly back to Boyd-Barrett's argument that news is a commodity, from which we can conclude that it must be packaged appropriately and that packaging will almost invariably position anti-capitalist activists as ideologically unsound. As Lee *et al.* argue 'television networks and the elite press, despite their fierce competition, play different variations on the same ideological themes. They operate within the same institutional relationship to the power structures and share the broadly similar ideological and cultural prisms' (2001: 352).

The norms of objectivity, the need to identify sources of conflict and the ideological values of the global news-making environment inevitably situate political protesters outside of normal social and political boundaries. The concern, however, is that the reasons behind the challenges activists pose are under- or mis-reported, so that a stereotypical presentation of political activism is given. Whilst perhaps somewhat galling for activists themselves, this is more significant in respect of its broader implications for participatory politics. If, as Bennett and Entman have argued, 'access to communication is one of the key measures of power and equality in modern democracies' (2001: 2), it is important to question whether the information we are receiving gives audiences enough insight to gain a full picture of the wider political landscape. Certainly – in developed countries at least – television, press and Internet reports provide many people with more information than they have ever had before. Whether this increased quantity of information is enough to present a balanced picture is, however, open to question.

Scheufele distils some of the most widely-accepted work on political participation and highlights key features of political awareness and expertise. Drawing from Zaller (1992), he suggests that political awareness is comprised of five areas: political information, political participation, media exposure, interest in politics and education (2002: 47). Then, referring to the work of Fiske, Lau and Smith, he suggests that there are also five core issues relating to political expertise: political knowledge, political activity, print media use, electronic media use and political self-schema (ibid.) In each case, media provision of information is a crucial feature of political understanding. Although Scheufele goes on to point out the relationships between individuals and their media experiences are extremely complex, it is fair to surmise that the ways political activism is framed in the mass media have an important impact on both how protests are understood by people not directly involved in such actions (which, of course, is the vast majority), and on whether people see these protests as having some relevance to their own lives. Or, more succinctly, if mass media are key components of political understanding – which in turn is related to political participation – the framing of political issues in the mass media is important in influencing how politics are interpreted and acted upon.

One useful example of media framing of protest is highlighted by coverage of the anti-capitalist demonstrations in Seattle and Genoa. Analysing the demonstrations against the WTO conference in Seattle, Smith found that:

> There was no clear consensus among protest groups about whether the WTO itself should be abolished or reformed. What was clear was that virtually all protesters on the streets sought to democratise and incorporate values other than profit-making into global institutions.
>
> (2001: 3)

That protesters do not operate as a homogeneous mass was not apparent in news coverage of this or similar events. During the G8 Summit in Genoa in July 2001, for example, CNN used banner headlines such as 'G8 summit braces for more violence' (CNN 2001a: online) and 'Protesters, problems and positions at the G8 summit' (CNN 2001b: online). Interestingly, a CNN reporter responded to viewer complaints about distorted coverage of protests at the summit in an open email exchange. In this, he stated that 'certainly the protesters come to raise legitimate points' (see ibid.) This exchange, however, appeared only online and so didn't receive mass media coverage in our current understanding of the term. So the negative coverage of the actions of protesters reached a global audience, while the acknowledgement of the legitimacy of the issues they sought to raise did not.

If the sharing of information is an important feature of political participation, negative or stereotypical coverage of activist practices within a narrow interpretative framework may undermine the potential to engage the public in political networks. Such considerations lead Gamson to ask if mass media 'provide a cultural tool for encouraging political engagement – to support and encourage the sense that by acting together grassroots constituencies can take actions that influence the policies and conditions that affect their daily lives' (2001: 59). Many activists would argue that whilst the mass media can provide a springboard for interest in an issue, more detailed information is necessary to promote active political engagement. For activists, the Internet provides an ideal mechanism for this type of detailed information.

For Tarrow, 'movements briefly, provisionally and often dramatically, "make news"; but they cannot make the media publish news the way they want it to be made' (1994: 129). That said, mass media representations have not stopped people becoming involved in political protests. Indeed, large-scale rallies against global institutions have now become fairly commonplace, with the interest of at least some of the participants presumably generated by mass media coverage of the issues. The inability to find an appropriate space on the mass media landscape of politics has, though, been one of the factors that has led to the flourishing of independent media organizations seeking to represent voices which are not generally heard in the mainstream media. Many of these organizations – such as Squall, IndyMedia and AlterNet – have chosen the Internet as their medium of choice for distribution. There are a variety of reasons for this, some of which are considered below.

The rise in independent media is not unrelated to broader structural change, with the rise of civil society, growth in the number of NGOs and so on seen as part of the broader pattern of political change. Bennett and Entman suggest that 'one of the hallmarks of the emerging culture, boosted no doubt by the profusion of communications channels, is the permeability of boundaries separating the political from the non-political and the private sphere from the public sphere'. (2001: 2). Independent media have, in some senses, positioned themselves at this nexus, where the public and private worlds of mass and interactive media intersect. Independent media should not, thus, be seen as operating in direct opposition to existing media output or animated purely by a certain rage against the machine of elite dominance. Not all independent media operate to left-wing, anti-establishment agendas. Some do, but one of the virtues – and great potential dangers – of the Internet is the ability for any group with access to the technology to find their voice. In this respect, neo-nazis stand alongside anarchists, advertisers and CNN as information providers.

Claims to 'represent the unrepresented' will always be met with a certain degree of scepticism, particularly in a global media environment. Who decides who is not being represented? How are decisions on appropriate forms of representation made? For Keck and Sikkink, it is the less powerful in society who are considered to need representation. For them, social networks – within which activist movements can be situated – seek to make the demands of the less powerful known in four ways: presenting issues in new ways (framing); seeking the most favourable arenas to fight their battles in; confounding expectations (disruption) and broadening the network's scope and density to supply necessary information (mobilizing social networks) (1998b: 218). The Internet offers at least a partial mechanism for fulfilling each of these objectives.

The Internet can offer new or alternative ways of framing issues and, whilst these pose no direct challenge to dominant representations, they provide information which would not otherwise be readily accessible to a general audience. There are at least five different ways in which online publication can be of use to political activists: cost, legitimacy, distribution, professionalization and archiving. The relatively low cost of establishing Internet sites has been an important factor in the growth of alternative media output. Distribution costs for hard copy publications – crippling for low budget operations – are drastically reduced by a shift to online production. So, while many 'cut and paste' publications still exist in activist circles, online publication provides a low cost, high return (in terms of potential readership) mechanism for reaching the widest possible audience. The Internet provides a 'professionalized' standard of output which low budget operations could not previously hope to match. This lends a legitimacy to the publications that offline output – in hard-copy magazine form, often on low-grade paper to keep costs down – could not achieve. Where online publishers use search engines effectively, independent news can achieve equal ranking in search results with mainstream publications. This gives online publishers access to the kinds of distribution networks that mainstream media organizations have. Whereas the costs of distribution of hard copies through commercial outlets can be crippling, the outlay for online publication, which can reach a far wider audience, is negligible. In this sense, 'distribution' becomes a meaningless term in relation to electronic publication (Atton 2002: 139).

Given advances in software and the lack of specific technical training now necessary to produce high-quality graphics, hyperlinks and so on ('everyone's a publisher on the net', as the old/new adage goes), the websites of volunteer and/or low budget organizations are now often comparable to those of major media organizations. This allows independent media to publish high-quality material at low cost, again something they are unable to do offline. Finally, independent media find in the Internet an opportunity to archive publications, while making them available to a wide audience. The costly distribution networks which have proved so difficult for independent organizations to access in the past, also limit their opportunities for the sale of previous editions. This problem is overcome by the ability to archive material on the net.

There is a paradox, of course, in that to get their point across the anti-capitalist networks need to make use of software and distribution systems provided by some of the most aggressive capitalist organizations. For Carey, the need to act strategically and fight on the fronts which will produce the greatest effect (2001: interview 1) is important. This reflects Keck and Sekkink's claim that activists need to chose favourable arenas to operate in (1998b: 218). Although the activities of Microsoft and similar companies may be anathema to many, the desire to provide information and contribute to the mobilization of political actors supersedes the need to boycott the facilities they can provide. Carey argues that the 'sleeping with the enemy' analogy is fallacious: 'This supposed "paradox" is used by media interviewers a lot to unbalance activist interviewees but I strongly feel it is a device to avoid more important issues … There is no end to it as an argument in the academic or philosophical sense' (2002: interview 2).

Few would argue with the claim that the mass media offer little room for non-conformist views. In addition, Mutz and Martin suggest that there are a number of indicators to suggest that our exposure to alternative political viewpoints is curtailed by both mass media constraints on such output and by our own changing living patterns. In the developed world at least, people increasingly live in environments segregated from people with oppositional views and tend to select 'politically like-minded discussion partners' (2001: 98). This means, in essence, that many people are exposed to characteristically homogenized views of the political landscape, both in their reading and viewing habits and in their lifestyles.

Independent media can do little to alter this. They attempt, though, to provide a counterbalance to what is often seen as the hegemony of large media corporations over news agendas. This is not to suggest that mass media coverage of political activism does not occur or that when it does it is uniformly negative. Tarrow suggests that the mass media have become something of an external resource for social movements and do provide a mechanism for generating initial attention in activist agendas (1994: 127). He also notes, though, that social movements have limited capacity to appropriate the media for their own purposes (ibid: 128); it is into this vacuum that the independent media now operating on the Internet have moved. If, as noted earlier, exposure to dissimilar political views is an important element of democratic growth, the Internet could be providing an important corrective to the dominant forms of media framing.

That mass and interactive audiences are now separate should not preclude investigation of the relative merits of Internet coverage of political events and, in particular, the representations of political actors not generally covered in mainstream media. Perhaps the last word on this matter should go to IndyMedia through an extract from their FAQ page:

Q   Should I believe news I read on IndyMedia?
A   Should you believe news you read on CNN.com? All reporters have their own biases; governments and massive for-profit corporations that own media entities have their own biases as well, and often impose their views on their reporters (or their reporters self-censor to conform their own biases to those of their employer). You should look at all reports you read on the IndyMedia site with a critical eye, just as you should look at all media before you in a discerning manner.

(IndyMedia 2001: online)

While we may not believe what we read on IndyMedia, we can be fairly sure that we wouldn't receive a similar recommendation from CNN.

Conclusion

The case studies in this chapter look at the Internet as a tool posing challenges to political structures. In the case of NGO use of the Internet, the applications of the technology reflect the strategies of the major international organizations they are. Their activities are planned, co-ordinated and designed to achieve specific objectives. Research is conducted to provide information on the effectiveness of their campaigns, and of the role their websites play in promoting access to political structures.

By contrast, the independent media organizations addressed in the second case study see their main role to be the provision of information which would not otherwise be available to a wide audience. Their challenge to the existing political order is less direct, in that they are not advocacy networks but information providers. In this sense, although these organizations are often more 'radical' in the traditional sense, their aim is to inform rather than to directly promote political engagement. In many instances, independent publishers are reporting on the same subjects as the mainstream media. Their aim, though, is to offer an alternative framing of events and to tell the stories from other angles.

It is easy to see already that 'Internet use' by 'activists' covers a broad range of actors and practices. It is clear too, that who is targeted and for what reasons influences how the technology is applied. These points will be picked up in Chapter 7, which applies spatial theories to these issues.

6 Activism case studies
Issue-specific protest

Introduction

The case studies in this chapter look at the classic 'single issue politics' that activists have become so closely associated with. The transnationalization of single issue politics often obscures the fact that, while there is a central core concern for activists, there can be quite significant differences to local campaigns. Two cases are considered, that of genetically modified (GM) foods and that of the US missile defense project. The first case study, on the GM foods issue, provides a useful insight into the ways international politics are spatialized. This operates at three levels: on the traditional mapping of politics where states act as domestic regulators; on the transnationalization of some areas of regulation; and on the internationalization of political protest.

Protests against GM foods are based on a tangible issue, food safety. This tangible concern is linked with the more nebulous issue of normative transnational values. The actors involved in the anti- and pro-GM lobbies comprise individuals, informal associations and collectives, formal social movement organizations, transnational institutions (such as the EU, the WTO and, obliquely but influentially nonetheless, the UN), scientists and researchers, farmers and agriculturalists and the major agro-chemical companies who mainly develop and sell both the GM technology and the resulting foodstuffs. The case study briefly examines the spread of GM production and distribution, particularly into European markets, some of the protests against genetic modification of foodstuffs and some of the ways the Internet is used by both protesters and GM companies to promote their respective causes.

The second case study, the US missile defense project was first mooted during the Reagan era, was sanctioned by the Clinton administration and taken up with vigour by the Bush government. It provides an interesting example of a dual transnationalization: of local and transnational protest against the foreign policy initiative of one government which has local as well as transnational implications. The landmine issue perhaps provides the closest comparison, generating as it has an international response to a security issue. The ongoing anti-landmine campaign resulted in the 1997 Mine Ban Treaty, which by November 2002 had been signed by 146 countries and ratified by 130 of them (ICBL 2002: online). The landmines campaign has been developed as a normative, transnational concern. The missile defence protests are similar but are less universal in some senses, as they require different foreign policy responses from different governments. The missile defence protest is considered here in the context of *local* activism and how campaigners in different regions respond to the project.

Case Study 6.1: Genetically modified foods

Introduction

The genetically modified (GM) foods issue[1] is a valuable case study for spatial theorizing, as it provides insights into the use of the Internet as a tool for transnational lobbying. In the case of GM crops, consumers, who may or may not be affiliated to formal campaigning organizations, have used the Internet to attempt to influence a range of actors, including governments, multinational corporations, the mass media and other consumers. It is within the myriad dimensions of cases such as this that the need for a mechanism for interpreting relationality becomes evident. The two parts of this case study address different aspects of the GM issue. The first section looks at the rise of the GM movement and examines the issues at the heart of debates about genetic modification of foodstuffs, while the second addresses some of the ways movement activists have been using the Internet to attempt to effect changes in policy and in the practices of the major MNCs involved in the development, sale and distribution of GM crops and foods.

These debates have arisen only since the late 1990s and opinions are still extremely divided. Commercial application of GM technology began in 1980 following a ruling by the US Supreme Court to extend patent protection to new types of plants and plant parts (Paarlberg 2000: 25). For years, the public in the USA have eaten GM foods without much complaint: 'Americans consume vast quantities of GMOs every day and would be hard pressed to avoid doing so' (Herring 2001: online). Food companies in the USA are not required by law to label foodstuff as genetically modified and the Food and Drug Administration (FDA) determined in 1992 that GM foods are 'substantially similar' to other foodstuffs and should not therefore be subject to special legislation or more rigorous labelling. This position was upheld in October 2000 by the US District Court in Columbia, when the claim of anti-GM campaigners that the lack of labelling and mandatory safety testing violated federal law was rejected (Chemical Market Reporter 2000: online). The US administration, as a strong supporter of its biotech industries, does not consider labelling of GM foods a 'material fact' for consumers. There are significant commercial implications behind this decision: one 1999 study found that 81 per cent of people surveyed in the USA felt that genetically engineered food should be labelled, but 58 per cent said they wouldn't buy it if it was (Time 1999: online).

GM became a major transnational political issue with the import of modified soya beans to Europe in the late 1990s, following the decision by US providers to stop separating GM crops from those grown using more conventional methods. This change in practice had a serious effect on the global distribution of USA-grown foodstuffs. Different legislative systems setting different standards meant that clashes between activists, US biotech companies and overseas regulators were inevitable. Some countries – most notably some European Union states – have been vociferous in their objections to the introduction of GM. Others have happily accepted the technology. These include China, Argentina and South Africa, some of the biggest developing world economies (see Mason 2002: 12). Some Eastern European states that may benefit from funding from GM producers are also keen to provide land to grow modified crops (see Kruszewska 2000: online). It has been suggested that GM producers are eager to take advantage of the more relaxed regulatory systems of countries outside of the EU in order to gain a foothold in the market (ibid.) The tensions generated by the issue have led to a somewhat bruising public relations battle between GM producers and anti-GM protesters for the hearts and minds of consumers.

The GM debate

The three key groups of actors in this debate – the GM producers, anti-GM campaigners and supranational organizations – have all made use of the Internet to promote their particular perspectives and to garner support for their causes. Although governments are important players in the regulation of GM distribution and in the licensing of field trials, they have not been subject to the same kind of pressures from the consumer lobby that GM producers have. The debate on GM on the Internet has been by and large between corporations and consumers. Many governments, although ultimately responsible for regulating the products and licensing test sites for experimental GM crops, have been able to take a back seat in the debate. These governments have been engaged in a difficult balancing act between demonstrating their willingness to listen to detractors by maintaining a precautionary approach and trying to maximize domestic economic advantage by allowing GM trials and sales. This is particularly true in Europe, where a series of food safety scares in recent years have resulted in an extremely cautious attitude to agricultural, or more specifically agri-business, developments.

In the case of GM, 'the enemy', the target of protest for movement activists, is not always clear. Although GM developers and growers are obviously seen as the bad guys by protesters, the multi-layering of regulations across institutions means that GM companies alone are not solely implicated in the testing and distribution of genetically modified organisms through the food chain. National governments, supranational organizations and MNCs all play different roles in the process of developing, regulating and facilitating the distribution of GM foods. Given the relationships between these various actors, the legitimate targets for protest are not always clear. Protests on the whole have tended to centre on the MNCs that produce, test and sell GM products, as their role in the promotion of the technology is clear. Although governments and supranational organizations have been challenged by protesters, it is MNCs which have borne the brunt of anti-GM campaigning.

GM food production begins with the transfer of traits between genes, a technological development which has produced a furious, and extremely polarized, debate. Usually a single gene from one organism is injected into another, introducing a desired trait from one to the other. Modification of genes in foodstuffs can take many different forms; some products have already been introduced into the food chain and many others are currently in development. 'Bt crops' produce their own insecticide without apparent harm to humans. Pests that feed on the crops die, while the plant remains healthy. Weed-killer-resistant plants allow farmers to spray herbicides without damaging crops. Protein-rich crops ostensibly designed to help fight malnutrition in developing countries have been produced, as has rice enriched with Vitamin A (so-called 'golden rice'), intended to help prevent the blindness caused by its deficiency (see Friends of the Earth 2002: online). 'Terminator seeds', perhaps the most controversial of all GM developments, result in the production of a biologically sterile grain. That is, the plant develops normally but does not produce seeds suitable for planting to grow new crops (see de la Perriere and Seuret 2000: Chapter 2). For protesters, the purported potential benefits of any of these products are outweighed by their unknown risks. It is thus the concept of GM that is seen as the problem.

The anti-GM arguments take several different tracks. Some of these are based on the scientific rigour, or otherwise, of the technology. First, opponents argue that the safety of GM foods has not yet been proved and that there has been insufficient testing of crops and foodstuffs to determine their safety. Second, they claim that cross-pollination could result in damage to other species. Cross-pollination, once it has occurred, is irreversible. Third, campaigners argue that building resistance to herbicides into plants will result in more pesticide residues entering water supplies, thus creating environmental damage and possible risks to human health. These arguments tend to be posed by the environmental lobby, which positions GM foods as 'unnatural' in some way. At the heart of this dimension of the anti-GM case is the claim that their introduction into the food chain could result in unknown and as yet unquantifiable damage.

Closely related – many campaigners would argue inextricably linked – to environmental concerns about GM is a concern about the power of multinational companies to control global food supplies. Many anti-GM lobbyists are concerned that the large agro-chemical MNCs will be in a position to dictate what kinds of food are grown where, and at what price, if the use of genetic modification becomes widespread. These fears relate, of course, to broader concerns about the spread of global capitalism and the lack of accountability of MNCs. For one commentator, 'society – at least European society – is beginning to view genetic science as a market-impelled juggernaut out of control and wearing moral blinders' (Walsh 1999). Berlan reflects the fears of campaigners regarding the rise of agro-business: 'farmers are slowly dying out – they have been transformed into agriculturalists, forever on the lookout for any kind of progress that could delay their inevitable elimination' (cited in de la Perriere and Seuret 2000: 26). For many campaigners, the power of a handful of large agro-chemical companies to control the world's food supplies is a very real prospect. The purchase of seed companies by GM producers has been another cause for concern (Corporate Watch 1999). It has been argued that the 'GM juggernaut' will position non-GM foods as a 'niche' product, for which consumers will be expected to pay a premium (see Branford 2002). In some senses, then, campaigners see the introduction of GM as a lose-lose situation: the products are considered to be ecologically unsound and the producers of them morally bankrupt.

The companies developing GM products counter these arguments by suggesting that not only is the technology safe but GM foods will help to solve some of the problems caused by poverty in the developing world. Biotechnology companies claim that GM foods will help to maximize productivity and increase crop yields for farmers and that seeds and crops will also have greater resistance to some common pests, resulting in savings on insecticide costs. The supply of livestock feeds could also be improved, which in turn will reduce costs across the whole of the food supply chain. Cost-efficiency and increased productivity have been central to the case promoted by GM producers. It is worth noting, though, that the issue of global poverty has become increasingly prominent on their communications agendas.

Supporters tend to view the benefits of GM as vastly outweighing their potential risks, and claim the 'real stakeholders in this debate are poor farmers and poorly fed consumers in Asia, Africa, and Latin America' (Paarlberg 2000: 24). Arguments that these advances are not significantly different to the hybridization and cross-breeding of plants that farmers have engaged in for centuries are also made. There is also a certain degree of bemusement about the violent reaction to GM foods, when there has been widespread acceptance of genetically modified vaccines such as insulin (Herring 2001). Herring characterizes the gulf between pro- and anti-GM campaigners as a fight between those who see GM as 'playing god' and 'those who see it as a continuation of a process of human manipulation of nature' (ibid.)

GM and the Internet

The US government treats challenges to its biotech companies as trading disputes, rather than as food safety or environmental issues, and uses the WTO as a settlement mechanism. At the level of production and distribution the GM issue is dominated by large transnational organizations with huge economic and political resources at their disposal. These mighty organs have, however, been subjected to considerable pressures from the anti-GM lobby and have responded accordingly. This has resulted in significant changes to the marketing and public relations strategies of the GM companies. Mass media coverage of the GM foods issue is interesting, as it provides media organizations with some of their favourite news standards: David and Goliath struggle between the 'little people' and the powerful multinationals, governments as a primary source of information, order versus anarchy and so on. For these reasons, it is one of the few activist concerns to have generated fairly substantial, and sometimes quite positive, media coverage, in Europe at least. While much of the debate has been aired in the mass media, a great deal of the organizing, lobbying and campaigning for and against GM has taken place on the Internet.

Anti-GM lobbyists include both the 'formal' and 'informal' types considered in Chapter 4. Some of the campaigns are led by major international NGOs, such as Greenpeace and Friends of the Earth, high profile organizations with well-structured campaigns. Information available on their sites tends to offer a 'scientific' explanation about the risks associated with genetic modification, alongside fairly emotive discussions about environmental and food hazards. The standard terms applied on these sites include 'scandal', 'danger', 'concern' and so on. The terms vary between organizations, of course, with some more measured than others. On the whole, however, there is a tendency to emphasize that the risks posed by GM require action on the part of campaigners. To this end, the major NGOs addressing the GM issue provide a wide range of targeted links to politicians, governments and international institutions. The electronic petition has come into its own in these campaigns, as the organizations focus their activity on achieving change through existing political hierarchies. Electronic letters to presidents, prime ministers and parliaments are common on these sites, as well as e-petitions to biotech companies and international policy-making bodies such as the World Trade Organization. The sites are seeking a mass response, with a certain strength-in-numbers logic to the design of the campaigns.

Some smaller activist groups use these same techniques on a lesser scale,[2] but many others operate on a much less formal or obviously structured basis and use the Internet to promote political action at the grassroots level.[3] The Internet becomes a public forum where ideas and information are exchanged as well as a technology applied specifically to facilitating direct action campaigns. The most successful example of this is the UK-originated GenetiX Snowball movement, which effectively established a set of ground rules for anti-GM activism.[4] The GenetiX sites provide an activists' handbook that details how to establish a diffused activist network and includes information on how to conduct and publicize actions such as supermarket 'decontamination' (that is, removing GM foodstuffs with maximum impact) and the destruction of GM crops.

Between these formal and informal organizations, their use of the Internet has prompted direct action worldwide.[5] The various forms these actions have taken, including crop burning, the dumping of GM crops at US embassies and the mass protest at the WTO meetings in Seattle in November 1999 have, in turn, prompted coverage by the mass media. This highlights the interplay between different media, a feature of Internet use that is often overlooked in media analysis. The relationship between the old media of broadcasting and the new media of the Internet signals a point of mediation between the 'real world' of reporting and the 'virtual world' of information used by activists, another dimension of political practice which we have yet to fully comprehend.

The major biotech companies which produce GM use Internet technology in a rather different way. Their framing of the issue, unsurprisingly, differs radically from that of the anti-GM campaigners. GM is portrayed by the companies who develop and produce it in two main ways – as a 'healthy' product and as something which will help to alleviate some of the suffering caused by global poverty. In this sense, the companies that produce GM seeds and foodstuffs promote themselves as having a strong sense of social duty. The GM companies are responding to, rather than challenging, the concerns raised by protesters. The position of GM providers has shifted subtly over the past few years: where once the talk was of cheap food, the safety and widespread availability of foodstuffs now dominates their public agendas. Syngenta suggests that 'the technology of our seeds division helps ensure growers a consistent and plentiful seed supply (2002: online), while Monsanto argues that the continually growing demand for food can be met only by improving agricultural output, which GM can do (ibid). As would be expected on corporate websites a good deal of space is given over to providing information relevant to investors but, in the information directed to a general audience, the dominant framing on their websites relates to good health and moral principles. As Monsanto put it: 'there are two primary choices in life: to *accept* conditions as they exist, or accept the responsibility for changing them' (2002: online).

Much of the material posted online by the biotech companies involved in production and development of seeds, crops and pesticides promotes this 'healthy' image of GM foods and tends to use terms such as 'enhanced flavour,' 'plentiful supply', and 'improved nutrition'. The sunny image of the benefits of GM contrasts sharply with the images of poison and toxicity used by anti-GM campaigners. The biotech companies tend to use the Internet as an information board that frames their activities as socially responsible and designed to contribute towards sustainable agricultural development. One company, AgrEvo, suggests that genetic engineering can be regarded as a form of accelerated evolution, which supersedes some of the rather lengthy processes plants go through naturally (see AgrEvo 2000: online). Most of these sites provide emailing lists for company updates and Monsanto, one of the largest biotech companies, provides a 'send comments' facility. Unlike on many of the anti-GM campaigners' sites, these comments are not available in the public domain, and none of the major biotech companies provides an online discussion forum.

On the whole, however, the sites of GM producers are mono-logical and are used largely as an informational tool, applying the patterns of sender–receiver practices employed by broadcast media. Whether the desired effect is to minimize interactivity and debate, this is the end result. This is relatively unusual now, even among the largest global corporations who have suffered adverse publicity. The response of GM companies to criticism is rather less overt than that of other companies who have been the subject of similar vociferous criticism. In response to challenges from the environmental lobby, for example, Shell now has a 'TellShell' platform on its website, and Nike, which has been criticized for worker exploitation, has a 'Global Citizenship' policy. GM companies may well be responding to their critics in similar ways but there is little in their online information to suggest that this is the case; the criticisms of detractors are given little, if any, coverage.

Conclusion

The main players in the pro- and anti-GM debate use the Internet in very different ways. Unsurprisingly, there are stark contrasts between the ways the two sides frame the issues; GM is either an extremely good or an incredibly bad idea, depending on which side is putting the argument. There is very little nuance or subtlety to this debate and very little in the way of common ground between the two sides. Anti-GM campaigners tend to make their sites much more interactive and are rather inventive in their use of the technology. Their aim is to generate mass public support for their campaigns and there is an imperative to provide access to both detailed information and a wide range of influential actors; hence the use of links to politicians, to traders, to GM producers, and so on. There is also a need to provide opportunities to engage with the GM debate: for anti-GM campaigners, it is not enough for people to be aware of the issue, it is important to promote action of some kind. There is almost a grading of possibilities for participation, from e-petitions to direct actions such as crop destruction and shop clearance.

The GM companies are aiming for a rather different constituency. They come from a position of strength, being both wealthy and having the weight of the political system (at least among the most powerful actors) behind them. In this respect, they use the Internet as a means of reaching a wide general audience, should such an audience be interested. There is no imperative for GM companies to generate public support, however: while anti-GM campaigns have undoubtedly led to some slight policy changes regarding how GM companies promote themselves, investment in the technology continues to rise. There is little evidence from the websites of GM companies, then, that they are making concerted efforts to use innovative techniques to capture new audiences.

Case Study 6.2: Missile defense

Introduction

Protests against the US missile defense project provide a useful case study of the interactions between activists and governments around national security issues and the ways different actors conceptualize political space. There is a long and complex history behind the project. In a nutshell, the Strategic Defense Initiative (SDI) of the Reagan years was renamed Ballistic Missile Defense (BMD) under the Clinton administration in 1993. BMD was given a variety of labels in the ensuing years – National Missile Defense (NMD), Anti-Ballistic Missile Defense (ABM) and the more media-friendly 'Son of Star Wars' among them. The project is now more commonly called simply 'missile defense' (the 'national' was dropped by the US administration in 2000, in an attempt to make it appear more of a co-operative project) and this is the term applied here.

Under the project, eight sites across the globe would be equipped with upgraded radar systems. These systems would provide early warning of nuclear attacks from 'rogue states', permitting the launch of US nuclear weapons intended to intercept the incoming warheads (Yorkshire CND 2000: online). The main sites have been chosen for their strategic value to the US and include Greenland, Alaska, the UK and South Korea. Two areas – Alaska and the UK – are considered in this case study. Both have fairly high Internet penetration but have very different demographics, cultural histories and economic infrastructures. Alaska is a US state; Britain historically has a 'special relationship' with America, dating back to the Second World War. Both use the lingua franca of the Internet, English, and have high literacy rates. The case study shows that, despite their similarities, the Internet is applied in different ways to protest around missile defense, as the objectives of activists are contingent upon local circumstances.

Anti-missile defense arguments

Campaigning against the missile defense project has a strong normative dimension. Detractors argue that the project could threaten a new arms race, damage international stability, risk environmental contamination and pour public funds away from public services and into private arms companies (CODE 2002: online). Co-ordinated in some areas through organizations like the Campaign for Nuclear Disarmament, No Nukes and GlobalNet, there is an underlying assumption of pacifism and anti-militarism to the campaigns. While many of the protesters do indeed hold such views, others – such as the Union of Concerned Scientists (UCS) – suggest that the practice, rather than the principle, of current missile defense development is problematic. UCS argue that the testing programme for the project depends on 'a-priori complete information about the nature of the attack' (Lewis *et al.* 2001: online), and that appropriate counter-measures (effectively, *un*predictable variables) have not been applied in tests.

For those who *do* hold an ideological position on the project, the ways actions are conducted in different areas suggest a pragmatic approach. The missile defense project covers enormous geographical distances but, perhaps more importantly in analysing how protest movements operate, it also crosses many social, political and cultural boundaries. The differences in history and circumstance in the various project sites results in both alternative styles of protest and, significantly in the spatialization of politics, different triggers for involvement. Plans to base a missile defense site in South Korea are seen as overtly hostile, for example. Greenlanders, meanwhile, see the proposed upgraded radar system at Thule as an extension of Danish colonialism and a continuation of Cold War power politics, with Greenland as a pawn.

Common to both sets of protesters is the claim that the technology simply does not and cannot work. Despite the vast funding that the project has received to date, there is little evidence that the system is workable. Although a number of tests have proved successful, in that incoming missiles were intercepted by US fire, critics remain unconvinced. The main criticism is that the tests are undertaken under controlled situations that would never be replicated in times of real conflict; real rogue states don't call to say a missile is on the way. Moreover, critics argue, even where all of the relevant information is available, not all of the tests are successful, making the technology, at best, inefficient and, at worst, dangerous. The US administration counters this by arguing that:

> Our test philosophy is to add, step-by-step over time, complexity such as countermeasures and operations in increasingly stressful environ-ments. This approach allows us to make timely assessments of the most critical design risk areas. It is a walk-before-you-run, learn-as-you-go development approach.
>
> (Kadish 2001)

Campaigns against missile defense have been established in every area where the technology is to be sited, as well as in other areas. The protests are characterized by a dominant normative framework that links activists, coupled with local contexts that demonstrate their differences. On the one hand, there is a unifying global technology, allowing campaigners world-wide to share ideas and information. On the other, specific local and regional concerns mean Internet technology, alongside others, is applied contingently. These two factors mean that protests are not undertaken in a uniform fashion.

Missile defense protests in Alaska

Alaska, which joined the USA in 1959, is often considered one of its most remote and inhospitable states. Its strategic value – it is the most northerly state and during the Cold War was closest to the USSR – has meant that its infrastructure has been developed in line with the broader military objectives of US governments. Alaska is treated as a foreign base by the USA, with military personnel being paid an overseas weighting while stationed there. There is in Alaska, as in many other areas where military bases are sited, a fairly ambivalent relationship between the local population and the soldiers stationed in the region. At the same time, the local economy is heavily dependent on the business and employment opportunities bases in Alaska provide. There are two key missile defense sites, one at Fort Greely, the other on Kodiak Island. The closure of the original Forty Greely base in 2000 dealt a blow to the local economy and the building of missile silos for the defense project has been welcomed by some of the population (Keefe 2002: online). Opposition to the missile defense project is much stronger on Kodiak Island, where the local economy is dominated by the fishing industry. The population of the area is therefore both less dependent on the army base and more suspicious of initiatives that could lead to environmental damage. Kodiak has been earmarked to act as a site for launching the missiles while Fort Greely will be used as a storage site. Work on bases in both areas began in 2002.

   Protesters in Alaska have had the tacit backing of the state legislature, which passed a resolution stating that 'Alaska's safety and security take priority over any treaty or obligation' (Swazo 2002: online). Protesters in Alaska are involved in the campaign at three levels: attempting to persuade the local population to support their case; challenging the US government (that is, their own government, making this both a domestic and a foreign policy issue); and linking in with global campaigns against missile defense. The use of the Internet in the Alaskan campaigns is intensive. Indeed, Stacy Fitz, one of the key co-ordinators, has argued that the campaign could not be conducted effectively without it (Interview 03/10/02). Linking Alaskan protests to global networks has become a key feature of the campaigning strategy. Alaska CODE (Citizens Opposed to Defense Experimentation) and NoNukesNorth, link to national and global campaigning sites, as well as to each other. Alaska CODE is a coalition of local campaigning organizations, while NoNukesNorth links anti-missile defense protests across the Arctic Circle.

Alaska CODE frames its campaign in local terms: 'if you care about the way your taxes are being spent, if you want the military to clean up its 648 toxic sites around Alaska before embarking upon another military experiment, then please join us' (2002: online). NoNukesNorth, while heavily involved in local protests, uses a slightly more international frame of reference and provides links to other campaigns, such as Space4Peace and the Stop the War (on Iraq) coalition, as well as to other US sites on missile defense.

There is a concerted and continuous local campaign of actions, with regular protest marches outside the missile defense bases, visiting speakers, questions in the legislature, public meetings and lectures, and talks in schools, colleges and universities. The Internet is seen as a key campaigning resource, both for publicizing events and in forming the infrastructure for direct action. The Internet keeps campaigners in remote areas connected to global protests, and many protesters have come to rely upon it as a central source of information on new initiatives. While the mass media do have a role to play in publicizing actions, the Internet, in a large but sparsely-populated area, is seen as the most important mechanism for both information provision and mobilization.

Missile defense protests in the UK

There are two US military bases in North Yorkshire. One of these, at Menwith Hill in the Yorkshire Dales – known locally as a 'spy base' – is 'the principle NATO theatre ground segment node for high altitude signals intelligence satellites' (Federation of American Scientists 2000: online). Menwith Hill is a listening post, where telephone calls, faxes and emails are intercepted, ostensibly for security purposes, by the US National Security Agency (See: Civil Liberties Committee of the European Parliament 2000: online). The other site, at Fylingdales on the North York Moors, is a ground-based early warning radar site, which would be used to provide midcourse tracking information on inbound missiles (Yorkshire CND 2000: online). The two stations are inextricably linked, strategically speaking, as information gathered at Menwith Hill, which is being expanded for the project, will be crucial to the efficient operation of NMD at Fylingdales.

What is particularly relevant to the study of Internet activism in this case is the history of protest around the sites and the profile of the NMD project on the international stage. There are two main issues to be taken into account here. First, activism against the NMD project has been going on for a long time, with little interest shown by the general public or by the mass media. There have been opposition movements to the Menwith Hill base since it was first proposed in the 1950s. In the UK, grassroots protest against the siting of NMD at Fylingdales has been taking place since the project was first proposed, building upon ongoing actions against other military activities at both bases. A core group of activists have set up vigils, illegally entered the bases to gather information, undertaken fundraising exercises and maintained frequent contact with local press to raise the profile of the issue. There is also a permanent women's peace camp at Menwith Hill, the only such camp in the UK still in existence. There is, therefore, a committed group of activists, operating within an established network of protesters, both locally and globally, against nuclear weapons in general and against the NMD project in particular.[6]

CND Yorkshire has been using the Internet to provide information on its activities since 1997,[7] providing links to a wide range of other anti-nuclear protesters. Their website originates with GreenNet, which links some 250 other non-profit organizations. The site provides comprehensive information on the Star Wars system and links to UK-based and international organizations, including peace movements in New Zealand, Australia, the USA, South Asia and India. In addition, the site provides a vast archive of information on missile defense, including briefings, the now effectively defunct ABM Treaty in full, US and UK policy documents, as well as documentation on the work of the Fylingdales and Menwith Hill sites and their proposed role in the development of NMD. A number of fairly prominent organizations, such as the Federation of American Scientists, also have anti-NMD campaign literature online, while organizations such as the Ballistic Missile Defense Organization, part of the Office of the US Under Secretary of Defense for Acquisition, Technology and Logistics, supplies evidence and information in support of the project. While the aim of the Yorkshire campaigners is quite clear, the counter-arguments to their case are given space.

A second point of note is that provision of information via the Internet is seen as only one part of the campaigning system, and then not necessarily as the most important. Campaigners use a range of different tactics to engage in both direct and indirect political actions. As well as the more traditional forms of protest, such as holding public meetings and demonstrations, a number of innovative on- and off-line actions are used. In late 2002, for example, a postcard and letter/fax campaign was available on the Yorkshire CND website. This provided addresses and templates for letters and cards to be sent to George Bush, Tony Blair and prominent politicians in other countries. There was also a 'Stop the Convoy' campaign running, asking motorists to monitor and report the movements of nuclear warhead convoys on roads in England and Scotland. A number of major international conferences on NMD have been held, largely publicized and planned making use of email and web facilities. Some elements of the movement against missile defense in the UK resolutely refuse to bother with email and web pages, preferring more conventional leafleting and telephone-trees to network and draw attention to their work. For direct action, the mobile 'phone is seen as the most important co-ordinating tool, as it permits contact between individuals on-site. The Internet is often used foremost as an informational resource, and only as a supplementary tool of direct action.

Despite long-term and comprehensive campaigning and online coverage of missile defence policies and actions against the project by local and international activists, the attention of the mass media was not captured until the stance of new US administration's stance on global defence became clear. The project has taken centre stage in the foreign policy initiatives of the Bush administration, with the impetus for a major defence build-up (already a major foreign policy) enhanced by the September 11 2001 attacks. In pushing the issue onto the political agenda, the Bush government has raised the project's profile considerably. There is strong resistance to the project among most member states of the European Union (Valasek 2000: online). China and Russia have both criticized the project, which they say threatens to halt the largely successful offensive arms control negotiations of the past twenty five years (Tisdall 2001). Although Russia has stated that it would like to see major arms reductions, missile defense is seen as a threat to its national security, with the potential to ignite a new arms race (Traynor 2001).

The heightened media profile of the issue finally brought it to the attention of a wider public, both local to Yorkshire and from a wider constituency. As the mass media began to cover missile defense, interest in and membership of Yorkshire CND and related organizations began to rise concomitantly. This is not to suggest that the websites were of little effect previously; they provided information and campaign details to people who were, by and large, already interested in issues relating to nuclear security. The role of the mass media has been crucial in raising the profile of this issue, however, and should not be overlooked. At the same time, the role of the telephone, both mobile and static, should not be ignored when we are attempting to understand the spatialization of activism against missile defense.

Perhaps most crucially, though, when addressing some of these questions of activism and political agendas, it is important to assess where debates originate and how public interest is stimulated. In the case of NMD, it is quite clear that information both on the missile defense project and on how to protest against it was readily available on the Internet. The growing campaign against the project did not, however, really start at grassroots level. Missile defense is a top-down issue, with the discourse of national and international security framing mass media conceptions of how to interpret it. In some ways, this is political protest in the IR traditional sense, in that it involves citizens and governments, rather than 'prosumers' and corporations or international organizations which lack recognizable figureheads. The campaigning movement against the project grew after governments and the mass media had already raised its profile.

Conclusion

Across the Alaskan and UK cases, there are some obvious similarities regarding the way the Internet is used. As an informational tool, the use on both sides of the Atlantic is dense, detailed and comprehensive. Activists in both areas make use of a wide range of links and direct readers to pro- as well as anti-missile defense sites. The project is identified as a global problem and is linked by both sides to broader concerns about the militarization of space and the escalation of arms sales and global violence. The provision of links to national governments, as well as to overseas protest networks, establishes a sense of both global connectivity and of transnational norms; the framing of missile defense online is of a common concern and a shared threat. In both areas, there is a mine of largely specialist information on what the project is about and the perceived dangers associated with it.

Campaigners in the two areas, though, tend to use the Internet rather differently in the local context. In Alaska, the Internet is seen as a vital resource. Web pages and email listserves are the key pillars of the campaigns, with the networking on local actions taking place largely online. As noted in Chapter 3, statistics on Internet use are notoriously unreliable. Going back to the ITU (which we might consider the best source), we find that Alaska has the highest Internet penetration of any US state: over 50 per cent of Alaskans use the Internet at home or work and 92 per cent of the state's schools have Internet access (Hudson and Pittman 2002: online).

Although campaigners in the UK use the Internet for similar purposes and in similar ways, there is much less reliance on it as a tool of mobilization. Web pages have become increasingly important as an informational resource and are used to publicize events. Much of the direct action in the UK is, however, co-ordinated through telephone networks and informal personal contacts, which are seen to serve the purposes of campaigners effectively. With lower access – less than 40 per cent of the population (Nielsen 2002: online) – and a more densely-populated territory, the UK campaigns are less dependent on the Internet. As a feature of missile defense campaigns, the Internet can be seen as a multi-platform tool, allowing different levels of access, various mechanisms for mobilization and a range of options for networking. Local use is dependent, however, on a range of factors, including the level of Internet access, the history of Internet use in the region and the patterns of use established by the campaigning organizations.

In both regions, the Internet is not superseding other communications media, but is being used in conjunction with them. The role of the press, television, and radio in framing politics for activists is still significant. In particular, the role of the mass media in triggering a response from people outside of protest networks needs to be considered. In the case of missile defense, it is evident that protest networks, though linked globally, had operated as fairly self-contained entities before the mass media picked up on the story. In turn, mass media interest was triggered by the raising of the missile defense profile by foreign policy elites. This gives us an interesting conjunction of old and new styles of politics, with the two running side by side.

The function of less visible communications media, notably the telephone, also needs to be taken into account. Although the Internet provides a powerful tool for communication and networking among people disenfranchised by the political elite and mainstream media, it does not yet provide a sufficiently visible platform for publicizing activities to those without access or without prior interest in an issue. In cases like the missile defense protests, the Internet still acts as a network which appeals to a fairly specialist audience. This is not because the information is inaccessible, in either technological or intellectual terms. Much of the material published online by campaigning organizations is designed to put the case against missile defense simply and clearly for a non-specialist audience. The problem in reaching a general audience seems to be related to the ways we currently use the Internet and the ways access to information are structured.

7 Spatializing activism

Introduction

This chapter draws together some of the issues outlined in previous chapters, and identifies issues which analysis of activist use of the Internet raises. These are manifest at three related levels: disciplinary divisions relating to research into network technologies; theoretical approaches to the study of political space; and questions of access to political processes through the use of the Internet. This chapter is divided into two sections which look at academic analysis of cyberspace and the application of spatial theories respectively. The aims of this chapter are twofold. First, by addressing the difficulties facing scholars in developing appropriate modes of analysis for Internet use, it highlights the necessity for more flexible theoretical approaches. Second, and obviously related to this, the application of spatial theories to activist use of the Internet provides an example of how one such flexible approach to analysis of the increasingly complex arena of political interactions can be developed.

Under the heading 'Internet ontologies', some of the key observations on the impact and effects of the use of this technology, as articulated by scholars across a range of disciplines, are outlined. These observations situate analysis of activist use of this form of communication within the context of broader debates on the nature of socio-technical change. The Internet constitutes and constructs social, political and cultural phenomena that do not lend themselves easily to interpretation through any analytical criteria currently used in the social sciences. For this reason, some of the difficulties facing scholars attempting to analyse the Internet are highlighted and the absence at present of a satisfactory theoretical framework for this area of study noted.

The second part of the chapter applies spatial theories to the case studies from previous chapters. This provides an interpretative framework rather than a definitive model. The application of spatial theories does, though, highlight how conceptualizations of space as dynamic and relational provide a fluid approach appropriate for analysis of these multi-layered political activities. Unlike more rigid conceptualizations of politics, spatial theories provide a mechanism for analysing multi-dimensional and rapidly changing phenomena. Using them to look at activism and the Internet provides a useful illustrative example of how this works.

In terms of methodological development, spatial theories provide a foundation for examining political practice from multiple levels, rather than the more obviously structure level approach of the hegemonic discourse. This presents the potential for an epistemological shift, by identifying a framework for relational analysis of political activity. Earlier chapters examined how the state serves as the point of reference for political practice in the discourse of IR and consequently acts, implicitly or explicitly, as the definitional focus for all other political actors. Despite acknowledgement of a broader range of actors and practices as influential in international affairs, analysis of social movements and political activism has been restricted by the discipline's discursive focus on state-related organizational structures.

Internet ontologies

Study of the Internet is necessarily transdisciplinary, as the intellectual divisions of labour that define the boundaries of academic disciplines are disrupted by the evolving computer-mediated, relational spaces it invokes. This relationality contradicts the conventional segregation of academic disciplines and challenges some of the intellectual boundaries applied in academia. For Gregory:

> It is always possible to provide reasons (historical reasons) for the boundaries being drawn this way rather than that. Once these boundaries are established, however, they usually become institutionalized. All the apparatus of the academy is mobilized to mark and, on occasion, to police them. But these divisions do not correspond to any natural breaks in the intellectual landscape; social life does not respect them and ideas flow across them.
>
> (1994: 11)

Within IR, the historical reasons for its intellectual boundaries are evident. The concept of the sovereign state as the autonomous embodiment of political legitimacy is enshrined in international convention and is embedded in cultural experience. States have historically been, and remain, potent political actors, and the boundaries that distinguish one territorial entity from another retain important practical implications and symbolic resonance for states and citizens alike. However, the alignment of state borders with conceptual boundaries of politics has been challenged from within and without the discipline, and patterns of political engagement that are not state-centred are recognized as significant to the organization of political space.

The intellectual divisions that distinguish IR from other disciplines, already undermined by intra-disciplinary critiques, and by some of the palpable effects of trans-national and globalizing activities, are further contravened by the use of the Internet as a tool of social and political engagement. Franklin has suggested that, for the researcher 'communications issues are, in their most prosaic sense, about the practical problems of sustaining a multidisciplinary approach in the face of the hegemonic demarcation lines of any respective paradigm(s)' (1998b: 5). This exposes a basic paradox in the discursive foundations of the discipline. On the one hand, IR is intrinsically interdisciplinary, in that it draws upon a range of contributory academic fields to satisfy its wide-reaching remit. On the other, its critical signifier, the equation of state territory with political legitimacy in the international arena, renders a multi-disciplinary approach problematic. This is particularly evident in relation to analysis of transcendent, non-state-centred political practices of the kind analysed here.

The Internet links with a host of factors which are not necessarily designed to directly threaten the authority of states, but which have a crucial impact on the defining principles of political legitimacy underpinning the discipline of IR: the sovereignty and autonomy of the state. Most pertinently for this research, the conjunction of the Internet and its use by social movement actors represents a dimension of political interaction that state-centric ontologies do not reflect adequately. If state sovereignty and autonomy *are* being affected by the trans-state political activity facilitated by the use of the Internet, current mainstream theories in the discipline provide no effective mechanism for analysis of this. The dynamic relationships between non-state actors and transcendent technologies suggest a multi-layering of socio-political practices that is alien to the differentiated epistemological approaches of the discipline. Or, to put it another way, the dichotomies and divisions in IR are too simplistic as defining features of a discourse to deal with the multi-dimensionality of contemporary politics.

Hirst and Thompson note that 'new communication and information technologies have loosened the state's exclusive control of its territory, reducing its capacities for cultural control and homogenization' (1995: 409). The Internet refutes the inside/outside distinction central to IR, by transcending state boundaries *and* disrupting internal systems of governance. In this respect, the ontologies of IR which situate the state as the definitional basis of political interaction, or the 'nodal point' of its discourse (Doty 1996: 125) are undermined, as both the international and domestic functions of states may be altered by the use of the Internet by states and by other actors. The potential impact of the Internet on the state and other actors cannot, therefore, be understood within the static state-spatial categories which remain hegemonic in IR (see Guzzini 1998).

In analysing the impact of this form of communication, it is problematic to assume the state to be either autonomous within the international system or to be the principal influence over decision-making within the confines of its own territory. In particular, the need for international and global forms of legislation and the influence of a few major economic players over the spread of communications technologies suggest that even powerful states have only limited autonomy regarding the distribution and use of these technologies within their borders (see Sassen 1999). Featherstone and Lash make this clear when they note that national governments still largely operate in a pre-digital era and do not have the capacity to regulate MNCs and the flows of capital across global markets (1999: 6).

The discipline of IR is not alone in struggling to reconceptualize its ontological premises in light of techno-social change; Poster suggested as early as 1990 that the rapid introduction of new communicational modes constituted a pressing field for theoretical development and empirical investigation (1990: 8). In this respect, the study of the Internet suggests that a fundamental re-imaging of the nature of enquiry in the social sciences is required, most specifically of the tendency towards division rather than linkage.

Kitchin has argued that the relationships between technology and society can no longer be framed within strict economic and political terms or in strict social and cultural terms but has to encompass both (1998: 71). One of the most obvious impacts of the Internet is to make even the broadest categories of analysis – economic, social, cultural and so on – inter-related, creating conceptual dilemmas for traditionally independent disciplines. Despite this, even where inter- or multi-disciplinary work is undertaken, distinct disciplinary boundaries remain. Historically, there have been some sound intellectual and pedagogical reasons for this. In many cases, there may still be. There is now, however, a widespread shift towards inter-disciplinarity that reflects, and is in part driven by, the changes wrought by the introduction of the Internet.

Lyon notes the frustration experienced in attempting to apply conventional theories to understanding of the social relations of online interactions:

> The forms of social interaction observable within CMC, especially on the Internet, appear to push social theory beyond the simple dichotomy of direct and indirect relationships ... [and] also beyond the scope of modern notions of self and society.
>
> (1997: 32)

These notions are particularly complex in IR, as the discipline has situated concepts of rationality and autonomy at state level, and has little real sense of self and society beyond the system of states. Thus the *self*, as rational, autonomous individual, has always been an *other* in IR, as individuals other than state leaders have effectively been located outside of interpretations of political legitimacy in the discipline. This dichotomy suggests that some of the foundational premises of IR also require radical reworking if emerging concepts of multi-dimensional political actors, operating within dis- and un-located spaces, are to be interpreted effectively. The use of the Internet by social movement actors suggests that a range of actors, not necessarily 'new' but currently inadequately accounted for in IR, are engaged in activities which are not imbued with political legitimacy within the discipline, but which can clearly have an impact on both other non-state, and state, actors.

Most academic disciplines have experienced some difficulty in incorporating the study of this form of communication within existing discursive parameters, since concepts of boundaries, both within academic disciplines and in social, economic and cultural existence, are disrupted. The Internet disrupts some of the fundamental constructs of social theory by reconfiguring agent/structure relations, most specifically by disputing the role of structure as the key determinant in defining agency. Though the choices available to actors will always be limited in some way or other, the availability of the Internet may provide one form of expression which operates outside of, but in relation to, the structural boundaries understood in IR.

Franklin highlights a key concern relating to analysis of the impact of the Internet in a discipline dedicated to investigating the international:

> there is an unarticulated conflict between traditional epistemological/ontological frameworks, of IR/IPE in particular, employed to critique Informatics and the experience of working and living in societies increasingly premised on this form of High-Tech infrastructure.
>
> (1998b: 1)

IR lacks analytical tools for interpreting the myriad effects and influences of this form of communication, at the level of either theory or of practice. The dichotomous logic underpinning the discipline, particularly in respect of definitions of political legitimacy, implies divisions between elements of political practice which may now be linked by the Internet, as well as by broader social and political changes. Linkages across social and political spaces, which are exemplified by the growth of social movements and appear to be extended through the growth of communications infrastructures, have important implications for the ontological foundations and epistemological directions of IR. From the case studies in the previous chapters it is clear that definitions of political activity prevalent in the dominant discourses of IR are inconsistent with some contemporary political practices. By situating the state as agent and the international system as structure, the impact of other actors and the validity of alternative interpretative mechanisms are frequently underplayed in the discipline.

Compounding this problem, communications media cannot simply be 'added in' to the discipline; Thompson points out that deployment of communications media does not consist simply of the establishment of new networks for the transmission of information between individuals where the basis of social relations remain intact (1994: 34). He suggests that 'on the contrary, the deployment of communications media establishes new forms of interaction and new kinds of social relations between individuals' (ibid.) The social relations engendered by network communications, coupled with the growth of trans-national, issue-based political activism, imply heterogeneous links and non-linear connections between actors, compromising historically conceived notions of autonomy and rationality, whether related to states or to citizens. These conceptualizations have already been dissected by feminist theorists, who have argued that notions of autonomy and rationality are culturally determined and exhibit masculine bias (see Sylvester 1994; Tickner 1992). Feminist theorists have thus played an important role in developing concepts of non-linear political agency, and have generated key critical insights into some of the givens in IR.

Rationality and autonomy are, of course, key elements of modernist conceptions of societal development, premised on notions of advance and progress. For Melucci, 'the historicist notion of change as global, homogeneous, and end-directed has ceased to apply to analysis of complex societies' (1996: 209). The Internet is becoming a fundamental component of complex societies, and cannot be considered in isolation from the wider effects of social change, in which it in turn indisputably plays a major role. Consequently, analysis of the use of the Internet by activists needs to be considered within the context of broader social effects, brought about in part by the introduction of these technologies. There is something of a 'chicken and egg' scenario here. As Loader points out:

> cyberspace can only be understood in relation to the techno-social restructuring which is occurring in the real world: ICTs are both driving that restructuring and responding to it; they are not creating an imagined realm separate from it.
>
> (1997a: 7)

In this respect, the inter-layering of social and political spheres, as well as the apparently inescapable role of new technologies in processes of change, places developments in theoretical approaches at the forefront of academic imperatives.

We are not talking here only about new forms of information exchange, but also about new forms of social interaction that cannot be interpreted effectively within a state-centric discourse. The application of spatial theories reflects Loader's conception of techno-social change, in that analysis of the ramifications of the use of the Internet does not centre upon the concept of a separate political sphere, but upon interpreting the ways these technologies are applied to existing and evolving practices. That is, activist use of the Internet, in common with that of other political actors, is embedded in existing practices, as well as implicit in the creation of new ones.

Research into the ways information is acquired and acted upon, and into how the agendas of political actors are formed and influenced requires acknowledgement of a broader picture of techno-social, as well as political, change. The ways activists – both formal and informal – produce and exchange information and the extent of their reach across the political spectrum are affected by the communications media they and the actors they engage with have access to. Street highlights the inextricable link between technology and social change in contemporary societies:

> technology is the embodiment of certain interests and possibilities, but ... it is also the bearer of effects: it changes what we can imagine and what we want, it alters our politics.
>
> (1997: 35)

He notes, moreover, that the relationships between actors and technologies are in constant flux, with political processes shaping technology, which in turn shapes politics (ibid.). The impact of technological change on political practices, therefore, relates not only to 'new' behaviours, but also to adjustments in actions and assumptions across the political spectrum, and through the whole of the political sphere.

Despite the complex relations underlying this area of investigation, it is possible to identify some of the most salient features of contemporary socio-political activity relevant to interpretation of political use of the Internet. In relation to one of the central propositions of the research undertaken for this book – that the Internet may provide new opportunities for access to political processes – the most pertinent concerns are essentially twofold. First, economic determinants, encompassing financial constraints on individuals through to the influence of various actors over decision-making processes on service provision, are significant. Second, the socio-political contexts within which activists operate, at micro and macro levels, have important implications for organizational and individual access to this form of technology. The cost of political participation – whether economic or social – is taken into account in individuals' decision-making processes (Brown and Svennevig 1999).

In respect of economic factors, there are a number of salient issues warranting brief examination. First, the diminished role of the state as chief regulator of telecommunications reduces the control of elected or imposed state representatives over decision-making processes on pricing and access (see Herman and McChesney 1997). Telecommunications systems, services and artefacts are increasingly regulated within the international and/or global arena and, as a consequence, major economic actors have a large degree of influence over policy direction. There is little real potential for states, or any other actors, to control either the infrastructures of ICTs or the content of transmissions effectively.

The influence of economic actors in the policy-making field, as well as in the distribution and provision of goods and services, has led many commentators to conclude that the interests of the most dominant telecommunications and media companies are both served by, and constitute a driving force for, the use of the Internet. Graham and Marvin suggest, for example, that ICTs are 'fully inscribed into the political, economic and social relations of capitalism' (1996: 94). They stress, too,

> the key role of telematics in reshaping the time and space limits that confine capitalist economic development, ... *in ways that directly favour those economic and political interests who already dominate society.*
>
> (ibid.: 100, emphasis in original)[1]

For some analysts there are three likely outcomes of the spread of network technologies: that current patterns of underdevelopment in some regions will persist; that networks will serve to reinforce existing inequalities; and that business imperatives will continue to be privileged over those relating to public access (see Franklin 1998b; Haywood 1998; May 1998). None of these eventualities is guaranteed, and the interweaving of social factors, technological change and global commercial interests precludes the identification of a single analytical baseline.

The emphasis placed by some analysts on the commercialization of the Internet in particular implies that the relatively unrestricted flows of information which many users currently experience are potentially threatened by the imposition of 'real' constraints, such as legislative or commercial restrictions, on virtual exchanges (see Haywood 1998; Holderness 1998). The WTO Agreement on Telecommunications which positions communications as a service comparable to banking and insurance, along with the increasing commercialization of the Internet, are the most obvious foundations for such fears.

The fundamental role of the Internet in facilitating the operational efficiency of the market is irrefutable, and their centrality to the mechanisms of global trading systems increasingly apparent. Despite the transcendent nature of network technologies and the multi-dimensional implications of the use of these technologies, capitalist economics are playing an important role in the current development of the Internet, as goods, as services and as an infrastructure of commercial endeavour. Much analysis of the impact of the Internet focuses exclusively on the role of either the market or the state, though, with the complex, multi-dimensional social relations constituted through their use unrecognized or underplayed. This takes us back again to the arguments about the need for relational rather than dichotomous approaches.

Claims about the use of the Internet as a tool for social and political participation remain situated to some degree within the dualistic debates of state versus market control. How people are actually *using* the Internet is, at best, a side-issue for many researchers. Although both states and markets are crucial variables within debates on access and provision, their dominance in discussions of the impact of the Internet reflects the power relations of public/private, elite-oriented interpretations of political participation. Franklin notes that new communications technologies 'reveal new sites and expressions of power/gender relations' (1998b: 7), and these are largely unconsidered in state/market debates. The Internet, as is obvious to anyone who uses it, does not exist within the exclusive province of either states or markets and cannot, therefore, be analysed from a deterministic perspective. These debates – about dualism, dichotomization, dominant actors and so on – demonstrate clearly what the Internet is not: it is not a technology which can be understood in isolation. Relationality – of actors and practices, of agency and structures – is evident in every aspect of Internet use. The spatial theories applied in the section which follows attempt to get a handle on this relationality. They tackle different aspects of the activist case studies and demonstrate how, if we move beyond dichotomy and division, we may be able to gain a closer understanding of how we can understand Internet politics.

Applying spatial theories

Statistics on Internet use and the data on growth rates for ICT use offer some indication of how rapidly network communications are spreading, both quantitatively and geographically (see ITU 2002: online). Although the vast majority of research in this field concurs with the notion that the Internet is affecting the lives of people worldwide, whether or not they actually come into direct contact with this form of communication (see McChesney 1997a), there is strong evidence to suggest that the impact of technologies depends to a significant degree on *how* they are applied. The apparently inexorable growth and relentless technological advancement of telecommunications systems in recent years cannot sufficiently explain the impact of the Internet across multiple dimensions of human existence. For academic analysts, the multi-dimensionality of the Internet is the most problematic aspect of this techno-social phenomenon. As discussed earlier in this chapter, the indivisibility of the Internet from its effects on social practices sits awkwardly with norms of inclusion and exclusion in academic discourse.

The spatial theories adapted from the work of Lefebvre, outlined in Chapter 1, provide a relatively fluid analytical schema, by permitting the impact of change on individual actors or organizations to be analysed. This contrasts with the top-down categorizations of political activity that dominate the discourse of IR. These theories also provide a mechanism for analysing the implications of this form of communication for non-state actors, viewed as political agents in their own right, whether as individuals or as part of broader collectives. The spatial categories applied here are by no means conclusive and do not provide a system of spatial classification. They are designed, rather, to promote the concept of space as a valid analytical construct within IR.

The spatial categories outlined in this book are both discrete and related. The three key headings applied below – spatial practice, representations of space and spaces of representation – highlight areas of analysis relevant to the complex issues of access to political processes, and for interpretation of the actions of non-state actors by reference to non-state, as well as to state, practices. Issues raised in Chapter 1 form the conceptual undercurrent to the application of spatial theories undertaken in this section. The notions that political practices cannot be mapped effectively against territorial interpretations of space, and that emphasis on the public spaces of politics in IR is analytically limiting, form a backdrop to the analysis that now follows.

Spatial practice

As stated in Chapter 1, spatial practice relates to the ways in which societies are organized, both by material environment and through the social behaviours of people within them. In looking at activist use of the Internet, two issues are most evidently germane: whether the Internet is changing the material environments of activists and the people they interact with; and whether any such change has an impact on the political behaviours of either group. These interwoven issues are addressed in this section.

The fundamental concern in respect of spatial practices relates to the availability or otherwise of network technologies, for the activists themselves and for the individuals, organizations and collectives they work with. It is somewhat easier to pin down the spatial practices of 'formal' activists than of their 'informal' peers, as the structuring of both their political opportunities and those that they facilitate for others is more evident. The spatial practices of large transnational NGOs can change quite dramatically when the Internet is introduced. The Internet and email can be used to enhance their internal bureaucracies, increase efficiency and lower the costs of intra- and extra-organizational transactions. Internally, the Internet provides a mechanism for improving the efficiency of large transnational organizations, facilitating more rapid and effective intra-agency communication. The relatively heavy outlay involved in providing network facilities to international offices is largely offset by the reduced costs of administration across borders and the increased speed of communication between different sectors of the organizations. Internal change is a given when the Internet is used by NGOs, with the technology fostering organizational change.

Externally, the Internet allows NGOs to publicize their concerns relatively inexpensively, using both email and websites. The potential to promote the interests, concerns and campaigns of the organizations across a wide geographical reach becomes available with the transcendence of national boundaries inherent to the technology. As we have seen, this information does not reach a mass audience in the traditional sense of the term. However, it can reach a range of different audiences: the general Internet user, specific targeted groups and those seeking specialist material. Whilst the availability of this kind of information is not in itself sufficient to fuel political change, the social conditions within which it exists indicate that such provision has the potential to have a significant impact on states and other actors. Most notable among these social conditions are the increased status of major NGOs on the international stage in recent years and the rapid spread of ICTs as a tool of social and political engagement across a broad range of actors.[2]

The spatial practices of formal activists are also affected by the ability the Internet provides to offer links to other organizations. Links to similar organizations help to promote a sense of transnational normative frameworks; organizations can be seen to be part of broader political collectives. The Internet is clearly not responsible for the introduction of normative frameworks – these have been evolving rapidly in recent decades. It is, though, largely responsible for their enhanced visibility. Links to 'official' institutions such as the UN, the EU and so on also influence the spatial practices of formal activists, by positioning them as equivalents on the political spectrum. Political hierarchies do still exist and, as earlier chapters showed, institutions still maintain a high level of control over access. That activist organizations can now direct their own audience to the resources of governments and international institutions offers a form of legitimization, and a sense that the hierarchies are of reduced impact.

For informal activists, the most profound effect of the Internet on their spatial practices is probably on their interactions with each other. The potential to extend networks and to share information has had a dramatic impact on the scale of activist communications in recent years. Changes to spatial practices have been experienced in two main ways. In open spaces, through their websites, activists extend communication between each other and with like-minded organizations and collectives. In closed (though I would hesitate to call them 'secret') discussions, activists make use of email, coded lists, etc., in some instances to plan direct actions, in others to share information which is not to be made available to a general audience.

Activists have always conducted these kinds of practices, of course – some in the public domain, some outside of it. What is different now is the *potential* geographic reach of the information. A global reach isn't always necessary; to plan the schedule for a sit-in against the upgrading of the missile defense site in Fort Greely in Alaska, for example, it isn't necessary to communicate with activists in other countries. What is useful, though, is the potential to gather – cheaply and quickly – information on similar actions at other bases. This was shown most clearly in the GM case study, where patterns of activism have been replicated in a number of different countries. The Internet affects spatial practices not only by facilitating global networking but also in allowing the sharing of expertise. As we find Internet analysis becoming more sophisticated, we may find that the replication of actions in different contexts constitutes new repertoires of contention in social movements.

For the individuals and groups activists seek to reach there remains the basic issue of availability or otherwise of appropriate technologies. Lack of access to the Internet does not preclude political participation, of course. Availability of the technologies, and the skills to use them effectively, however, may have a domino effect in relation to informational resources available, and to the range of other easily-accessible actors. If political activity is premised on access to relevant information, the Internet appears to be becoming the *sine qua non* of contemporary activism. This applies both to formalized activism, relating to engagement with 'official' political institutions, and to the activities of informal collectives. In addition, the phenomenon of 'downloaders,' well-informed individuals who use specialist information from the Internet to lobby politicians, local authorities and so on, suggests the potential for the development of an information underclass.

The concept of an information underclass is important in terms of spatial practice, as the new ways activists organize themselves through their use of the Internet may exclude some groups of actors from non-state political processes. The more formalized 'Internet protest' becomes, the more the potential for such exclusions increases. This begs the question of the negative effects increased use of the Internet may have on those who do not have access to this form of communication. This cannot be answered entirely satisfactorily by a response which suggests that the 'information rich' will dominate the 'information poor'. Although this position has been widely argued (see Holderness 1998; Stallabrass 1995), it is problematic because it situates economic determinants at the crux of access issues that, as we have seen, can be rather limiting. Moreover, the 'digital divide' is widely perceived to be a North/South, developed/developing world imbalance. This, too, is an oversimplified spatialization; there are many disadvantaged groups within developed countries with little access to these technologies. Although economic factors do play a significant role in the availability of Internet access to individual actors, the reductionist logic of the economically deterministic position pays inadequate regard to the broad social, cultural and political dimensions of the use of this technology.

It *is* evident from much recent research that, despite rapid growth, people in developing countries, and in less developed regions within advanced industrial societies, have far fewer opportunities to use the Internet than their wealthier counterparts (see Hamelink 1997). In terms of the spatial practices of activists, however, these disparities in access serve to highlight the significance of this form of communication to their political activities. Pruett has suggested that NGOs have a critical role to play in providing access to the Internet in less developed regions:

> Sufficient demand for the Internet exists even in the poorest countries to make it a viable, indeed a highly profitable venture. If the market is ensuring rapid Internet growth, ... NGOs may need to focus on ensuring access and benefits for the less advantaged.
>
> (1998 online)

The lack of basic telecommunications provision in some areas could emphasize the role of activists, particularly those involved in umbrella networks, as political actors. This appears to be true insofar as these organizations can increase their profile, both locally and in the wider political arena, through the use of this form of communication.

Besette has noted the disjuncture between provision of information at global level and its value for local actors:

> Facilitating access to information is important, in the global sense as part of the communication process, but we also need to facilitate the production and circulation of information at the local level. ... This means using technology not only to validate local knowledge, but even more importantly, to place users in an active role.
>
> (1997: 22)

Resources are never unlimited, and the wisdom of prioritizing information technology provision is contested by both theorists and practitioners (see Pharoah and Welchman 1997). Besette has suggested, though, that one important role of the Internet is in facilitating feedback and enhancing participation in decision-making (1997: 23), a function which may justify greater investment.

As the use of the Internet increases, methods of communication between activists and other political actors are adjusting to make use of this technology. That is, the spatial practices of all political actors are adjusted by the introduction of this form of communication as, for example, the use of multi-level communications between state agencies, international institutions, formal and informal activists becomes increasingly common.

Representations of space

Representations of space, as noted in Chapter 1, relate to conceptualized spaces which, for Lefebvre, constitute control over knowledge, signs and codes. Thus the ways societies represent space are articulated in dominant discourses and theories, through the lexicons of academic disciplines, through accepted codes of social behaviour and so on. As previous chapters have shown, understandings of political practice in IR have traditionally been dominated by state-spatial characterizations of politics. All of the movement actors in the case studies use their websites to stress, to greater or lesser degrees, individual empowerment, local and regional communities and what could be termed 'partnership politics' between individuals, NGOs, businesses and governments.

The erosion of state control over media output and telecommunications infrastructures in recent years has now been exacerbated by the introduction of the s/elective technologies of the Internet. Consequently, the opportunities for states to structure the codes of political engagement, and in turn to influence academic interpretations of the constituents of politics, are undermined by the use of the Internet by a wide range of actors. The activists considered here are all non-state, *transnational* actors, whether they are formally associated with organizational networks or not, and the kinds of normative politics they engage in can be promoted easily through the Internet. Even where their activism is about local issues – for example the expansion of a military base for the missile defense programme in Yorkshire or Alaska – the Internet allows activists to draw upon global expertise to position their actions in broader political contexts.

Looking at the case studies, it is clear that multi-level politics are taking place. For most, if not all, of the movement actors considered the context of political engagement is defined by a normative approach, rather than through state referents of the validity of non-state practices. The value systems which many movement actors claim to represent are articulated through a discourse which is based on normative rather than territorial interpretations of politics. Although the state system has a structuring effect on the role of movement actors in the international arena, the various factors which contribute to a diminution of state authority over representations of space suggest that perceptions of political space are being disrupted. The Internet is one of these factors, and activist use of this form of communication another; these are transnational actors using largely geographically unconstrained technologies in a system often regulated with reference to regional and global, rather than national, econo-political spaces.

In addition, the use of the Internet to promote campaigns radically increases the potential audience for their resources, including archives, publications and publicity material. One of the most important effects of this is to extend the reach of the organizations, providing the opportunity to deliver more information on their activities to much wider audiences. In this respect, despite the uneven distribution of the Internet across social groups, the potential to influence the actions of key publics is enhanced. Hirst and Thompson note the importance of the link between movement actors and key publics in influencing state and international policy-making, and suggest that:

Such influence is the more likely if the populations of several major states are informed or roused on an issue by the world 'civil society' of trans-national NGOs.

(1995: 431)

Providing information which may influence the opinions of key publics is a function of the Internet which some movement actors are in a fairly strong position to capitalize upon. This is most obvious with the large NGOs, particularly at major international conferences where a specialist normative voice is often welcomed by both governments and the media. NGOs also provide a useful counter to governmental perspectives and fit well within the framework of 'point counter point' that news production relies upon. Formal activists may therefore gain media coverage by virtue of, rather than despite, their non-governmental perspective. There is a problem for activists, though, in that they are *not* the agenda-setters for the global media. Their voice may be heard but not always in the way they would like it to be (cf. Tarrow 1994).

Some activists, particularly those involved in direct action, are still likely to be cast in the role of rebel and the nuances of their arguments are likely to go unheard. Mass media representations frequently cast activists in a negative light and the introduction of the Internet allows them to tackle this framing of their activities in two ways. First, the introduction of the Internet has an impact on the opportunities for activists to publicize their activities. The organization of mass media structures in many societies curtails access for many non-state actors, as their activities generally fall outside the remit of news producers. Although using the Internet doesn't invoke political participation – as we have seen, it doesn't make people political – it does broaden the networks through which information can be exchanged. In this sense, the organizing of our understanding through mass media structures is challenged. The ways politics as a field is framed are disrupted, as information which counters 'official' versions becomes more readily available. Which framing may be right or wrong is not the issue here – what is important is the fact that the ways political space is represented to us are less easily dominated by one group of actors than previously.

The second way activists can disrupt dominant representations of space is seen in the growth of online independent media, where a concerted effort is made to overcome the standard ways of depicting political activism. Movements like Squall and IndyMedia use the Internet *as* mass media and apply the technology to pose a direct counter to mass media framings. In this respect, they are among the first actors to use the Internet specifically and strategically as a mass media technology; many actors treat the Internet as a supplementary technology but for online independent media organizations, it has become the only feasible mechanism for mass distribution of their material.

In some respects, the provision of information on local, regional, national and international issues, and the links made between actors and across issues, have been key strengths of activists in establishing a distinctive and influential voice on the international stage. Agendas which posit individuals, local and regional collectives and other actors marginalized within traditional interpretations of international politics as significant players essentially disrupt dualistic impressions of politics. High/low, public/private, exclusionary political ontologies, already undermined by the proliferation of non-state actors staking claims on the realm of the political, can be further undercut by the use of the Internet. This form of communication blurs the boundaries of political activity and interpretation, by responding to neither geographical demarcations regarding the sites of politics, nor discursive demarcations on its content. In this respect, the structural basis of IR, which is premised on the concept of states as discrete units, albeit ones which have increasingly complex relations with other actors, is weakened. The codification of politics in IR is, as a consequence, challenged.

The Internet also affects representations of space by emphasizing challenges posed to the state as the embodiment of political community. This is evident both in the limited ability of states to control the use and development of this form of communication, and through the potential non-state actors have to use the Internet to engage in forms of political activism conceptualized as issue- rather than state-based. The ability of any single group of actors, such as states or MNCs, to hegemonically influence the content or flow of information via the Internet is compromised by the nature of the technology. Opportunities to dominate definitions of political practice are consequently limited. Communication between political actors, constituted for most activists of far more diverse groups than state-centred interpretations recognize, extends discursive parameters by forcing new issues onto high political agendas.[3]

The use of the Internet to publicize campaigns, moreover, provides a mechanism for promoting non-state political agendas into the social arena. The diminishing control of states over these crossover socio-political agendas is highlighted by the use of the Internet, with activists shifting information up, down and through the spectrum of political actors. The use of information technologies can consolidate some of the operational features upon which activists have capitalized in recent decades, most notably their ability to link practical aspects of political activism to the promotion of universal social concerns. For 'informal' movement actors, the potential to promote alternative visions of the political arena is important. The extension of the concept of politics – what it is or can be – rather than direct challenge to governments is often central to their representations of space.

Activist use of the Internet depends to an important degree on a capacity to communicate freely and openly, unfettered on the whole by external constraints on the distribution and exchange of information, whether from political or commercial sources. Indeed, one of the most valuable attributes of the Internet for non-state political actors is their potential to circumvent restrictions on open exchange of ideas and information. To date, states and other actors have generally been unable or unwilling to impose constraints on the information flows which ICTs facilitate, and Moore suggests that, although actors have followed different policy directions, most are consistent in their desire to see an 'information society' develop (1998: 152). At present there is no evidence to indicate that any emergent public sphere will be hindered by restrictive legislation on information exchange. In relation to the development of this new form of public sphere, the Internet is not the *basis* of an activist challenge to high political discourse. It may, though, provide a tool for building on some of the gains non-state organizations have made in expanding the agendas set by high political actors and in drawing social concerns into the political arena.

Chapter 1 suggested that all non-state actors are marginal to the discourse of IR, as the hegemony of state-spatial conceptions continues to dominate analysis in the discipline. The Internet can be seen, however, to express many of the changes already witnessed in international political practice; it transcends borders, can foster non-state political communities and facilitate non-state political activism, and can be used as a tool of activism at multiple levels. In these respects, the use of the Internet may represent a significant development in the role of activists as agents of social change. In addition, the marginalization of non-state actors in IR has been reduced in recent years as the impact of social movements has filtered through to state agendas.

Representations of space in both political practice and theory are reflecting a shift towards collective endeavour and the increasingly important role of communications technologies in political practices. The decreasing marginality of non-state actors is not necessarily experienced at the expense of states as political players. The analytical approaches of most spatial theorists, which reject binarized conceptualizations of politics, acknowledge that politics is a multi-faceted realm and that states remain important players, both in defining some of the rules of engagement and regulating some aspects of citizen behaviour. For many theorists critical of the discursive hegemony of the state in IR, the major point of dissent has not been the presence of states as key players in international affairs but the relative absence and influence of other significant actors. Representations of political space in IR, influenced among other things by the two transnational trends of increased activist prominence and the spread of the Internet are slowly beginning to reflect the inter-relationships between states and other actors.

Spaces of representation

As noted in Chapter 1, spaces of representation equate most closely with concepts of agency and particularly with the possibilities for political action available to individuals. These possibilities are framed by the real and metaphoric demarcations of spatial practices and representations of space. That is, the perceived and conceived spaces of human existence, as defined by Lefebvre, have important implications for actors in terms of the choices available to engage in political activity.

Activist use of the Internet which affects spatial practices has implications for access to political processes by individuals and social groups. The potential for political participation has, in many respects, traditionally been equated almost exclusively with the notion of representations of space. Historically, the notion of political participation has focused upon the structural level, defining political practices through the auspices of the state. This is, of course, the model of politics which both political science and IR have applied as the standard for interpretation of the role of the individual in political practice. In the domestic arena, individuals are represented *by* the state, and on the international stage, are subsumed *to* the state. While the state does provide, and can deny, access to political processes, it is its role as definitional of political legitimacy which is brought into question here. To decide not to buy genetically modified food, for example, is a political act, whatever one's government's perspective on the matter. Such a decision may or may not be felt directly by legislators; it is, regardless, an act with political impact, whether for other governments, for agro-chemical multinationals, for farmers, for international organizations and so on.

Access to political processes is increasingly structured not only by the political system within which activists reside but also by other factors such as available economic resources, and by the presence or absence of technological artefacts and information provision (see Frederick 1997; Walch 1999). The spaces of representation of individuals are consequently as influential over the opportunities for political participation as the state-political system within which they reside. Access to the Internet is part of the complex of factors which now influence the choices available to individuals as political actors. The introduction of the Internet into the political arena alters the spaces of representation for many non-state actors, as individuals and social groups who have access to this technology undoubtedly have an increased range of options for political engagement. Opportunities for political activism and dissent may be increased. Or, as social movement theorists would put it, political opportunity structures are altered by enhanced access to a wider range of actors.

Regarding increased access, this relates not so much to access to individuals (though some political elites have, one could say, thrown open the virtual doors of their offices to make themselves available online). The point relates more particularly to access to information. Activists can both draw on a vast range of previously unavailable (or difficult to obtain) resources and can provide access to this, framing it within their own parameters. This structuring of information provides a resource for both specialist and general audiences and large NGOs have been particularly successful in enhancing their global 'branding' by using this technology. Smaller and/or informal activist groups have benefited too. In the case studies, this was clearest in respect of Squall, where the cost of reaching an audience – any audience – offline was a constant challenge.

The speed of information exchange and supply of specialist information on the Internet may all serve to enhance the potential of individuals and social groups to 'act politically'. Online political action parallels conventional campaigning methods, such as producing and distributing publicity material, mobilizing activists, lobbying government agencies and other decision-making bodies and so on. The advantages of the Internet in this respect are the speed of communication and the potential for theoretically infinite reproduction of data. Things that activists *already* do can, with the Internet, be done with greater intensity and efficiency. For example, missile defense activists in the UK and Alaska have a long history of co-operation but the scale of their interactions and the opportunities to share information have been vastly increased by the Internet. Organizations like Amnesty International and Friends of the Earth have long been able to target both specialist and general audiences but have adapted their operations to accommodate the wider reach of the Internet. In this sense, the Internet is not providing a new process but is enhancing existing functions.

Activists use the Internet both to enhance their existing operational techniques and to find new ways of facilitating political participation. Rather than directly increasing access by providing communications facilities to marginalized groups, activists are using the Internet to distribute, receive and exchange information and to forge links up and down the political spectrum and between political actors. Most do not aim to 'create' new actors or to empower marginalized groups directly. Those who do aim to provide access to technologies – such as APC WSNP and OneWorld – do so through education and training, rather than through provision of hardware.

The provision of information is a necessary element of the development of activist politics and the Internet provides a mechanism for increasing their potential to reach geographically, if not necessarily socio-economically, diverse audiences. In this respect, the limitations which geographical barriers place upon political participation are of reduced significance. Other barriers, such as technical and economic problems in gaining access to the Internet, persist, but the constraints of territory appear to be diminished.

The use of the Internet by activists also contributes to a form of political activity which is premised on non-linear agency. This reflects a general trend in patterns of political practice. Where, until fairly recently, the political impact of individuals was largely experienced through representative authorities, the forms of activism which the Internet permit can reduce the relevance of public/private boundaries and makes exclusion from political processes more difficult for 'official' institutions to effect.

Access to information is a prerequisite of political campaigning. Much of the material placed online by activists is designed to encourage response from users, utilizing the interactive potential of the technology to elicit specific practical effects, such as raising funds, encouraging supporters to lobby governments and MNCs, or taking part in on- and off-line campaigns. Organizations like Amnesty International and Friends of the Earth have developed online campaigning tools, which create links to named actors to allow direct lobbying of governments, international institutions and commercial organizations. Like many other transnational NGOs, they have also introduced facilities for direct membership subscriptions and/or donations via the Internet. As the case study on transnational NGOs showed, enhancing political opportunities in this way brings with it potential problems. Although large organizations of this kind operate on a global scale, their membership systems and their budgets still tend to be managed at national level. In creating global membership democracies, as it were, they shift their interpretation of their own political spaces; while their approach to politics may be normative and global, their functional infrastructures are only just beginning to reflect this.

The absence of mass media-style gatekeeping on the Internet also opens up possibilities for new forms of political engagement and thus extends spaces of representation. As noted in Chapter 3, the gatekeeping function of mass media serves to filter information for audiences, effectively deconstructing complex issues and reconstituting them in more digestible forms for transmission. The absence of a gatekeeping mechanism on intersecting networks of activists online, where access to output is user-led, has both advantages and drawbacks. On one hand, users can access information which has not been pre-digested for mass consumption, and which often reflects specialist opinion on complex issues. In addition, the Internet can only indirectly be used to promote hegemonic societal norms and values, as governments and other dominant actors lack any real system for encoding multi-logical interactions. On the other hand, however, the diffuse nature of network communications effectively renders all information of equivalent merit, and no effective filtering system exists for distinguishing between online documents. As most Internet users have found, it can be difficult to distinguish between 'good' and 'bad' sources, and between reliable and unsubstantiated information.

This is dealt with in two ways by activists. Perhaps somewhat paradoxically, big name organizations such as Oxfam and Greenpeace, who are well known as credible political actors, attract huge amounts of online traffic. The high profile of these organizations is seen as a valuable attribute as users seek out familiar names among the proliferation of sites online. This could place smaller organizations at a disadvantage, with the big getting bigger at the expense of less well-known organizations. This is where social networks, as a key part of movement activism, come into play. Both offline and online networks influence Internet use by activists: sites recommended by friends and acquaintances promote new use, as do sites vetted by trusted activist groups.

Conclusion

The Internet does not fit neatly, as we have seen, into any academic framework. Nor, for that matter, do spatial theories. Relationality can be a rather untidy concept. Spatial theories help to link some of the more abstract practices of Internet use by allowing us to identify a loose theoretical framework through which relationality can be better understood. The term framework is itself used loosely, of course. Lefebvre's conceived, perceived and lived spaces are subjective and therefore open to interpretation. They do, however, highlight the relationships between the real, imagined and potential constraints on political activists, at the levels of both structure and agency.

The three areas of spatial theorizing outlined here do not operate in isolation from each other. They are relational too. The introduction of the Internet to activist practices will have an impact on their material existence – on their spatial practices. In affecting material conditions, the Internet may in turn influence the discursive structures – representations of space – within which political actors operate, and so on. This cannot be characterized as a causal relationship but must be seen as a series of shifting and mutable ones. Despite this, spatial theories provide some access to answers to the most tricky 'what if?', 'how do?' and 'what impact?' questions that the use of the Internet in the international arena throws up.

The ultimate concern of research of this kind, which aims to develop new forms of theorizing, must lie in analysis of the efficacy of the theoretical framework adopted. The utility of this form of spatial methodology for research into use of the Internet in particular, and in analysis of political practice in general, is assessed in the concluding chapter. Any interpretative model has both strengths and weaknesses, and defining criteria for analysis, however flexible, inevitably leads to occlusions. The validity of the method of analysis based on the spatial theories outlined in Chapter 1 and applied in this chapter is examined next and possible ways to improve upon it are considered.

Conclusion

Introduction

What is new with the Internet is that the newly-mobilizing public are able to counter the hegemonic discourse of governments and the mass media by turning to the websites of specialist protest organizations. As Shell's Internet manager has noted, the balance of power has shifted and activists are no longer entirely dependent on the existing media (Klein 2000: 394). It is true that 'the Internet is facilitating a grassroots communications revolution in the international sphere where more and more individuals and groups ... are communicating, campaigning and community-building' (Youngs 2002: 79). It is also true that individuals as political actors have been badly under-represented in analysis of international politics, and that the current surge of interest in Internet use by activists is helping to redress the balance on this issue. Research challenging structure-level conceptualizations of politics is valuable in promoting alternative interpretations of 'the international'. In this light, it becomes possible to argue that the at least partial existence of a global civil society is contributing to the development of a global public sphere, where interactions between states and non-state actors find expression (Devetak and Higgott 1999: 491).

This chapter has two, related aims. First, a brief interpretation of the application of spatial theories undertaken in Chapter 7 is made, outlining how activist use of the Internet may be influencing political practices. The chapter focuses initially on whether there is any evidence from this research that new forms of political engagement are emerging through activist use of the Internet. One of the primary concerns when identifying any new approach to theorizing must be to assess the benefits and drawbacks thereof so, following this discussion, the chapter examines the effectiveness of the spatial theories that have been applied here.

To examine the indications of new forms of political engagement that may emerge from this research, we need to revisit the assumptions about agency upon which the research has been based. Although this research has extended across disciplinary boundaries, the central focus of critique lies in the ontologies of IR. In particular, the discipline's assumptions of state-centred political processes are subject to scrutiny. Political activists are marginalized in the discourse of mainstream IR, as the attributes of these actors are framed within the dominant discourse by reference to their relations with states, rather than in direct relation to their own interpretations of political practice.

This research challenges these assumptions and suggests that political activists engage in forms of activity that, although they are not legitimized by the discourse of IR, are having a perceptible impact on the international political system. To this extent, the forms of political engagement outlined here relate more specifically to the impact of the use of the Internet on activists, than to their influence upon state practices. The focus of the following analysis is therefore upon the potential impact of Internet use upon activists and not on other actors. Any changes to activist practices, however, are likely to have an impact on other political actors.

The Internet, activists and political change

Activism that does not take the state as a defining site of political engagement – a phenomenon discussed in detail in earlier chapters – is difficult to situate within the context of the discourse of the international adopted in IR. There is, moreover, no clear consensus among scholars in IR on the structure of the contemporary international system; contradictory perspectives on globalization, neo-liberal institutionalism, North–South relations and so on, suggest that system-level analysis can produce only a partial impression of political change. This is not to suggest that there *should* be a consensus among IR scholars. The point is, rather, that there are now a number of interpretations of the field of politics which dominate the discourse of IR but that these generally adopt system-level interpretations. Although some aspects of activist practices can be qualitatively assessed, and their influence on policy-making processes loosely determined, many other dimensions of their operations, including their impact on access to political processes for individuals and for non-state collectives through the use of the Internet, cannot be analysed with any real effectiveness from system-level. The Internet as a communications medium is inherently non-state, in that it is not confined within geographical state borders and much of its content and flow is controlled by customary law, rather than through formal legal frameworks (Kitchin 1998: 103). The social conditions and technological advances which have fuelled the spread of the Internet, such as the introduction of relatively inexpensive modems, standardized protocols, widespread use of computers in the home and workplace, and so on, also render state borders of diminished consequence in terms of control over output and infrastructures.

With current analytical frameworks within IR, the uses and impacts of the Internet cannot be analysed as multi-dimensional or relational phenomena because interpretations of the *international* are dominated by a focus on trans-state politics and the role of trans-national institutions. Access to the Internet *is* located, in that users are real and not virtual. The pre-configured spatial units of IR cannot, however, adequately reflect the multi-dimensionality of this form of location, such as the social and economic contexts of use. In these respects, use of spatial theories that permit analysis of international affairs from multiple levels can provide a more effective mechanism for analysing complex phenomena than the prevalent top-down interpretative methods.

To this extent, this research illustrates four changes to the nature of political practice in the international system effected, at least in part, through activist use of the Internet. First, the spatial determinants of political community appear to be altering as activists extend their reach across territorial boundaries. As activist networks provide organizational frameworks for other individuals – activists or otherwise – to do the same, political interactions become characterized by multi-dimensional links when this form of communication is used. In this sense, the hierarchical distinctions made between actors in the discourse of IR underplay the impact of non-state actors in the field of political interactions. This is not to suggest that non-state actors are either more or less important than states. The suggestion is, rather, that activist use of the Internet is facilitating links between a wide range of actors into the political arena and that the impact of these links needs to be explored.

Second, the use of the Internet by activists poses a challenge to concepts of boundaries in the political arena, chiefly through their espousal of normative agendas. Where interpretations of political activity in IR have assumed the primacy of territory, and have consequently elevated states to the role of principal actor, the influence of NGOs and other activists in the international arena, and upon the policies of states, is now widely acknowledged. The use of the Internet by movement activists poses a challenge to the significance of territory as a repository of political meaning by facilitating the exchange of normative agendas across and beyond territorial confines. As a result, transnational activism on the Internet may extend the concept of political identification beyond the state, continuing trends apparent in recent decades through the spread of issue-based politics in which these organizations have played a key role.

A third change to political practices with the Internet is seen in the way it provides activists with a medium through which they can provide and develop an informational resource. For individuals, this may provide an opportunity to access information less readily available from other sources. Probably more significantly in terms of changing political practices, however, this provision may limit the opportunities for any category of actor to hegemonically influence the discourse of political legitimacy through this evolving form of communication.

Finally, the use of the Internet by activists suggests that a public sphere that operates outside of the confines of states, in both spatial and discursive terms, could be developing. The platform for public debate that the Internet is being used to provide situates states as one of many categories of actor, rather than as the principal and definitional focus of political legitimacy. Although some scholars have argued that the commercialization of the Internet is detrimental to its potential as a public network (see Herman and McChesney 1997: 135), the capacity for information provision and exchange which this technology provides indicates that the potential for any group of actors to dictate the development of this form of communication is limited.

Access to political processes for individuals is undoubtedly influenced by activist use of the Internet. In some aspects, this influence can be experienced as an extension of existing opportunities. For example, while the ability to access information on direct actions or NGO campaigns is not new, the amount of specialist data available through the Internet is. Other aspects of activist use of the Internet apparently offer new dimensions of political engagement. Synchronous (or near-synchronous) communication with large groups of people who share similar concerns, for example, is a feature no other technology offers. The role of social movement actors in these evolving political practices is to provide the structures that can facilitate these forms of political interaction.

Validity of spatial theories

All methodological decisions have ramifications for research findings. Arguing that the discourse of IR restricts the potential to analyse political change on the lives of non-state actors, this research is based on the application of spatial theories which aim to provide an alternative approach to the analysis of international affairs. As the first such attempt to adopt spatial theories as a methodological foundation for a specific research project, the research highlights a number of issues pertinent to the development of research of this kind. This section will first outline the disadvantages of approaching research in this manner that have been identified during the course of this analysis. There are strengths to this form of theorizing too, though, and these will also be addressed.

The application of spatial theories to a specific project encounters the problems inherent in categorization of any complex research issue. Categorization inevitably incurs occlusions. The separation of categories is particularly problematic in relation to the complex issues relating to the use of communications technologies by political actors. The spatial categories applied here offer a framework for exploring changing political practices but may not allow the opportunity to illustrate the inter-relation of actors and activities effectively.

The epistemological limitations of academic analysis of ICTs generally, and the Internet in particular, are highlighted by this research. Attempts to transcend the norms of academic discourse by seeking to avoid oppositional categories and adopt a fluid and relational approach ironically fall victim to the very norms they challenge. That is, existing norms of academic analysis require a linear logic of coherence to which neither the Internet nor spatial theories conform. Categories of analysis are inevitably and unavoidably *not* inter-relational, and the Internet and spatial theories *are*. Thus to separate spatial practices, representations of space and spaces of representation under separate headings automatically serves to disrupt the sense of the interplay between these aspects both of spatial theorizing and the use of this technology.

Despite the limitations identified above, there are some clear strengths to the use of spatial theories in analysis of political practice. Analysis of the application of spatial theories identifies seven ways in which they may contribute to the development of new forms of political analysis that can be related to contemporary practices. The listing of seven different issues is perhaps not the most elegant approach to identification of key concerns but, given the multi-layering of spatial analysis, it provides the most coherent framework possible. First, and most significantly, the use of spatial theories permits analysis of activists as political entities. It is possible to assess continuity and change in the material environment, in the dominant discourse and in opportunities for dissent by applying spatial theories. This constitutes a critical development in the nature of theorizing on international politics, as discursive constraints have previously served to preclude effective analysis of the impact of non-elite individuals on political processes.

Second, and related to the potential to analyse the impact and actions of individuals, spatial theories overcome some of the gendered limitations of mainstream theorizing in IR. As noted in Chapter 1, the oppositional categories that characterize the dominant approaches to analysis in the discipline are frequently based upon assumptions of inclusion and exclusion that validate one subject position and negate another. The use of spatial theories permits interpretation that acknowledges rather than seeks to diminish relationality.

Third, spatial theories can provide an important tool for measuring political change contemporaneously, contrary to the norm in IR. Spatial theories provide a potential to analyse *current* conditions rather than to examine change retrospectively. The spatial theories used here have also allowed analysis of how activists are using the Internet *now*, rather than to attempt to predict how this form of communication *will* affect the political arena. This is particularly significant for IR as its self-defined remit necessitates expertise in international interactions. The pace of technological change in recent years requires analytical tools that can be applied to contemporary conditions and practices if effective interpretation of international affairs is to be achieved within the discipline.

Fourth, the spatial theories used allow analysis of the interface between the two dominant aspects of activism in the international arena: ideological intent and material influence. The linkages between spatial practices, representations of space and spaces of representation illustrate the connections and discontinuities between the organizations' objectives and their actions. This is achieved by highlighting how changes to the material environment may affect the discourse of politics and, in turn, how such changes may provide new opportunities for political activism.

Fifth, the types of spatial theory used can be applied to any actor or group of actors in the political arena. The main benefit of this aspect of spatial theorizing is that actors need not be analysed by reference to others, but through direct examination of their own actions and activities. A recurring theme has been the problem of analysing the activities of non-state actors within the discourse of IR, since an implicit hierarchy situates states as the definitional focus of international politics. Although the activities of actors such as the activists studied may have an impact on states and state practices, this is not always their primary or sole aim. Spatial theories provide an analytical framework that does not necessarily situate the state as the focus of non-state activity.

Sixth, spatial theories of the kind applied here provide a mechanism for transcending the territorial norms that have proved restrictive in developing the discipline of IR. As discussions in Chapter 1 noted, although the territorial state remains a valid and significant agent in international politics, the complex, multi-dimensional interactions that now characterize global politics are difficult to analyse within a state-centric discourse. Consequently, the need to develop analytical tools that provide a mechanism for acknowledging and interpreting a broad range of actors and practices is evident. Spatial theories provide one such tool.

Finally, spatial theories of the kind applied here are not dependent upon or restricted by a specific disciplinary framework. Although the research outlined has focused upon a critique of some of the limitations of IR as a field of study, it is possible to apply spatial theories across disciplinary boundaries because analysis operates at the level of agency rather than of structure. Consequently, the framework for analysis is not determined by disciplinary givens but through interpretation of action. This renders spatial theories particularly significant for analysis of the impact of the Internet which, as noted earlier in this chapter, transcends many of the disciplinary divisions which prevail in academic analysis.

Thus, despite their current limitations, spatial theories can be seen to offer an important analytical tool of relevance to contemporary IR. Many of the ontological and epistemological concerns that have been raised in the discipline in recent years are at least partially addressed by the application of this approach to analysis of international affairs.

This, to the best of my knowledge, represents the first work in IR to link specific spatial theories to specific practices in international politics. Although other scholars have produced important critiques of the ways politics are spatialized in IR, none has yet developed specific conceptual categories that may be applied to specific political practices. Some important benefits to this mode of theorizing have been identified, not least the potential for agency-level analysis. As the first piece of research of this kind, however, it is subject to some of the pitfalls associated with the development of new forms of analysis. Much more work is required to develop spatial theories that are readily applicable to analysis of political practices in the international and other arenas.

Conclusion

This concluding conclusion, as it were, briefly summarizes the core concerns of this book and identifies related areas that warrant further investigation. Analysis has centred on three key issues: spatial theories, the impact of ICTs on political processes, and their use by NGOs and other political collectives as actors in the international arena. Of these areas, the development of spatial theories has been the key concern of the book, since the central aim of this research has been to provide an analytical tool that transcends the limitations of the public/private, state-centric interpretations of space that dominate the discourse of IR.

Theses on the impact of the Internet are constantly evolving, as both the capacities of these technologies and the range of actors making use of them increase. The roles, functions and relevance of new communications technologies in international politics are now widely acknowledged but little clear evidence on their impact has been produced. The book has, therefore, addressed what could be termed the moving target of the Internet in the international arena by seeking to develop spatial theories to provide a more flexible analytical tool than the extant discourse of the discipline permits.

The increase in the range and scope of movement activism in recent decades suggests that impressions of politics which do not centre on states are now commonplace. There is a need to reiterate that states remain important players, since they retain a significant degree of power, resources and legitimacy in the international arena. Non-state politics co-exist with state politics, however, and can have crucial relevance for many marginalized groups, and for individuals and collectives in circumstances not prioritized on state agendas. In this respect, the impact of social and political change, such as the introduction of new technologies, can be assessed through the use of spatial theories. People existing at the margins of a state-centric discourse, including many women and the groups with whom many activists interact, are frequently overlooked by structure-level analysis. Spatial theories can provide an opportunity to explore their activities, and the impact of the actions of other actors upon them.

Perhaps the most important contribution of the book has been to highlight an under-explored aspect of social theorizing, since very little work on spatial *methodologies* has been undertaken by scholars in the social sciences to date. Although there has been much discussion of the nature of space, and the power relations embedded in its organization and categorization, there has been little research into the development of methodological approaches which permit closer examination of the constraints spatial categories impose. The book has attempted, therefore, to develop a form of theorizing that extends the parameters of the discipline to incorporate complex interactions and a range of actors more readily. The spatial categories applied in the book could, even at this early stage of development, be used to address any form of political practice. In particular, they would be a valuable tool for shedding light on the activities of non-state actors as political participants in their own right. The spatial theories used are slightly over-simplified, and tend to compartmentalize actors and their behaviours. An important strength of these theories, however, is their value in analysing complex phenomena and, though their application in the book does present a mechanism for analysing political practices at the level of individual agency, the need to identify spatial methodologies that can illustrate intersecting relations effectively is evident.

As a first attempt to *apply* spatial theories to specific practices in the international arena, the book has largely achieved its objectives, by producing an analytical tool that can be applied to complex phenomena in IR. In developing spatial theories, it also highlights the limitations of the extant discourse and identifies ways in which spatial theories can be adapted to provide agency-level analysis. An attempt has been made here to move beyond abstract spatial theorizing, and towards some form of assessment of the real effects of the organization of space. Although they can be applied to most situations in the international arena, spatial theories, by providing a potential to assess political change contemporaneously, are particularly apposite to analysis of new communications technologies. Political analysts have struggled in recent years to incorporate rapid technological development into their epistemologies; the spatial method used here represents an attempt to develop theoretical approaches that respond to such changes.

Notes

Introduction

1 It should be noted that this book is not about 'virtual geographies' (see Crang *et al.* 1999), that is the relationship between the 'real' and the virtual (cyber) worlds. It sweeps both more broadly and more narrowly than that. On the one hand, it is about socially-constructed spatial relations – between actors, institutions, structure and technologies – in general. On the other, its focus is on the opportunities afforded by the Internet for non-state actors to engage in political activity – that is, on specific aspects of spatial change.
2 They usually *are* loose collectives rather than formal organizations.
3 Chapters 1 and 2 will make the relevance of these headings more apparent.

1 Space in international relations

1 Analysis in this book focuses upon the *conceptual* terrain of IR and not upon national boundaries. It is recognized, of course, that national borders are important for all sorts of reasons. Their mythical position as encapsulators of power is a source of scholarly concern for many spatial theorists, however (see Agnew and Corbridge 1995; Agnew 1998).
2 The spatial theories applied here also represent a form of discursive closure, of course, but they are designed to provide a flexibility which is currently lacking in the frameworks available for analysis of complex political interactions.
3 See Chapter 2 for further detail on feminist approaches to space and politics.
4 Note that I have identified these categories as a framework for analysis. Lefebvre used these headings simply as alternative ways of viewing space but did not apply them as a method of analysis.

2 Feminists and space

1 This point refers back to the work of bell hooks mentioned in the previous chapter, with feminist scholars clearly occupying both the margins and the mainstream of IR simultaneously.
2 This point relates to both gender politics and to the discursive delegitimization of other, non-state, 'unofficial' political practices.
3 See Mouffe (1992: Chapter 5) and Bryson (1992) on the approaches of different feminist schools of thought regarding political processes.
4 Peterson and Runyan use a rather startling table to demonstrate gender inequalities in the political arena showing, among other things, that women make up less than one per cent of heads of state but more than 60 per cent of illiterates and people living in poverty (1999: 6)

4 Activism and the Internet

1 In a study of women and social movements, Rowbotham challenged the impression of 'newness', pointing out that 'certain of these forms of social protest are not absolutely new, they simply lack recorded histories' (1992: 294).
2 McAdam *et al.* distinguish the following as 'constituted collective political actors': agents of government, polity members (who have routine access to governments), challengers (who do not have such access), subjects (people and groups not organized into constituted political actors) and outside political actors (including other governments) (2001: 12).
3 In looking at the use of the Internet by social movements, we may find that the pace of change has quickened. This point will be picked up in the concluding chapters.
4 There are exceptions to this general principle, with some NGOs reflecting the political and economic status quo: 'Sometimes, powerful and well-to-do persons and groups in various countries form transnational organizations to formulate policies that they believe will benefit their interests and values' (Kriesberg 1997: 12)
5 As social organizations, NGOs are not gender-neutral. However, many NGOs, including some of those surveyed, place gender-awareness high on their agendas, arguing that women's human rights must be taken into account at both grassroots and policy-making levels.

5 Activism case studies: structural challenges

1 The interviewees are all web developers who consider themselves to be committed activists within their respective organizations.
2 To protect the privacy of the interviewees, their names and contact details have not been given, though they may be made available on request, with their permission.
3 Interview 2, 13th August 2002.
4 Carey, in common with Starr (2000), suggests that 'anti-corporatisation' would be a more appropriate term (ibid.) Indeed, it could be argued that the 'anti-globalization' label is another example of the way the mass media casts activists in a negative light.
5 Interview 1, 7th March 2002.

6 Activism case studies: issue-specific protest

1 Genetically modified foods are various referred to as GM foods, GMOs ('genetically modified organisms') and, occasionally in the US, LMOs (living modified organisms). GM foods is the term most commonly used and thus applied here.
2 See, for example, Organics Direct, a UK based company which promotes and lobbies supermarkets to sell non-GM foods – www.organicsdirect.co.uk
3 See, for example, the artactivist and purefood sites which publicize direct actions against biotech companies and provide information on crop test sites, forthcoming actions and so on – www.artactivist.com and www.purefood.org
4 See www.genetix.org
5 Greenpeace records details of the actions of governments, MNCs and protesters on GM issues in various countries on its website. See www.greenpeace.org/ ~geneng
6 Interview, Dr David Webb, Yorkshire CND, 9th February 2001.
7 Ibid.

7 Spatializing activism

1 The role of major economic actors in the policy-making field is important. The degree of resistance to this dominant-actor model, both in research and practice, should be noted, however. See, for example, Smith and Kollock (1999), Slevin (2000) and Walch (1999).
2 The effects of geographical concentrations of both NGO activity and of ICT networks warrant further investigation.
3 The ways NGO activity have extended the discursive boundaries of politics have been widely discussed. The most obvious impact has been in the field of environmental politics but other areas, such as gender, development and animal rights causes, have all benefited from the consciousness- raising of activists.

References

Abbate, Janet (1999), *Inventing the Internet*, Cambridge MA, MIT Press.

Adam, Alison and Eileen Green (1998), 'Gender, Agency, Location and the New Information Society', in Brian D. Loader (ed.), *Cyberspace Divide: Equality, Agency and Policy in the Information Society*, London/New York, Routledge, 83–97.

Agnew, John A. (1994), 'Timeless Space and State-Centrism: The Geographical Assumptions of International Relations Theory', in Stephen J. Rosow *et al.* (eds), *The Global Economy as Political Space*, Boulder CO, Lynne Rienner, 87–106.

Agnew, John (1998), *Geopolitics – Revisioning World Politics*, London/New York, Routledge.

Agnew, John (1999), 'Mapping Political Power Beyond State Boundaries: Territory, Identity, and Movement in World Politics', *Millennium: Journal of International Studies*, vol. 28, no. 3, 499–521.

Agnew, John and Stuart Corbridge (1995), *Mastering Space: Hegemony, Territory and International Political Economy*, London, Routledge.

AgrEvo (2002), www.agroevo.com/biotech (accessed 08/01/02).

Alcoff, Linda and Elizabeth Potter (1993), *Feminist Epistemologies*, New York/ London, Routledge.

Allan, Peter (1999), *News Culture*, Buckingham, Philadelphia, OU Press.

Alternatives, vol. 18, no. 4, *Special Issue – Feminists Write International Relations*, winter 1993.

Ang, Ien (1991), *Desperately Seeking the Audience*, London, Routledge.

Ang, Ien (1996), *Living Room Wars – Rethinking Media Audiences for a Postmodern World*, London/New York, Routledge.

Atton, Chris (2002), *Alternative Media*, London/Thousand Oaks/New Delhi, Sage.

Axford, Barry and Richard Huggins (eds) (2001), *New Media and Politics*, London/ Thousand Oaks/New Delhi, Sage.

Ayish, Muhammed I. (1992), 'International Communication in the 1990s: Implications for the Third World', *International Affairs*, vol. 68, no. 3, 487–510.

Bailie, Mashoed and Dwayne Winseck (eds) (1997), *Democratizing Communication – Comparative Perspectives on Information and Power*, Cresskill NJ, Hampton Press Inc.

Baker, Gideon (1999), 'The Taming of the Idea of Civil Society', *Democratization*, vol. 6, no. 3, autumn, 1–29.

Ballistic Missile Defence Organization (2000), http://www.acq.osd.mil/bmdo (accessed 11/03/03).

Banks, Karen (2000), 'The APC WNSP – Pioneering Women's Electronic Networking', in K. Banks, S. Burch, I. Leon, S. Boezak and L. Probert, *Networking for Change*, Philippines, APC WNSP Women in Sync/Toolkit for Electronic Networking, 1–29.

Banks, Karen *et al.* (2000), *Networking for Change – The APC WNSP's First 8 Years*, Philippines, APC WNSP Women in Sync/Toolkit for Electronic Networking.

Barnett, Steven (1997), 'New Media, Old Problems – New Technology and the Political Process', *European Journal of Communication*, vol. 12, no. 2, 193–218.

Bennett, W. Lance and Robert Entman (eds) (2001), *Mediated Politics – Communication in the Future of Democracy*, Cambridge/New York, Cambridge University Press.

Bennett, W. Lance and Robert Entman (eds) (2001), 'Mediated Politics: An Introduction', in W. Lance Bennett and Robert Entman (eds) *Mediated Politics – Communication in the Future of Democracy*, Cambridge/New York, Cambridge University Press, 1–29.

Besette, Guy (1997), 'Empowering People Through Information and Communication Technology: Lessons From Experience?', *The Journal of Development Communication*, vol. 8, no. 1, June 1997, 1–26.

Biersteker, Thomas and Cynthia Weber (eds) (1996), *State Sovereignty as Social Construct*, Cambridge, Cambridge University Press.

Boese, Wade (2002), 'December Missile Defense Test Yields One Success, One Failure', *Arms Control Association*, Jan/Feb 2002, http://www.armscontrol.org/act/2002_01-02/misdeftestjanfeb02.asp (accessed 10/10/02).

Booth, Ken and Steve Smith (eds) (1995), *International Relations Theory Today*, Cambridge, Polity.

Boyd-Barrett, Oliver and Terhi Rantanen (1998), *The Globalization of News*, London/Thousand Oaks/New Delhi, Sage.

Brah, Avtar, Mary J. Hickman and Mairtin Mac an Ghaill (eds) (1999), *Global Futures – Migration, Environment and Globalization*, Basingstoke, Macmillan.

Branford, Sue (2002), 'Brazil's Battle over GM Crops', *The Ecologist*, http://www.theecologist.org/archive_article.html?article=303&category=58 (accessed 01/12/02).

Bromley, Hank (1995), 'Gender Dynamics Online: What's New About the New Communication Technologies?', *Feminist Collections*, University of Wisconsin, vol. 16, no. 2, winter.

Brooks, James and Iain A. Boal (eds) (1995), *Resisting the Virtual Life: The Culture and Politics of Information*, San Francisco, City Lights.

Brown, Robin (1997), 'Think Local, Act Global: Political Strategy and Transnational Conflict'. Paper presented to 'Non-State Actors and Authority in the Global System Conference', University of Warwick, 31 October – 1 November 1997.

Brown, Robin (1998), 'All Change or No Change? Evaluating the Impact of New Communications Technologies on World Politics'. Paper presented to International Studies Association Annual Convention, Minneapolis, 17–21 March 1998.

Brown, Robin and Michael Svennvig (1999), 'Waiting for the Great Leap Forward? New Information and Communications Technologies and Democratic Participation'. Paper presented at the Political Studies Association Conference, University of Nottingham, 1999.

Brunn, Stanley D. and Thomas R. Leinbach (1991), *Collapsing Space and Time – Geographic Aspects of Communication and Information*, London, Harper Collins.

Bryson, Valerie (1992), *Feminist Political Thought – An Introduction*, Basingstoke, Macmillan.

Butler, Judith and Joan W. Scott (1992), *Feminists Theorise the Political*, London/ New York, Routledge.

Camilleri, Joseph A. and Jim Falk (1992), *The End of Sovereignty? – The Politics of a Shrinking and Fragmented World*, Aldershot, Edward Elgar Publishing Ltd.

Campbell, Rebecca (1995), 'Weaving a New Tapestry of Research – A Bibliography of Selected Readings on Feminist Research Methods', *Women's Studies International Forum*, vol. 18, no. 2, March–April, 215–222.

Carey, Jim (2001), 'The Story of Squall', http://www.squall.co.uk/papes.html (accessed 11/03/03).

Carnegie Endowment for International Peace (2000), 'Contending Views: Coming to Terms with Civil Society', http://www.ceip.org/files/news/csevent.asp (accessed 11/03/03).

Carothers, Thomas (1999), 'Civil Society: Think Again', *Foreign Policy* 117, winter 1999–2000, 18–29.

Carruthers, Susan L. (2001), *The Media at War*, Basingstoke/London, Macmillan.

Carvell, Terrell, Molly Cochran and Judith Squires (1998), 'Gendering Jones: Feminisms, IRs, Masculinities', *Review of International Studies*, vol. 24, no. 2, 283–297.

Castells, Manuel (1996), *The Rise of Network Society*, Oxford/Cambridge MA, Blackwell.

Castells, Manuel (1997), *The Power of Identity*, Oxford/Cambridge MA, Blackwell.

Charlton, Roger, Roy May and Tony Cleobury (1995), 'NGOs in the Politics of Development: Projects as Policy', *Contemporary Politics*, vol. 1, no. 1, spring 1995, 19–42.

Chemical Market Reporter (2000), 'Biotech Welcomes Dismissal of GM Case', New York, October 2000.

Cherny, Lynn and Elizabeth Reba Weise (eds) (1996), *Wired Women – Gender and New Realities in Cyberspace*, Seattle, Seal Press.

Citizens Opposed to Defense Experimentation (Alaska CODE) (2002), 'Stop the Deployment of National Missile Defense in Alaska', http://www.alaskacode.org/ index.php?section=about (accessed 06/09/02).

Civil Liberties Committee of the European Parliament (2000), 'Assessing the Technologies of Political Control', http://mprofaca.cronet.com/atpc2.html (accessed 01/11/01).

Clarke, Paul Barry (1996), *Deep Citizenship*, London/Chicago, Pluto Press.

Claval, Paul (1995), 'The Impact of Modern Communications Systems Worldwide', *International Political Science Review*, vol. 16, no. 3, 305–308.

CNN (2001a), 'G8 summit braces for more violence', http://www.cnn.com/2001/ WORLD/europe/07/21/genoa.violence.0548/index.html0 (accessed 20/02/02).

CNN (2001b), 'Protesters, problems and positions at the G8 summit', http://www.cnn.com/2001/WORLD/europe/07/21/king.scene.otsc/index.html (accessed 20/02/02).

Cockburn, Cynthia (1994), 'The circuit of technology: gender, identity and power', in Roger Silverstone and Eric Hirsch (eds), *Consuming Technologies – Media and Information in Domestic Spaces*, London/New York, Routledge, 32–47.

Cockburn, Cynthia and Susan Ormrod (1993), *Gender and Technology in the Making*, London/Thousand Oaks/New Delhi, Sage.

Collin, Matthew (2001), *This is Serbia Calling – Rock'n'Roll Radio and Belgrade's Underground Resistance*, London, Serpent's Tail.

Comor, Edward A. (1996), *The Global Political Economy of Communication*, Basingstoke/London, Macmillan.

Connell, R. W. (1996), *Masculinities*, Cambridge, Polity Press.

Coole, Diana H. (1988), *Women in Political Theory – From Ancient Misogyny to Contemporary Feminism*, Brighton, Wheatsheaf Books Ltd.

Corbridge, Stuart, Ron Martin and Nigel Thrift (eds) (1994), *Money, Power and Space*, Oxford/Cambridge MA, Blackwell.

Corporate Watch (1999), 'AgrEvo on (Farm-Scale) Trial', *Corporate Watch Magazine*, 9, autumn 1999, http://www.corporatewatch.org.uk/magazine/issue9/cw9gm1.html (accessed 12/01/00).

Cox, Robert W. (ed.) (1997), *The New Realism*, Basingstoke/New York, Macmillan Press/St Martin's Press.

Crang, Mike, Phil Crang and John May (1999), *Virtual Geographers – Bodies, Space 7 Relations*, London/New York, Routledge.

Crowley, David and David Mitchell (eds) (1994), *Communication Theory Today*, Cambridge, Polity Press.

Curran, James (ed.) (2000), *Media Organisations in Society*, London/New York, Oxford University Press.

Dahlgren, Peter (2001a),'The Transformation of Democracy?', in Barry Axford and Richard Huggins (eds), *New Media and Politics*, London/Thousand Oaks/New Delhi, Sage, 64–88.

Dahlgren, Peter (2001b), 'The Public Sphere and the Net: Structure, Space, and Communication', in W. Lance Bennett and Robert Entman (eds) *Mediated Politics – Communication in the Future of Democracy*, Cambridge/New York, Cambridge University Press, 33–55.

Damarin, Suzanne K. (1993), 'Where is Women's Knowledge in the Age of Information?', in Cheris Kramarae and Dale Spender (eds), *The Knowledge Explosion – Generations of Feminist Scholarship*, New York/London, Harvester Wheatsheaf, 362–370.

Darby, Philip (ed.) (1997), *At the Edge of International Relations – Postcolonialism, Gender and Dependency*, London/New York, Continuum, 197–213.

December, John (1996), 'Units of Analysis for Internet Communication', *Journal of Communication*, vol. 46, no. 1, winter 1996, 14–38.

Deibert, Ronald (1996), 'Typographica: the medium and the medieval-to-modern transformation', *Review of International Studies*, vol. 22, no. 1, January 1996, 29–56.

Deibert, Ronald (2001), 'Shift → Public Sphere – Towards a Field Guide to Planetary Network Studies'. Paper presented to International Studies Association Convention, Chicago, February 2002.

de la Perriere, R. A. B. and Frank Seuret (2000), *Brave New Seeds: The Threat of GM Crops to Farmers*, London, Zed.

Della Porta, Donatella and Mario Diani (1999), *Social Movements – An Introduction*, Oxford/Malden, Blackwell.

Devetak, Richard and Richard Higgott (1999), 'Justice Unbound? Globalization, States and the Transformation of the Social Bond', *International Affairs*, vol. 75, no. 3, 483–498.

Doty, Roxanne Lynn (1996), 'Sovereignty and the Nation – Constructing the Boundaries of National Identity', in Thomas Beirstecker and Cynthia Weber (eds), *State Sovereignty as Social Construct* Cambridge, Cambridge UP, 121–147.

Drainville, Andre C. (1995), 'Of Social Spaces, Citizenship, and the Nature of Power in the World Economy', *Alternatives*, vol. 20, no. 1, January–March, 51–77.

Dutton, William H. (ed.) (1996), *Information and Communication Technologies – Visions and Realities*, Oxford, Oxford University Press.

Dutton, William H. *et al.* (1996), 'The Politics of Information and Communication Policy: The Information Superhighway', in William H. Dutton, (ed.), *Information and Communication Technologies – Visions and Realities*, Oxford, Oxford University Press, 387–405.

Dyson, Kenneth and Peter Humphreys (eds) (1986), *The Politics of the Communications Revolution in Western Europe*, London, Frank Cass.

Dyson, Kenneth and Peter Humphreys (eds) (1990), *The Political Economy of Communications – International and European Dimensions*, London/New York, Routledge.

Elshtain, Jean Bethke (1987), *Women and War*, Brighton, Harvester Press.

Elshtain, Jean Bethke (1991), *Public Man, Private Woman: Women in Social and Political Theory*, Oxford, Robertson.

Elshtain, Jean Bethke (1995a), 'International Politics and Political Theory', in Ken Booth, and Steve Smith (eds), *International Relations Theory Today*, Cambridge, Polity, 263–278.

Elshtain, Jean Bethke (1995b), 'Exporting Feminism', *Journal of International Affairs*, vol. 48, no. 2, winter, 541–558.

Enloe, Cynthia H. (1988), *Does Khaki Become You?: the Militarisation of Women's Lives*, London, Pandora.

Enloe, Cynthia H. (1989), *Bananas, Beaches and Bases: Making Feminist Sense of International Politics*, London, Pandora.

Enloe, Cynthia H. (1993), *The Morning After: Sexual Politics at the End of the Cold War*, Berkeley, University of California Press.

Enloe, Cynthia H. (2000), *Maneuvers – The International Politics of Militarizing Women's Lives*, Berkeley/Los Angeles/London, University of California Press.

Entman, Robert (1996), 'Manufacturing Discord: Media in the Affirmative Action Debate', *Harvard International Journal of Press/Politics*, vol. 1, no. 3, 77–92.

Esser, Josef and Ronald Noppe (1996), 'Private Muddling Through as a Political Programme? The Role of the European Commission in the Telecommunications Sector in the 1980s', *Western European Politics*, vol. 19, no. 3, July, 547–562.

Farrands, Chris (1996), 'The Globalization of Knowledge and the Politics of Global Intellectual Property: Power, Governance and Technology', in Eleonore Kofman and Gillian Youngs (eds), *Globalization – Theory and Practice*, London/New York, Pinter, 175–187.

Featherstone, Mike and Scott Lash (eds) (1999), *Spaces of Culture*, London/ Thousand Oaks/New Delhi, Sage.

Featherstone, Mike, Scott Lash and Roland Robertson (eds) (1995), *Globalising Modernities*, London/Thousand Oaks/New Delhi, Sage.

Federation of American Scientists (2000), 'Menwith Hill Station, UK', http:// www.fas.org.frp/facility/menwith.htm (accessed 21/05/02).

Federation of American Scientists (2002), http://www.fas.org.frp (accessed 16/11/02).

Ferdinand, Peter (ed.) (2000a), *The Internet, Democracy and Democratization*, London/Portland, Frank Cass.

Ferdinand, Peter (2000b), 'Conclusion', in Peter Ferdinand (ed.), *The Internet, Democracy and Democratization*, London/Portland, Frank Cass, 174–182.

Fischer, Claude S. (1992), *America Calling – A Social History of the Telephone to 1940*, Berkley/Los Angeles/Oxford, University of California Press.

Fitz, Stacey (2002), 'Star Wars and Space Pork: The Kodiak Launch Complex', http://www.nonukesnorth.net/Starwarsspacepork.htm (accessed 15/11/02).

Flichy, Patrice (1995), *The Dynamics of Modern Communication – The Shaping and Impact of New Technologies* (Trans. Liz Libbrecht), London/Thousand Oaks/ New Delhi, Sage.

Fonow, M. and J. Cook (1991), *Beyond Methodology: Feminist Scholarship as Lived Research*, Indiana, Indiana University Press.

Fonow, M. and J. Cook (1991), 'Back to the Future – A Look at the Second Wave of Feminist Epistemology', in M. Fonow and J. Cook, *Beyond Methodology: Feminist Scholarship as Lived Research*, Indiana, Indiana University Press, 1–15.

Franklin, M. I. (1998a), 'The Political Economy of Informatics – Global-Speak and Gender-Power Relations'. Paper presented at the ISA-ECPR Conference, Vienna, 16–19 September.

Franklin, M. I. (1998b), 'This is not a Telephone: FAQ for a Critical Researcher in the Informatic Age'. Paper presented at the ISA-ECPR Conference, Vienna, 16–19 September 1998.

Frederick, Howard H. (1997), 'Mexican NGO computer Networking and Cross-Border Coalition Building', in Mashoed Bailie and Dwayne Winseck (eds), *Democratizing Communication – Comparative Perspectives on Information and Power*, Cresskill NJ, Hampton Press Inc., 255–286.

Freeman, Carla (2001). 'Is Local:Global as Feminine: Masculine? Rethinking the Gender of Globalization', *Signs: Journal of Women in Culture and Society*, vol. 6, no. 4, 1007–1037.

Friends of the Earth (2002), 'Golden Rice and Vitamin A Deficiency', www.foe.org/ safefood/rice.html (accessed 10/10/02).

Frissen, Paul (1997), 'The Virtual State: Postmodernisation, Informatisation and Public Administration', in Brian D. Loader (ed.), *The Governance of Cyberspace*, London/New York, Routledge, 111–125.

Frissen, Valerie (1995), 'Gender is Calling: Some Reflections on Past, Present and Future Uses of the Telephone', in Keith Grint and Rosalind Gill, *Gender and Technology: Contemporary Theory and Research*, London, Taylor & Francis, 79–94.

Fuchs, Gerhard and Andrew M. Koch (1996), 'The Globalization of Telecommunications and the Issue of Regulatory Reform', in Eleonore Kofman and Gillian Youngs (eds) (1996), *Globalization – Theory and Practice*, London/New York, Pinter, 163–174.

Gamson, William A. (1991), 'Commitment and Agency in Social Movements', *Sociological Forum*, vol. 6, no. 1, 27–50.

Gamson, William A. (1995), 'Constructing Social Protest', in Hank Johnston and Bert Klandermans (eds), *Social Movements and Culture*, London, UCL Press, 85–106.

Gamson, William A. (2001), 'Promoting Political Engagement', in W. Lance Bennett and Robert Entman (eds), *Mediated Politics – Communication in the Future of Democracy*, Cambridge/New York, Cambridge University Press, 56–74.

Gauntlett, David (ed.) (2000), *Web Studies – Rewiring Media Studies for the Digital Age*, London, Arnold.

Gauntlett, David and Jayne Rodgers (2002), 'Teenage Intercultural Communications Online: A Redeployment of the Internet Activist Model'. Paper presented at IAMCR Conference, Barcelona, 21–25 July 2002.

Gitlin, Todd (1980), *The Whole World is Watching*, Berkeley, University of California Press.

Gould, Peter (1991), 'Dynamic Structures of Geographic Space', in Stanley D. Brunn and Thomas R. Leinbach *Collapsing Space and Time – Geographic Aspects of Communication and Information*, Harper Collins, 3–30.

Graber, Doris A. (1996), 'The 'New' Media and Politics: What Does the Future Hold?', *PS – Political Science and Politics*, vol. XXIX, no. 1, March, 33–36.

Graham, Stephen and Simon Marvin (1996), *Telecommunications and the City – Electronic Spaces*, Urban Places, London/New York, Routledge.

Grant, Rebecca (1991), 'The sources of gender bias in international relations theory', in Rebecca Grant and Kathleen Newland (eds), *Gender and International Relations*, Milton Keynes, OU Press, 8–26.

Grant, Rebecca and Kathleen Newland (eds) (1991), *Gender and International Relations*, Milton Keynes, OU Press.

Gregory, Derek (1994), *Geographical Imaginations*, Oxford/Cambridge MA, Basil Blackwell Ltd.

Gretz, Anne Marie (1986), 'Information Capacity and Power in North–South Relations: Transborder Data Flow and the Example of Brazil', *Millennium*, vol. 15, no. 1, 48–72.

Grint, Keith and Ross Gill (eds) (1995), *The Gender-Technology Relation: Contemporary Theory and Research*, London/Bristol, Taylor & Francis Ltd.

Grint, Keith and Ross Gill (1995), 'The Gender-Technology Relation: Contemporary Theory and Research – An Introduction', in Keith Grint and Ross Gill (eds), *The Gender-Technology Relation: Contemporary Theory and Research*, London/Bristol, Taylor & Francis Ltd, 1–28.

Groom, A. J. R. and Margot Light (eds) (1994), *Contemporary International Relations: A Guide to Theory*, London/New York, Pinter.

Groom, A. J. R. and Dominic Powell (1994), 'From world politics to global governance – a theme in need of a focus', in A. J. R. Groom, and Margot Light (eds), *Contemporary International Relations: A Guide to Theory*, London/New York, Pinter, 81–90.

Grosz, Elizabeth (1995), 'Women, CHORA, Dwelling', in Sophie Watson and Catherine Gibson (eds), *Postmodern Cities and Spaces*, Oxford UK/Cambridge MA, Blackwell, 47–58.

Guzzini, Stefano (1998), *Realism in International Relations and International Political Economy – The Continuing Story of a Death Foretold*, London/New York, Routledge.

Hamelink, Cees J. (1997), 'World Communication: Business as Usual?', in Mashoed Bailie and Dwayne Winseck (eds), *Democratizing Communication – Comparative Perspectives on Information and Power*, Cresskill NJ, Hampton Press Inc., 407–425.

Haraway, Donna (1990), 'A Manifesto for Cyborgs: Science, Technology, and Socialist Feminism in the 1980s', in Linda J. Nicholson (ed.), *Feminism/Postmodernism*, New York/London, Routledge, 190–233.

Haraway, Donna (1997), Modest_Witness@Second_Millennium.FemaleMan_Meets_OncoMouse: *Feminism and Technoscience*, London/New York, Routledge.

Harcourt, Wendy (ed.) (1999), *Women@Internet – Creating New Cultures in Cyberspace*, New York/Sydney/London, Zed Books.

Harding, Sandra (1986), *The Science Question in Feminism*, Milton Keynes, Open University Press.

Harding, Sandra (ed.) (1987), *Feminism and Methodology*, Milton Keynes, Open University Press.

Harding, Sandra (1990a), 'Feminism, Science and the Anti-Enlightenment Critiques', in Linda J. Nicholson (ed.), *Feminism/Postmodernism*, New York/London, Routledge, 83–106.

Harding, Sandra (1990b), 'Feminist Theories and Scientific Knowledge', Women, no. 1, 87–98.

Harding, Sandra (1991), *Whose Science? Whose Knowledge? Thinking from Women's Lives*, Milton Keynes, Open University Press.

Harding, Sandra and Merrill Hintikka (eds) (1983), *Discovering Reality: Feminist Perspectives on Epistemology, Methodology and the Philosophy of Science*, Dordrecht, Netherlands, D Reidel.

Harvey, David (1990), *The Condition of Postmodernity*, Oxford/Cambridge MA, Blackwell.

Haywood, Trevor (1998), 'Global Networks and the Myth of Equality: Trickle Down or Trickle Away?', in Brian D. Loader (ed.), *Cyberspace Divide: Equality, Agency and Policy in the Information Society*, London/New York, Routledge, 19–34.

Hedges, Chris (1996), 'Milosevic Caught in Vibrant Web of New Technology', *Guardian*, 10/12/96, p. 7.

Herman, Edward S. and Robert McChesney (1997), *The Global Media – The New Missionaries of Corporate Capitalism*, London/Washington, Cassell.

Herring, Ronald J. (2001), 'Promethean Science, Pandora's Jug and Areal Studies: Globalization Makes Strange Bedfellows', The 2001 Mary Keating Das Lecture, Columbia University, http://216.239.51.100/search?q=cache:2H3EjZksUuMC: www.einaudi.cornell.edu/southasia/workshop/pdf/columbia2001b.pdf+promethean+%22ronald+j+herring%22&hl=en&ie=UTF-8 (accessed 01/07/02).

Herrmann, Anne C. and Abigail J. Stewart (eds) (1994), *Theorising Feminism: Parallel Trends in the Humanities and Social Sciences*, Boulder/Oxford, Westview Press.

Hettne, Bjorn (1997), 'The Double Movement: global market versus regionalism', in Robert W. Cox (ed.), *The New Realism*, Basingstoke/New York, Macmillan Press/St Martin's Press, 223–242.

Higgins, Andrew (1996), 'China Attempts to Control Internet', *Guardian* online, http://online.guardian.co.uk/ (accessed 04/02/96).

Hills, Jill (1994), 'Dependency theory and its relevance today: international institutions in telecommunications and structural power', *Review of International Studies*, no. 20, 169–186.

Hirst, Paul and Sunil Khilnani (1996), *Reinventing Democracy*, Oxford/Cambridge MA, Blackwell Publishers Ltd.

Hirst, Paul and Grahame Thompson (1995), 'Globalization and the Future of the Nation-State', *Economy & Society*, vol. 24, no. 3, 408–442.

Hogan, Hank (1997), 'Lightning Speed', *New Scientist*, no. 2073, 15 March, 32–35.

Holderness, Mike (1998), 'Who are the World's Information-poor?', in Brian D. Loader (ed.), *Cyberspace Divide: Equality, Agency and Policy in the Information Society*, London/New York, Routledge, 35–56.

hooks, bell (1984), *Feminist Theory – from Margin to Center*, Boston MA, South End Press.

hooks, bell (1991), *Yearning – Race, Gender and Cultural Politics*, London, Turnaround.

Hopkinson, Nicholas (1995), 'The Impact of New Technology on the International Media and Foreign Policy', *Wilton Park Paper 97*, UK, HMSO.

Hourigan, Niamh (2001), 'New Social Movement Theory and Minority Language Television Campaigns', *European Journal of Communication*, 16/1, 77–100.

Hudson, Heather E. and Theda S. Pittman (2002), 'Rural Telecommunications for Development: Lessons from the Alaskan Experience', ITU, http://www.itu.int/ITU-D/fg7/case_library/documents/ptc001.html (accessed 11/03/03).

Huff, Chuck and Thomas Finholt (1994), *Social Issues in Computing – Putting Computing in its Place*, New York, McGraw-Hill Inc.

Hughes, Donna M. (1995), 'Significant Differences: the construction of knowledge, objectivity and dominance', *Women's Studies International Forum*, vol. 18, no. 4, July–August 1995, 395–406.

Hurrell, Andrew (1995), 'International Political Theory and the Global Environment', in Ken Booth and Steve Smith (eds), *International Relations Theory Today*, Cambridge, Blackwell, 129–153.

IndyMedia (2002), 'IndyMedia FAQ', http://process.indymedia.org/faq.php3 (accessed 11/03/03).

Inglehart, Richard and Pippa Norris (2003), *Rising Tide – Gender Inequalities and Cultural Change around the World*, New York, Cambridge University Press.

International Campaign to Ban Landmines (2002), http://www.icbl.org (accessed 01/11/02).

International Telecommunications Union (2002), *World Telecommunications Indicators 2001*, www.itu.int/it/publications/YB2001/index.htm (accessed 20/10/02).

James, Lucy (1998), 'Problematising Gender and Methodology in IR', University of Manchester, unpublished manuscript.

Johnston, Hank and Bert Klandermans (eds) (1995), *Social Movements and Culture*, London, UCL Press.

Jones, Adam (1996), 'Does "Gender" Make the World Go Round? Feminist Critiques of International Relations', *Review of International Studies*, vol. 22, no. 4, 405–429.

Jones, Adam (1998), 'Engendering Debate', *Review of International Studies*, vol. 24, no. 2, 299–303.

Jones, S. G. (ed.) (1995a), *Cybersociety: Computer-Mediated Communication and Community*, London, Sage.

Jones, S. G. (1995b), 'Understanding Community in an Information Age', in S. G. Jones (ed.), *Cybersociety: Computer-Mediated Communication and Community*, London, Sage, 10–35.

Kadish, Ronald (2001), 'Missile Defense Director Outlines Evolving Program – Says no to Single Architecture Designated for Missile Defense', Ballistic Missile Defense Organization (BMDO), July 12 2001, http://www.uspolicy.be/issues/nmd/kadish.071201.htm (accessed 11/03/03).

Kahin, Brian and James Keller (eds) (1995), *Public Access to the Internet*, London/Cambridge MA, MIT Press.

Katz, James E. (1997), 'The Social Side of Information Networking', *Society*, March/April 1997, 9–12.

Keck, Margaret E. and Kathryn Sikkink (1998a), *Activists Beyond Borders – Advocacy Networks in International Politics*, Ithaca/London, Cornell University Press.

Keck, Margaret E. and Kathryn Sikkink (1998b), 'Transnational Advocacy Networks in the Movement Society', in David S. Meyer and Sidney Tarrow (eds), *The Social Movement Society – Contentious Politics for a New Century*, Lanham, Maryland/Oxford, Rownan and Littlefield, 217–238.

Keeble, John (1998), 'Called to account – When charity begins at Net access', *Guardian*, 23/7/98, pp. 4–5.

Keefe, Bob (2002), 'Missile Defense Taking Shape on Alaskan Army Base', Cox Washington Bureau, 28/07/02, http://www.coxnews.com/washingtonbureau/staff/b.../0/2802alaska-starwars.html (accessed 11/03/03).

Keith, Michael and Steve Pile (eds) (1993), *Place and the Politics of Identity*, London/New York, Routledge.

Keohane, Robert (1984), *After Hegemony: Co-operation and Discord in the World Political Economy*, Princeton, Princeton University Press.

Kirkup, Gill and Laurie Smith Keller (eds) (1992), *Inventing Women – Science, Technology and Gender*, Cambridge, Polity/Open University Press.

Kitchin, Rob (1998), *Cyberspace*, Chichester, John Wiley & Sons Ltd.

Klein, Naomi (2000), *No Logo*, London, Flamingo.

Knutsen, Torbjorn L. (1992), *A History of International Relations Theory – An Introduction*, Manchester, Manchester University Press.

Kobrin, Stephen (1998), 'The MAI and the Clash of Globalization', *Foreign Policy*, Fall 1998, 97–109.

Kofman, Eleonore and Gillian Youngs (eds) (1996), *Globalization – Theory and Practice*, London/New York, Pinter.

Kramarae, Chris and Dale Spender (eds) (1993), *The Knowledge Explosion – Generations of Feminist Scholarship*, New York/London, Harvester Wheatsheaf.

Kriesberg, Louis (1997), 'Social Movements and Global Transformation', in Chatfield Smith and Ron Pagnucco (eds), *Transnational Social Movements*, 3–18.

Kruszewska, Iza (2002), 'Sustainable Production and Consumption: Genetically Modified Organisms', APNED, http://www.anped.org/index.php?a=4&b=4100 (accessed 01/09/02).

Kuumba, M. Bahati (2001), *Gender and Social Movements*, Lanham/Oxford, Rowman & Littlefield.

Laccy, Nick (2002), *Media Institutions and Audiences – Key Concepts in Media Studies*, Basingstoke/New York, Palgrave.

Lash, Scott and John Urry (1994), *Economies of Signs and Space*, London/Thousand Oaks/New Delhi, Sage.

Lebkowsky, Jon (1999), 'A Few Points About Online Activism', *Cybersociology*, Issue 5, http://www.socio.demon.co.uk/magazine/5/5jon.html (accessed 10/12/99).

Lee, Chin-Chuan *et al.* (2001), 'Through the Eyes of US Media: Banging the Democracy Drum in Hong Kong', *Journal of Communication*, June, 344–365.

Lefebvre, Henri (1991), *The Production of Space*, Oxford/Cambridge MA, Blackwell.

Lefebvre, Henri (1996), *Writings on Cities*, Oxford/Cambridge MA, Blackwell (translated and edited by Eleonore Kofman and Elizabeth Lebas).

Lekhi, Rohit (2000), 'The Politics of African America On-Line', in Peter Ferdinand (ed.), *The Internet, Democracy and Democratization*, London/Portland, Frank Cass, 76–101.

Lewis, George, Lisbeth Gronlund and David C. Wright (2001), 'Will Missile Defense Work? Only Realistic Testing Will Tell', *Inside Missile Defense*, vol. 7, no. 22, 2001, http://www.uscusa.org/global_security/missile_defense/page.cfm?pageID=561 (accessed 08/11/02).

Libicki, Martin C. (1995), 'What Is Information Warfare?', Washington DC, National Defense University, Centre for Advanced Concepts & Technology/Institute for National Strategic Studies, August.

Libicki, Martin C. (1996), 'The Emerging Primacy of Information', *ORBIS*, spring, 261–276.

Libicki, Martin C. (1997), 'Defending Cyberspace and Other Metaphors', Washington DC, National Defense University, Centre for Advanced Concepts & Technology/Institute for National Strategic Studies.

Lie, Marete (1995), 'Technology and Masculinity – The Case of the Computer', *The European Journal of Women's Studies* – Special Issue on Technology, vol. 3, no. 2, August, 379–394.

Light, Margot and Fred Halliday (1994), 'Gender and International Relations', in Groom A. J. R. and Margot Light (eds), *Contemporary International Relations: A Guide to Theory*, London, Pinter, 45–55.

Linklater Andrew (1998), *The Transformation of Political Community*, Cambridge, Polity Press.

Lipschutz, Ronnie D. (1992), 'Reconstructing World Politics: The Emergence of Global Civil Society', *Millennium*, vol. 21, no. 3, winter, 389–420.

Lipson, Michael and Jeffrey T. Gayton (1998), 'The Internet and Global Governance: Globalization, Territoriality, and Political Authority'. Paper presented to 38th International Studies Association Annual Convention, Minneapolis, 17–21 March.

Loader, Brian D. (1997a), 'The Governance of Cyberspace: Politics, Technology and Global Restructuring', in Brian D. Loader (ed.), *The Governance of Cyberspace*, London/New York, Routledge, 1–19.

Loader, Brian D. (ed.) (1997b), *The Governance of Cyberspace*, London/New York, Routledge.

Loader, Brian D. (ed.) (1998), *Cyberspace Divide: Equality, Agency and Policy in the Information Society*, London/New York, Routledge.

Luke, Timothy W. (1995), 'New World Order or Neo-World Orders: Power, Politics and Ideology in Informationalizing Glocalities', in Mike Featherstone *et al.* (eds), *Globalising Modernities*, London/Thousand Oaks/New Delhi, Sage, 91–107.

Lyon, David (1997), 'Cyberspace Sociality: Controversies over Computer-mediated Relationships', in Brian D. Loader (ed.), *The Governance of Cyberspace*, London/New York, Routledge, 23–37.

McAdam, Doug (1996), 'Conceptual Origins, Current Problems and Future Directions', in Doug McAdam *et al., Comparative Perspectives in Social Movements – Political Opportunities, Mobilizing Structures and Cultural Framings*, Cambridge, Cambridge University Press, 23–40.

McAdam, Doug, Sidney Tarrow and Charles Tilly (2001), *Dynamics of Contention*, Cambridge, Cambridge University Press.

McAdam, Doug, John D. McCarthy and Mayer N. Zald (1996), *Comparative Perspectives in Social Movements – Political Opportunities, Mobilizing Structures and Cultural Framings*, Cambridge, Cambridge University Press.

McChesney, Robert W. (1996), 'The Internet and US Communication Policy-Making in Historical and Critical Perspective', *Journal of Communication*, vol. 46 no. 1, winter, 98–124.

McChesney, Robert W. (1997a), 'Contradictions in the Democratization of International Communication', *Media, Culture & Society*, London/Thousand Oaks/New Delhi, Sage, vol. 19, 219–246.

McChesney, Robert W. (1997b), 'The Communication Revolution: The Market and the Prospect for Democracy', in Mashoed Bailie and Dwayne Winseck (eds), *Democratizing Communication – Comparative Perspectives on Information and Power*, Cresskill NJ, Hampton Press Inc., 57–78.

McDowell, Linda and Joanne P. Sharp (eds) (1997), *Space, Gender, Knowledge – Feminist Readings*, London/New York, Arnold.

McQuail, Denis (2000), *Mass Communication Theory: An Introduction (Fourth edition)*, London, Sage.

McQuail, Denis and Sven Windahl (1993), *Communications Models for the Study of Mass Communication (Second edition)*, London/New York, Longman.

Manning, Tony (1995), 'Left on the Net', *Red Pepper*, March, 33–35.

Mansell, R. (ed.), (1993), *Information, Control and Technological Change*, London, Aslib.

Marchand, Marianne H. and Anne Sisson Runyan (2000a), *Gender and Global Restructuring – Sightings, Sites and Resistances*, London/New York, Routledge.

Marchand, Marianne H. and Anne Sisson Runyan (2000b), 'Introduction. Feminist Sightings of Global Restructurings: Conceptualizations and Reconceptualizations', in Marianne H. Marchand and Anne Sisson Runyan, *Gender and Global Restructuring – Sightings, Sites and Resistances*, London/New York, Routledge, 1–22.

Margetts, Helen (1996), 'The Implications for Democracy of Computerisation in Government', in Paul Hirst and Sunil Khilnani, *Reinventing Democracy*, Oxford/Cambridge MA, Blackwell Publishers Ltd, 70–84.

Mason, John (2002), 'Gaining Ground', *Financial Times*, 27 March 2002, p. 12.

Massey, Doreen (1992), 'Politics and Space/Time', *New Left Review*, 196, November–December, 65–84.

Massey, Doreen (1994), *Space, Place and Gender*, Cambridge, Polity.

Massey, Doreen (1995), *Spatial Divisions of Labour – Social Structures and the Geography of Production (Second edition)*, Basingstoke/London, Macmillan.

Massey, Doreen (1999), 'Imagining Globalization: Power-Geometries of Time-Space', in Avtar Brah, Mary J. Hickman and Mairtin Mac an Ghaill (eds), *Global*

Futures – Migration, Environment and Globalization, Basingstoke, Macmillan, 27–44.

Massey, Doreen and Pat Jess (eds) (1995), *A Place in the World?*, Milton Keynes, Open University Press.

Mattelart, Armand and Michele Mattelart (1995/1998), *Theories of Communication – A Short Introduction*, London/Thousand Oaks/New Delhi, Sage.

May, Christopher (1998), 'Capital, Knowledge and Ownership – Preface to a Critique of the Information Society', *Information, Communication and Society*, vol. 1, no. 3, autumn.

Maynard, Mary and Jane Purvis (eds) (1994), *Researching Women's Lives from a Feminist Perspective*, London/New York, Taylor & Francis.

Melody, William (1994), 'Electronic Networks, Social Relations and the Changing Structure of Knowledge', in David Crowley and David Mitchell (eds), *Communication Theory Today*, Cambridge, Polity Press, 254–273.

Melucci, Roberto (1996), *Challenging Codes – Collective Action in the Information Age*, Cambridge, Cambridge University Press.

Meyer, David S. and Sidney Tarrow (1998) (eds), *The Social Movement Society*, Lanham MA/Oxford: Rowman & Littlefield.

Michael, Keith and Steve Pile (eds) (1993), *Place and the Politics of Identity*, London/New York, Routledge.

Miles, Ian (1996), 'The Information Society: Competing Perspectives on the Social and Economic Implications of Information and Communications Technologies', in William H. Dutton (ed.), *Information and Communication Technologies – Visions and Realities*, Oxford, Oxford University Press, 37–52.

Miller, Danny and Don Slater (2000), *The Internet: An Ethnographic Approach*, New York, New York University Press.

Miller, Laura (1995), 'Women and Children First: Gender and the Settling of the Electronic Frontier', in James Brooks and Iain A. Boal (eds), *Resisting the Virtual Life: The Culture and Politics of Information*, San Francisco, City Lights, 49–57.

Minges, Michael (2002), 'Counting the Net: Internet Access Indicators', ITU, www.isoc.org/isoc/conferences/inet/))/cdproceedings/8e/8e_1.htm (accessed 10/01/02).

Mitter, Swasti (1994), 'What Women Demand of Technology', *New Left Review*, 205, May/June, 100–110.

Mobbs, Paul (2002a), *Campaigning Online – Using the Internet to Get Your Point Across*, GreenNet Civil Society Internet Rights Project, http://www.gn.apc.org/action/csir/index.html#briefing (accessed 11/03/03).

Mobbs, Paul (2002b), *Media Regulation and Convergence – The Impact of the New Digital Media on Society*, GreenNet Civil Society Internet Rights Project, http://www.gn.apc.org/action/csir/index.html#briefing (accessed 11/03/03).

Monsanto (2002) www.monsanto.com/monsanto/layout/products/popup1.asp (accessed 31/11/02)

Moog, Sandra and Jeff Sluyter-Beltrao (2001), 'The Transformation of Political Communication?', in Barry Axford and Richard Huggins (eds), *New Media and Politics*, 30–63.

Moore, Nick (1998), 'Confucius or Capitalism? Policies for an Information Society', in Brian D. Loader (ed.), *Cyberspace Divide: Equality, Agency and Policy in the Information Society*, London/New York, Routledge, 149–160.

Morley, David and Kevin Robins (1995), *Spaces of Identity – Global Media, Electronic Landscapes and Cultural Boundaries*, London/New York, Routledge.

Morris, Merrill and Christine Ogan (1996), 'The Internet as Mass Medium', *Journal of Communication*, vol. 46, no. 1, winter, 39–50.

Mosco, Vincent (1993), 'Free Trade in Communication: Building a World Business Order', in Kaarle Nordenstreng and Herbert I. Schiller (eds), *Beyond National Sovereignty: International Communication in the 1990s*, Norwood NJ, Ablex Publishing Corporation, 193–209.

Mouffe, Chantal (ed.) (1992), *Dimensions of Radical Democracy – Pluralism, Citizenship, Community*, London, Verso, 63–85.

Mowlana, Hamid (1997), *Global Information and World Communication (Second edition)*, London/Thousand Oaks/New Delhi, Sage.

Murphy, Alexander B. (1996), 'The Sovereign State as Political-Territorial Ideal', in Thomas Biersteker and Cynthia Weber (eds), *State Sovereignty as Social Construct*, Cambridge, Cambridge University Press, 81–120.

Murphy, Craig N. (1996), 'Seeing women, recognizing gender, recasting international relations', *International Organization*, vol. 50, no. 3, summer, 513–538.

Mutz, Diana C. and Paul S. Martin (2001), 'Facilitating Communication across Lines of Political Difference: The Role of the Mass Media', *American Political Science Review*, vol. 95, no. 1, March, 97–114.

National Research Council NRenaissance Committee (1994), *Realizing the Information Future – The Internet and Beyond*, Washington DC, National Academy Press.

Nielsen Media Research (2002), 'Nielsen/NetRatings Reports a Record Half Billion People Worldwide Now Have Home Internet Access', www.eratings.com/news/2002/20020306.htm (accessed 11/03/03).

Niemann, Michael (2001), 'The Spatial Dialectics of IR Theory'. Paper presented at British International Studies Association Conference, University of Edinburgh, December.

Nordenstreng, Kaarle and Herbert I. Schiller (eds) (1993), *Beyond National Sovereignty: International Communication in the 1990s*, Norwood NJ, Ablex Publishing Corporation.

Noveck, Beth Simone (2000), 'Paradoxical Partners: Electronic Communication and Electronic Democracy', in Peter Ferdinand (ed.), *The Internet, Democracy and Democratization*, London/Portland, Oregon, Frank Cass Publishers, 18–36.

Nueman, Johanna (1996), *Lights, Camera, War – Is Media Technology Driving International Politics?*, New York, Saint Martin's Press.

Nye, David E. (1997), 'Shaping Communication Networks: Telegraph, Telephone, Computer', *Social Research*, vol. 64, no. 3, fall, 1067–1091.

Nyugen, Dan Thu and John Alexander (1996), 'The Coming of Cyberspacetime and the End of Polity', in Rob Shields (ed.), *Cultures of Internet – Virtual Spaces, Real Histories, Living Bodies*, London/Thousand Oaks/New Delhi, Sage, 99–124.

O'Sullivan, Cathie (2002), '10% of the World's Population Now Have Internet Access', Europamedia.net, www.europamedia.net/shownews.asp?ArticleID=12003, (accessed 13/08/02).

Ormrod, Susan (1995), 'Feminist Sociology and Methodology: Leaky Black Boxes in Gender/Technology Relations', in Keith Grint and Rosalind Gill (eds), *The Gender-Technology Relation: Contemporary Theory and Research*, London/Bristol, Taylor & Francis Ltd, 31–47.

Paarlberg, Robert L. (2000), 'The Global Food Fight', *Foreign Affairs*, vol. 79, no. 3, 24–38.

Parker, Ian C. (1996), 'Myth, Telecommunication and the Emerging Global Information Order: The Political Economy of Transitions', in Edward A. Comor, *The Global Political Economy of Communication*, Basingstoke/London, Macmillan, 37–60.

Parker, Geoffrey (1994), 'Political geography and geopolitics', in A. J. R. Groom and Margot Light, *Contemporary International Relations: A Guide to Theory*, London/New York, Pinter, 170–181.

Parpart, Jane L. Shirin M. Rai and Kathleen Staudt (eds) (2002), *Rethinking Empowerment: Gender and Development in a Global/Local World*, London, Routledge.

Peterson, V. Spike (ed.) (1992a), *Gendered States – Feminist (Re)Visions of International Relations Theory*, Boulder/London, Lynne Rienner.

Peterson, V. Spike, (1992b), 'Security and Sovereign States: What is at stake in taking feminism seriously', in V. Spike Peterson, *Gendered States – Feminist (Re)Visions of International Relations Theory*, Boulder/London, Lynne Rienner, 31–64.

Peterson, V. Spike (1996a), 'The Politics of Identification in the Context of Globalization', *Women's Studies International Forum*, vol. 19, nos. 1 & 2, January–April, 5–15.

Peterson, V. Spike (1996b), 'Shifting Ground(s): Epistemological and Territorial Remapping in the Context of Globalization(s)', in Eleonore Kofman and Gillian Youngs (eds), *Globalization – Theory and Practice*, London/New York, Pinter, 11–28.

Peterson, V. Spike and Anne Sissan Runyan (1999), *Global Gender Issues* (Second edition), Boulder CO, Westview.

Pettman, Jan Jindy (1996), *Worlding Women – A feminist international politics*, Sydney/London, Allen & Unwin/Routledge.

Pharaoh, Cathy and Rosemary Welchman (1997), *Keeping Posted – A Survey of Current Approaches to Public Communications in the Voluntary Sector*, West Malling, Kent, Charities Aid Foundation, Research Report One.

Pharaoh, Cathie (2002), 'Who Pays the Piper?', *Global Policy Forum*, www.global policy.org/ngos/role/globdem/indiy/2002/0902piper.htm (accessed 01/08/02).

Phillips, Anne (1992), 'Universal Pretensions in Political Thought', in M. Barrett and A. Phillips (eds), *Destabilizing Theory: Contemporary Feminist Debates*, Cambridge, Polity, 10–30.

Phillips, Anne (1991), *Engendering Democracy*, Oxford/Cambridge, Polity.

Phillips, Louise (2000), 'Mediate Communication and the Privatization of Public Problems', *European Journal of Communications*, vol. 15, no. 2, 171–207.

Pickerill, Jenny (2000), 'Weaving a Green Web? Environmental Activists' Use of Computer Mediated Communication in Britain', University of Newcastle: PhD thesis. Summary at www.angelfire.com/electronic/greenweb (accessed 01/06/01).

Pool, Ithiel de Sola (1990), *Technologies Without Boundaries – On Telecommunications in a Global Age*, Cambridge MA/London, Harvard University Press.

Poster, Mark (1990), *The Mode of Information*, Cambridge, Polity Press.

Pruett, Duncan with James Deane (1998), Panos Media Briefing no. 28, Panos Communications and Social Change Programme, April 1998, http://www.igc. apc.org/ia/mb/panos.html (accessed 11/06/01).

Raab, Charles *et al.* (1996), 'The Information Polity: Electronic Democracy, Privacy and Surveillance' in William H. Dutton (ed.), *Information and Communication Technologies – Visions and Realities*, Oxford, Oxford University Press, 283–299.

Rideout, Vanda and Vincent Mosco (1997), 'Communication Policy in the United States', in Mashoed Bailie and Dwayne Winseck (eds), *Democratizing Communication – Comparative Perspectives on Information and Power*, Cresskill NJ, Hampton Press Inc., 81–104.

Rinehart, Sue Tolleson (1992), *Gender Consciousness and Politics*, New York/London, Routledge.

Rodgers, Jayne (1998a), 'Bosnia, Gender and the Ethics of Intervention in Civil Wars', *Civil Wars*, vol. 1, no. 1, April 1998, 103–116.

Rodgers, Jayne (1998b), 'NGO use of Computer-Mediated Communication: Opening New Spaces of Political Representation?' Paper presented to International Studies Association Annual Convention, Minneapolis, 17–21 March 1998.

Rodgers, Jayne (1999), 'NGOs, New Communications Technologies and Concepts of Political Community', *Cambridge Review of International Affairs*, vol. 12, no. 2, summer 1999.

Rodgers, Jayne (2001a), 'Mainstreaming the Marginalized: Conceptualizing Activism on the Internet'. Paper presented at the International Studies Association Annual Convention, Chicago, 20–24 February 2001.

Rodgers, Jayne (2001b), 'Bosnia, Kosovo and the Gendered Dimensions of Intervention', in Colin McInnes and Nicholas J. Wheeler (eds), *The Military Dimensions of Intervention*, London, Frank Cass.

Rodgers, Jayne (2003), 'Spatializing International Activism: Genetically Modified Foods on the Internet', in Cynthia Weber and Francois Debrix (eds), *Mediating Internationals*, Minneapolis, University of Minnesota Press.

Rose, Gillian (1993), *Feminism and Geography – The Limits of Geographical Knowledge*, London, Polity.

Rosenau, James (1997), 'The Person, the Household, the Community, and the Globe: notes for a theory of multilateralism in a turbulent world', in Robert W. Cox (ed.), *The New Realism*, Basingstoke/New York, Macmillan Press/St Martin's Press, 57–80.

Rosow, Stephen J. (1994), 'Introduction: Boundaries Crossing – Critical Theories of Global Economy', in Stephen J. Rosow *et al.* (eds), *The Global Economy as Political Space*, Boulder CO, Lynne Rienner, 1–13.

Rosow, Stephen J., Naeem Inayatullah and Mark Rupert (eds) (1994), *The Global Economy as Political Space*, Boulder CO, Lynne Rienner.

Rowbotham, Sheila (1992), *Women in Movement – Feminism and Social Action*, New York/London, Routledge.

Sassen, Saskia (1999), 'Digital Networks and Power', in Mike Featherstone and Scott Lash (eds), *Spaces of Culture*, London/Thousand Oaks/New Delhi, Sage, 49–63.

Sassi, Sinikka (2001), 'The Transformation of the Public Sphere?', in Barrie Axford and Richard Huggins (eds), *New Media and Politics*, London/Thousand Oaks/New Delhi, Sage, 89–108.

Schiller, Herbert I. (1996), *Information Inequality – The Deepening Social Crisis in America*, London/New York, Routledge.

Scheufele, Dietram A. (2002), 'Examining Differential Gains From Mass Media and their Implications for Participatory Behaviour', *Communication Research*, vol. 29, no. 1, February, 45–65.

Schoenbaach, Karl (2001), 'Myths of Media and Audiences', *European Journal of Communication*, vol. 16, no. 3, 361–376.

Shade, Leslie Regan (1996), 'Is there Free Speech on the Net? Censorship in the Global Information Infrastructure', in Rob Shields (ed.), *Cultures of Internet – Virtual Spaces, Real Histories, Living Bodies*, London/Thousand Oaks/New Delhi, Sage, 11–32.

Shields, Rob (ed.) (1996a), *Cultures of Internet – Virtual Spaces, Real Histories, Living Bodies*, London/Thousand Oaks/New Delhi, Sage.

Shields, Rob (1996b), 'Introduction: Virtual Spaces, Real Histories and Living Bodies', in Rob Shields (ed.), *Cultures of Internet – Virtual Spaces, Real Histories, Living Bodies*, London/Thousand Oaks/New Delhi, Sage, 1–10.

Silber, Ian Friedrich (1995), 'Spaces, Fields, Boundaries: The Rise of Spatial Metaphors in Contemporary Sociological Theory', *Social Research*, vol. 62, no. 2, summer, 323–355.

Silver, David (2000), 'Looking Backwards, Looking Forwards: Cyberculture Studies 1990–2000', in David Gauntlett (ed.), *Web Studies – Rewiring Media Studies for the Digital Age*, London, Arnold, 19–30.

Silverstone, Roger and Eric Hirsch (eds) (1994), *Consuming Technologies – Media and Information in Domestic Spaces*, London/New York, Routledge.

Singh, J. P. (1999), *Leapfrogging Development? The Political Economy of Telecommunications Restructuring*, New York, State University of New York/ Wantage University Press.

Slevin, James (2000), *The Internet and Society*, Cambridge/Oxford, Polity.

Smith, Jackie (1997), 'Characteristics of the Modern Transnational Social Movement Sector', in Jackie Smith *et al.* (eds), *Transnational Social Movements and Global Politics – Solidarity Beyond the State*, New York, Syracuse University Press, 42–59.

Smith, Jackie (2001), 'Globalizing Resistance: The Battle of Seattle and the Future of Social Movements', *Mobilization*, vol. 6, no. 1, 1–20.

Smith, Jackie, Charles Chatfield and Ron Pagnucco (eds) (1997), *Transnational Social Movements and Global Politics – Solidarity Beyond the State*, New York, Syracuse University Press.

Smith, Marc A. and Peter Kollock (eds) (1999), *Communities in Cyberspace*, New York, Routledge.

Smith, Neil and Cindi Katz (1993), 'Grounding Metaphor – Towards a Spatialized Politics', in Keith Michael and Steve Pile (eds), *Place and the Politics of Identity*, London/New York, Routledge, 67–83.

Smith, Steve (1995), 'The Self-Images of a Discipline: A Genealogy of International Relations Theory', in Ken Booth and Steve Smith (eds), *International Relations Theory Today*, Cambridge, Polity, 1–37.

Smith, Steve, Ken Booth and Marysia Zalewski (1997), *International Theory: Positivism and Beyond*, Cambridge, Cambridge University Press.

Smythe, Elizabeth and Peter J. Smith (2001), 'New Technologies and Networks of Resistance: Reframing the Globalization Discourse'. Paper presented at the International Studies Association Convention, Hong Kong, 28 July 2001.

Soja, Edward W. (1989), *Postmodern Geographies – The Reassertion of Space in Critical Social Theory*, London/New York, Verso.

Soja, Edward W. (1995), 'Heterotopologies: A Remembrance of the Other Spaces in the Citadel-LA', in Sophie Watson and Catherine Gibson (eds), *Postmodern Cities and Spaces*, Oxford/Cambridge MA, Blackwell, 13–33.

Soja, Edward W. (1996), *Thirdspace – Journeys to Los Angeles and Other Real-And-Imagined Places*, Oxford/Cambridge MA, Blackwell.

Soja, Edward and Barbara Hooper (1993), 'The Spaces that Difference Makes – Some Notes on the Geographical Margins of the New Cultural Politics', in Keith Michael and Steve Pile (eds), *Place and the Politics of Identity*, London/New York, Routledge, 183–205.

Stallabrass, Julian (1995), 'Empowering Technology: The Exploration of Cyber-space', *New Left Review*, no. 211, May/June 1995, 3–32.

Starr, Amory (2000), *Naming the Enemy – Anti-Corporate Movements Confront Globalization*, London/New York, Zed.

Stavenhagen, Rodolfo (1997), 'People's Movements: the Antisystemic Challenge', in Robert W. Cox (ed.), *The New Realism*, Basingstoke/New York, Macmillan Press/St Martin's Press, 20–37.

Stavropoulos, Pam (1997), 'Women in Colonial Africa: Agency, Theory and Literature', in Philip Darby (ed.), *At the Edge of International Relations – Postcolonialism, Gender and Dependency*, London/New York, Continuum, 197–213.

Strange, Susan (1996), *The Retreat of the State – The Diffusion of Power in the World Economy*, Cambridge, Cambridge University Press.

Street, John (1997), 'Remote Control? Politics, Technology and Electronic Democracy', *European Journal of Communication*, vol. 12, no. 1, London/Thousand Oaks/New Delhi, Sage, 27–42.

Street, John (2001), *Mass Media, Politics and Democracy*, Basingstoke/New York, Palgrave.

Stromer-Galley, Jennifer (2000), 'Democratizing Democracy: Strong Democracy, US Political Campaigns and the Internet', in Peter Ferdinand, (ed.), *The Internet, Democracy and Democratization*, London/Portland, Frank Cass, 36–58.

Sundin, Elizabeth (1995), 'The Social Construction of Gender and Technology – A Process with No Definitive Answer', *The European Journal of Women's Studies – Special Issue on Technology*, vol. 3, no. 2, August, 335–353.

Sunstein, Cass R. (1990), *Feminism and Political Theory*, London/Chicago, University of Chicago Press.

Swazo, Norman K. (2002), 'For "Just Results": Questioning National Missile Defense Research in Alaska', *Journal of Philosophy, Science & Law*, vol. 2, July, www.psljournal.com/archives/papers/swazo.htm (accessed 11/03/03).

Sylvester, Christine (1994), *Feminist Theory and International Relations in a Postmodern Era*, Cambridge, Cambridge University Press.

Tarrow, Sidney (1994), *Power in Movement – Social Movements, Collective Action and Politics*, Cambridge, Cambridge University Press.

Tarrow, Sidney (1996), 'States and Opportunities: The Political Structuring of Social Movements', in Doug McAdam *et al.*, *Comparative Perspectives in Social Movements – Political Opportunities, Mobilizing Structures and Cultural Framings*, Cambridge, Cambridge University Press, 41–46.

Taylor, Peter J. (1985/1993), *Political Geography – World Economy, Nation-State and Locality (Third edition)*, Essex, Longman.

Taylor, Peter J. (1993), *Political Geography of the Twentieth Century – A Global Analysis*, London, Belhaven Press.

Taylor, Verta and Nancy Whittier (1999), 'Guest Editors' Introduction: Special Issue on Gender and Social Movements: Part 2', *Gender and Society*, vol. 13, no. 1, 5–7.

Thrift, Nigel (1996), *Spatial Formations*, London/Thousand Oaks/New Delhi, Sage.

Thompson, John B. (1994), 'Social Theory and the Media', in David Crowley and David Mitchell (eds), *Communication Theory Today*, Cambridge, Polity Press, 27–49.

Thomson, Janice E. (1995), 'State Sovereignty in International Relations: Bridging the Gap Between Theory and Empirical Research', *International Studies Quarterly*, no. 39, 213–233.

Thussu, Daya Kishan (2000), *International Communication – Continuity and Change*, London/New York, Arnold.

Tickner, J. Ann, (1992), *Gender in International Relations – Feminist Perspectives on Achieving Global Security*, New York, Columbia University Press.

Tickner, J. Ann (1997), 'You Just Don't Understand: Troubled Engagements Between Feminists and IR Theorists', *International Studies Quarterly*, no. 41, 611–632.

Tilly, Charles (1986), *The Contentious French*, London/Cambridge MA, Belknap Press.

Tisdall, Simon (2001), 'Fear of Attack Triggers Arms Build-up', *Guardian*, 23 January, p. 3.

Traynor, Ian (2001), 'Russia Halts Military Cuts as Hawks Take Over in US', *Guardian*, 18 January, p. 12.

Vakil, Anna C. (1997), 'Confronting the Classification Problem: Towards a Taxonomy of NGOs', *World Development*, vol. 25, no. 12, 2057–2070.

Valasek, Tomas (2000), 'Europe's Role in National Missile Defense', *Weekly Defense Monitor*, vol. 4, issue 23, 8 June, http://www.cdi.org/weekly/2000/issue23.html (accessed 11/03/03).

Verstraeten, Hans (1996), 'The Media and the Transformation of the Public Sphere – A Contribution for a Critical Political Economy of the Public Sphere', *European Journal of Communication*, vol. 11, no. 3, London/Thousand Oaks/ New Delhi, Sage, 347–370.

Vincent, Richard C. (1997), 'The New World Information and Communication Order (NWICO) in the Context of the Information Superhighway', in Mashoed Bailie and Dwayne Winseck (eds), *Democratizing Communication – Comparative Perspectives on Information and Power*, Cresskill NJ, Hampton Press Inc., 377–406.

Wakeford, Nina (2000), 'New Media, New Methodologies: Studying the Web', in David Gauntlett (ed.), *Web Studies*, London, Arnold, 31–42.

Walch, Jim (1999), *In the Net – An Internet Guide for Activists*, London/New York, Zed.

Walsh, James (1999), 'Brave New Farm', *Time*, vol. 153, no. 1, 11 January, http://www.time.com/time/magazine/articles/0,3266,1/698,00.htm (accessed 06/04/99).

Walker, R. B. J. (1990), 'Security, Sovereignty, and the Challenge of World Politics', *Alternatives*, vol. 15, 3–27.

Walker, R. B. J. (1991), 'State Sovereignty and the Articulation of Political Space/ Time', *Millennium*, vol. 20, no. 3, 445–461.

Walker, R. B. J. (1992), 'Gender and Critique in the Theory of International Relations', in V. Spike Peterson (ed.), *Feminist (Re)Visions of International Relations Theory*, London/Boulder CO, Lynne Rienner, 179–202.

Walker, R. B. J. (1993), *Inside/Outside: International Relations as Political Theory*, Cambridge Studies in International Relations 24, Cambridge, Cambridge University Press.

Walker, R. B. J. (1995), 'The Concept of the Political', in Ken Booth and Steve Smith (eds), *International Relations Theory Today*, Cambridge, Polity, 306–327.

Walker, R. B. J. and Saul Mendlovitz (eds) (1990), *Contending Sovereignties – Redefining Political Community*, Boulder CA/London, Lynne Rienner.

Wallerstein, Immanuel (1991), *Geopolitics and Geoculture – Essays on the Changing World System*, Cambridge, Cambridge University Press.

Warkentin, Craig (2001), *Reshaping World Politics – NGOs, the Internet and Global Civil Society*, Lanham/Boulder/New York/Oxford, Rowman & Littlefield.

Warleigh, Alex (2001), 'Europeanizing Civil Society: NGOs as Agents of Political Socialization', *Journal of Common Market Studies*, 39/4, November, 619–639.

Watson, Sophie and Catherine Gibson (eds) (1995), *Postmodern Cities and Spaces*, Oxford/Cambridge MA, Blackwell.

Weber, Cynthia (1992), 'Reconsidering Statehood: Examining the Sovereignty/Intervention Boundary', *Review of International Studies*, vol. 18, no. 3, July, 199–216.

Weber, Cynthia and Francois Debrix (eds) (2003), *Mediating Internationals*, Minneapolis, University of Minnesota Press.

Whitworth, Sandra (1994/1997), *Feminism in International Relations*, Basingstoke/London, Macmillan.

Wilhelm, Anthony G. (2000), *Democracy in the Digital Age – Challenges to Political Life in Cyberspace*, New York/London, Routledge.

Willetts, Peter (1996), 'From Stockholm to Rio and Beyond: the Impact of the Environmental Movement on the United Nations Consultative Arrangements for NGOs', *Review of International Studies*, vol. 22, no. 1, January, 57–68.

Winseck, Dwayne (1997a), 'Contradictions in the Democratization of International Communication', *Media, Culture and Society*, London/Thousand Oaks/New Delhi, Sage, 219–246.

Winseck, Dwayne (1997b), 'The Shifting Contexts of International Communication: Possibilities for a New World Information and Communication Order', in Mashoed Bailie and Dwayne Winseck (eds), *Democratizing Communication – Comparative Perspectives on Information and Power*, Cresskill NJ, Hampton Press Inc., 343–376.

Wolcott, Peter *et al.* (2001), 'A Framework for Assessing the Global Diffusion of the Internet', *Journal of the Association of Information Systems*, vol. 2, article 6, November, http://mosaic.unomaha.edu/2001_GDI_Framework.html (accessed 10/02/02).

Wyatt, Sally (2000), 'From the Net to the Web and Beyond: Actors and Interests in the Construction of the Internet', *Virtual Society? The Social Science of Electronic Technologies*, http://virtualsociety.sbs.ox.ac.uk/projects/wyatt.htm (accessed 11/03/03).

Yorkshire CND (2000), 'Fylingdales – The Proposed Upgrade System for the US NMD System', http://www.gn.apc.org/cndyorks/fdales/fd2000.htm (accessed 11/03/03).

Youngs, Gillian (1996a), 'Dangers of Discourse: The Case of Globalization', in Eleonore Kofman and Gillian Youngs (eds), *Globalization – Theory and Practice*, London/New York, Pinter, 58–71.

Youngs, Gillian (1996b), 'Political Economy of Spatiality: Gender, Power and Conceptualizing Globalization'. Paper presented at 37th Annual Convention of the International Studies Association, San Diego, 16–20 April 1996.

Youngs, Gillian (1998), 'Virtual Voices: Real Lives', in Wendy Harcourt (ed.), *Women@Internet – Creating New Cultures in Cyberspace*, New York/Sydney/London, Zed Books.

Youngs, Gillian (2000), 'Breaking Patriarchal Bonds – Demythologizing the Public/Private', in Marianne H. Marchand, and Anne Sisson Runyan, *Gender and Global Restructuring – Sightings, Sites and Resistances*, London/New York, Routledge, 44–58.

Youngs, Gillian, (2001), 'Globalization, Communication and Technology: Making the Democratic Links', *Politica Internazionale*, vol. 1, no. 2, 2001, 217–226. Special issue 'This Major-Minor World', published in Italian and English by IPALMO (Institute for Italy's Relations with the Countries of Africa, Latin America and the Middle East), in cooperation with SID (Society for International Development).

Youngs, Gillain (2002), 'Feminizing Cyberspace: Rethinking Technoagency', in Jane L. Parpart, Shirin M. Rai and Kathleen Staudt (eds), *Rethinking Empowerment: Gender and Development in a Global/Local World*, London, Routledge, 79–94.

Yuval-Davis, Nira (1996), 'Women and the Biological Reproduction of "The Nation"', *Women's Studies International Forum*, vol. 19, nos. 1/2, 17–24.

Yuval-Davis, Nira (1997), 'Women, Citizenship and Difference', *Feminist Review*, 57, autumn, 4–27.

Zalewski, Marysia (1995), 'Well, What is the Feminist Perspective on Bosnia?', *International Affairs*, vol. 71, no. 2, April, 339–356.

Zalewski, Marysia and Cynthia Enloe (1995), 'Questions about Identity in International Relations', in Ken Booth and Steve Smith (eds), *International Relations Theory Today*, Cambridge, Polity, 279–305.

Zalewski, Marysia and Jane Parpart (1998), *The 'Man' Question in International Relations*, Boulder CO/Oxford, Westview.

Zaller, John (1992), *The Nature and Origins of Mass Opinion*, New York, Cambridge University Press.

Index